LONDON PUBLIC LIBRARY
20 E FIRST ST
LONDON OH 43140

09/20/2006

THE BOOK OF
MARTIAL POWER

THE BOOK OF
MARTIAL POWER

THE UNIVERSAL GUIDE TO THE COMBATIVE ARTS

Steven Pearlman

THE OVERLOOK PRESS
Woodstock & New York

First published in the United States in 2006 by
The Overlook Press, Peter Mayer Publishers, Inc.
Woodstock & New York

Woodstock:
One Overlook Drive
Woodstock, NY 12498
www.overlookpress.com
[for individual orders, bulk and special sales, contact our Woodstock office]

New York:
141 Wooster Street
New York, NY 10012

Copyright © 2006 by Steven J. Pearlman

All Rights Reserved. No part of this publication may be reproduced or
transmitted in any form or by any means, electronic or mechanical,
including photocopy, recording, or any information storage and
retrieval system now known or to be invented without permission in
writing from the publisher, except by a reviewer who wishes to quote
brief passages in connection with a review written for
inclusion in a magazine, newspaper, or broadcast.

The paper used in this book meets the requirements for paper
permanence as described in the ANSI Z39.48-1992 standard.

Cataloging-in-Publication Data is available from the Library of Congress

Book design and type formating by Bernard Schleifer
Manufactured in United States of America
ISBN-10 1-58567-635-7 / ISBN-13 978-1-58567-635-4
1 3 5 7 9 8 6 4 2

Contents

SECTION II: PHYSIOKINETIC PRINCIPLES 75

SECTION III: PRINCIPLES OF TECHNIQUE 175

Acknowledgments

THANKS TO ALL THOSE INSTRUCTORS WITH WHOM I HAVE CROSSED PATHS formally and informally, including Mike Krivka, Jack Ling, Joe Mansfield, "Brian" Wu, and to the countless other martial artists who have taught me so much in the informal exchanges that have been the mainstay of my education to date.

It is also important to recognize other authors who have contributed to the promotion of principles in the martial arts world and to the multiplexity of overlapping terms, concepts, definitions, and interpretations: Don Angier, Tony Annesi, Richard Behrens, Bruce Juchnik, Bob Klein, Bob Orlando, Peter Ralston, Marc "Animal" MacYoung. I try to acknowledge them individually if they serve as a particular source for a particular point but most principles simultaneously emerge from so many arts that particular attribution, at least for me, is impossible.

Thanks to April and Matt Bristow-Smith and Henry Caporoso for offering valuable feedback, and to Patrick Hussey.

Thanks to mom and dad for encouraging me to take up martial arts.

Thanks to my agent, Ed Knappman and everyone at NEPA.

Thanks, of course, to the students who have shared this journey with me, including the original AU group, especially Chuck and Mike, and the later AU'ers, especially Bruce Bernstein, Mark Geary, "Sonny" Lewis, Kirill Reznick, and Mr. & Mrs. Eric & Angie.

Thanks to all the students in Saratoga, especially those who shared my journey there the most: Howie Austin, Nicole Biamonte, Jess Fredican, Mike Haftel, Zach Hastings, Stephanie Kvam, Andrew Matusiewicz, Max Poppel, Erica Sexton, Dan "Sharkey" Sharkey, Joe Seggio, Dan Walfield, Andrew Williams, Natty Veytsel, and Frank "Superheavinesspunch" Won.

Special thanks to those students closest to my heart and in whom my vision has truly come to life. You are not only friends; you are family: Asa

Snyder, Brandi Collesides, Ed Dewey, Chris "Haseman" Haseman, Bob Horsman, Ted "The Skeptic" Marr, and Ryan "Bubi" Merrick.

An extra thanks to Ed for making the trip for the photo shoot.

Special thanks Brett McCormick: You know my journey better than anyone. This book would not exist without you. Thanks for all those late night discussions—you know the ones I mean. Who would have thought we would end up here?

Deepest thanks to my wife, Terrylynn, for the unwavering love and support that made this book possible. I love you!

MARTIAL PRINCIPLES

IN RECENT YEARS THERE HAS BEEN MUCH DISCUSSION IN THE MARTIAL ARTS world about principles and principle-based teaching. Modern times and advancements in the understanding of the mechanics of the human body have changed the way we think about martial arts. Contemporary martial artists often strive to define and understand these ancient teachings with the mind and eyes of modern sciences. The choice of weapon not withstanding, we all have the same tool to use, the human body, and are subject to its limitations and the laws of physics. Yet among the different systems there is no cohesive or consistent understanding of just what principles are in relation to the martial arts in general.

Principles within martial arts are, or should be, the common denominators between anatomy, physics, kinesiology, biomechanics and psychology in the context of martial arts. They guide us and teach us understanding of ourselves, our bodies and how they/we relate to others and to movement in general.

In the past understanding of such principles and insight was reserved knowledge, highly guarded secrets bestowed only upon the most trusted disciples of the art. They were and are sometimes couched in the cryptic writings or scrolls, or sayings within the oral traditions of the art. But sometimes these little bits of understanding made a vast difference and gave one an edge over adversaries that lacked such knowledge.

But this isn't the feudal age anymore, and there is much cross-pollination between the different styles and teachings in the martial arts. And it's about time someone defined and put into writing some of the common denominators.

Steven Pearlman, in this work, has broken ground in doing just that. And considering the vast differences in the use of the human body between all the styles of martial arts around the world, that is no small undertaking.

Principles can be compared with our alphabet. There are only twenty-six letters, but look how many words can be made from them. The same holds true for the principles. Each technique within a system is made up of many different principles. Sometimes more than one will be occurring at the same time, or possibly repeating themselves throughout the course of a single technique. Some techniques will seem focused around the application of a particular principle, with the others only having incidental or supportive roles in defining the movements inherent to the form.

One should not become overly conscious of any particular principle, unless that is the focus of your training at the time. Simply try to recognize them when they occur, when they are applicable, and take advantage of their inherent qualities. They are a guide, there to provide technical precision, understanding, and to assist in the clean and efficient application of technique.

Trying to recognize and define a set of principles that is applicable to all martial arts regardless of stylistic differences is exhaustive work. But if you look deeply within your own system you will find what is in all of the others. Steven has recognized this and gone in-depth putting into words aspects of the arts that have often defied more elementary explanations. Not just the "what's and when's", but also the "how's and why's," the definitions behind the definitions, so to speak. Regardless of the system you study or its origins, I believe all martial artists will find value in this work that will provide insight applicable to your own art, and martial arts in general.

Valentino (Richard) Elias
Yoshida ha Shidare Yanagi ryu
Takamura ha Shindo Yoshin ryu

Introduction

And We're Not Doing it Because . . . ?

FIRST TOOK UP MARTIAL ARTS IN MY EARLY TEENS. MY PARENTS THOUGHT it a good idea because my slim build made me a ripe target for school bullies, a problem inflamed by my unknowing, occasional big mouth. Yet while my parents wanted me to learn to defend myself, I wanted to study martial arts because of my fascination with their mystique, a fascination born of Saturday afternoon "Kung Fu Theater" and ice breaking exhibitions on *The Wide World of Sports*.

Unfortunately, studying *Tae Kwon Do* at my local "Y" failed quite completely to deliver the mystique I desired. I had prepared myself to become the humble disciple of a wizened old Asian man with a long white beard and bushy white eyebrows, one who spoke in fortune cookie riddles, and who would put me through secret and obscure training rituals. What I got didn't quite live up to that expectation: a pot-bellied, middle-aged Caucasian man in a school classroom. To be honest, I probably would have overlooked his non-Asian stature and continued *Tae Kwon Do* training were I not the only student still around by the second class and were we not training in sweat pants and tee shirts. (Perhaps the other students also were driven off by his inability to live up to the same kung fu movies I watched.) In hindsight, I was a fool for passing up private instruction from a credible instructor.

Honoring my distaste for the classes at the "Y," my parents switched me to a "real" martial arts school, one where students wore uniforms, and one that taught *Shorin-Ryu Karate*. Despite the chief instructor's failure to be Asian, the general atmosphere still offered enough of the "mystique" I desired. But "mystique" goes only so far. It lost its charm when I found myself doing arm toughening exercises against men with forearms nearly as thick as my calves. They took it easy on me, or at least most of them did, but I lacked the maturity and discipline to tolerate the pain and the bruises. I dropped out but my closet passion for martial arts remained.

A year later, when two close friends revealed their intentions to join a *dojo* near our high school, I jumped at the chance. Having two friends with whom to enter the frightening and mysterious world of the martial arts was too sweet a deal to pass up. It not only gave me the confidence of strength in numbers, it also provided me with instant training partners.

What sweetened the prospect even more was that the school in question purported to teach something superior to the average martial art. The school claimed to teach "the best of all martial arts"—an "eclectic" mixture of *karate, jujitsu, aikido, chi na, tae kwon do, hapkido, kung fu*, and other styles. I was ecstatic. While the instructor, whom I shall call "John Doe," once again failed to be Asian, the school certainly appeared mysterious. Subconsciously, I reasoned that if martial arts had mystique compared to Western pursuits, John Doe's school held mystique when compared to most martial arts! After all, what could be better than "the best of all styles"?

Keep in mind that at the time, around the mid-1980s, the hybridization we see today proved neither popular nor common. Thus, John Doe not only seemed unique, but he also appeared to be some kind of renegade—defying tradition by blending styles—and that appealed to whatever sense of teenage rebellion I possessed. Furthermore, I reckoned that John Doe's ability to combine ancient art forms must have made him (1) exceptionally knowledgeable, (2) exceptionally wise, and (3) exceptionally skilled (I believe the phrase I used at the time was "bad ass").

It would not be for a few years, however, long after my friends stopped attending, that I would discover just how inherently problematic his teachings were. While on a certain level I wish I could reclaim the time I spent devoted to John Doe's style, ultimately I would not trade even a part of the experience, and I say that for three reasons: First, that if not for John Doe's school, I would not have met my wife, Terrylynn. Second, because it was in John Doe's school that I met my great friend, Brett. Third, if John Doe's school had not been so utterly problematic, I doubt I would have discovered the path I am on today.

This statement requires some explanation. I had been at the school for some years and had, along with Brett, attained the rank of sandan—third degree black belt. We became the highest ranking students in the school and not only believed its rhetoric, we taught it. We espoused the "best of all systems" slogan quite well, often better than our instructors.[1] We did it so well that we never thought to take a critical look at the style we both cherished. That luxury would not last long.

While away at college, where I ran a John Doe's style martial arts club, I met another martial artist, a black belt, and one who practiced one of the

---

1. I should note that while we both feel foolish for having bought into the rhetoric to begin with, our true disappointment is in having espoused it and taught it to other members of the school.

styles supposedly included in John Doe's system. We decided to workout together and, as I knew my style to be "the best," I assumed that *I* would be showing *him* a thing or two. How wrong I was! No sooner had we bowed to one another than he asked, "What would you do against one of these?" and lashed out with the hardest, fastest haymaker I had ever encountered (a feat not difficult to achieve because I had never encountered a hard or fast anything). In response, after years of training in "the most effective self-defense system," I essentially froze. I feebly managed to block the attack without being knocked too far off balance, and after a moment or two of pause and bewilderment summoned the wherewithal to counter with a single punch that did not carry force enough to wrinkle his *gi*.

In contrast to my own feeble attempts at anything resembling actual martial arts, he displayed a myriad of techniques, all of which he performed well—fast, hard, and to their completion. He tossed me around quite proficiently and, in more ways than one, taught me quite a bit. He certainly made me aware of the true nature of what I had been "learning."

Though a sucker punch, his attack revealed that I possessed virtually no martial arts ability or knowledge. I could not react instinctively. I did not know many techniques. I could not apply to fruition the few techniques I did "know." Instead, as both Brett and I eventually realized, we were in the habit of excusing ourselves from actually applying techniques on the grounds that "they would cause injury" or that they would not work "until the adrenaline factor kicked in." We did not intend to make excuses. We thought, from John Doe's tutelage, that we actually *were* doing martial arts. In reality, however, we lacked both the knowledge and the training to even resemble functionality.

To offer an example of what our training looked liked, when we practiced a "technique," let's say a throw, it involved a fully complicit partner, one "weakened" or "distracted" enough by *theoretical* counterstrikes to pretty much fall down on his or her own. We never encountered or created even a modicum of resistance, to the point where we would jump over our partners to help create the effect of being thrown. Furthermore, we always executed throws somewhat gently to "guard our partner's safety," if not simply because John Doe never expected anything else. It would be accurate to say that we *simulated* techniques instead of actually executing them: we did not realize we were faking it, we just were.

The light of that one haymaker made me question everything about John Doe's style, which in turn revealed a plethora of other inconsistencies. Amongst the many, one stood out in particular. At the time, I did not realize how great an effect it would come to have on my vision and practice of the martial arts. In fact, it took me years to appreciate its importance.

One day, while I was practicing "counter punching," John Doe made the point that blocking and striking simultaneously proved more efficient than blocking first and striking second, even in rapid succession. As we had never blocked and punched in simultaneity before, this struck me as pure genius.

"And so that is what we are going to do from now on?" I asked, assuming of course that it would be.

"No," John Doe replied, and without further explanation.

We never practiced it again. He never even spoke of it again.

While I am not at this point in the text interested in opening discussion about the relative merits of simultaneity in defending and countering, I do want to point out the inconsistency in John Doe's own logic. To (1) advocate something as useful and (2) fail to do it (3) seems inescapably foolish. The merits of simultaneous blocking and striking aside, John Doe violated his *own* logic.

In the months to come, the inconsistencies and failings we discovered in John Doe's style multiplied faster than Brett and I could tally. Consequently, although it hurt to leave what had become a second family to us, Brett and I resigned our ranks and left the school. This was particularly difficult for me because John Doe's school had given me quite a bit. I felt a real friendship with John Doe and the other senior instructor, so leaving John Doe's school was even more complicated because it was personal. The school and the people in it meant a great deal to me. Furthermore, being an instructor at John Doe's school showed me that I loved teaching. I have to think it is one of the reasons I am a teacher by trade today. Leaving that school was one of the hardest things I had to do up to that point in my life.

Yet I was not entirely free of John Doe's style. I still ran a John Doe's club at college. It probably would have been wisest for me to terminate the club with humble apologies and seek out an instructor of quality, but I felt an obligation to my students and I believed that many of John Doe's "techniques" could prove useful *if actually trained well and applied.* (I was wrong about that but it would take me a while to discover it.) Furthermore, many of my students lacked alternatives, if only because they lacked the funds to train offcampus.

Motivated by my responsibility to my students, my love of the arts, as well as my love of teaching, I began my quest for martial knowledge. I learned from instructors, fellow students at the college, and even books and magazines. I finally began my serious journey in the real world of the martial arts, and I proceeded voraciously. As a result, my knowledge grew exponentially, something I loved personally but that caused friction between me and my students. I began to change my entire curriculum at least every six months, if not every three, and my club shrank as a result. And who could blame students for leaving. After all, I did *not* know what I was doing. But I was doing my best, teaching with integrity, and occasionally offering something of value. As I was not profiting from the club, it seemed a fair exchange. Thus, and in spite of dwindling numbers, I stiffened my resolve to seek out substantive martial arts.

I studied varying amounts of many different systems—hard systems, soft systems, linear systems, circular systems, Chinese, Japanese, Korean, Malaysian and Western systems. Most were wonderful in their own regard and I respected them greatly. Had I found one that fully satisfied my passion (without purging my wallet), I might have devoted myself to it alone. Instead, I continued exploring, taking what I could from different sources.

As my proficiency in different styles developed, I came to find inherent problems in them together. Each style worked in its own context but I lacked a mechanism by which to compare them and unite them. For example, the *judoka* I met advocated grappling on the grounds that most fights converged into short range after a brief time. A sound theory. I also met kicking stylists who advocated keeping one's distance from the attacker while using the body's largest weapons—the legs—to do the fighting. Also a sound theory. I found equally sound theories for trapping, ground fighting, striking, etc. At first, I thought the solution entailed training for both kicks and grappling (and trapping and ground fighting and hand strikes and . . .). But that amounted to training for so many *different* things. *Wing Chun, Kali,* boxing, *Kenpo, Kempo*—they all exercise sound theories for striking range. *Wing Chun* says hold the centerline, *Kali* often favors triangulating the opponent, boxing favors dodging and jabbing, *Kenpo* wins with rapid strikes, and *Kempo* focuses on vital points. Are they all right, I wondered. Do they all work equally? Each certainly holds its own and works in its own context but to which should I devote my time? Is it healthy to train so many *different* things?

By the same token, how was I to choose between *judo's* version of a hip throw and *jujitsu's, ninjutsu's, Shuai Chiao's,* etc.? To be sure, there were similarities; all were hip throws. But some put the hip here instead of there, or entered this way instead of that way, or stepped one way instead of the other.

Likewise, I practiced trapping in different ways based on different arts, such as *Wing Chun, Kali, Silat, Tai Chi,* and others. Some worked in vertical circles, some in horizontal circles, and some at triangulated angles. Which is better? Should I train in all of them? What did they have in common despite the differences? What difference did the differences make?

Was there no basis for determination?

Before too long, I realized that I could not continue training without first resolving two pre-eminent questions:

1. What was the underlying connection between so many seemingly *different* approaches?
2. By what standard of measure could one approach be evaluated against another?[2]

---

2. I want to make it very clear that evaluating one against another does not mean trying to determine which is empirically better. Instead, I consider it a matter of weighing qualities. Gold can be measured to be heavier than steel but it is far too soft, to say nothing of expensive, to use for I-beams.

Looking at so many seemingly *different* yet internally sound approaches to the martial arts drove me to realize that there must be underlying factors that make *all* martial arts function. In short, every style, though different, must work from a similar set of *principles*. That single realization fully and irrevocably altered my approach to the martial arts, and ultimately led to this book. I stopped looking at martial arts in terms of techniques and styles, and started instead to examine the factors common to all styles.

This book explains in detail that very premise. If we can understand the principles that our arts express and manifest then we can, I hope, both (1) improve the practice of our own art and (2) acquire a common language through which to dialogue with practitioners of other arts.

It requires wisdom to understand wisdom:
the music is nothing if the audience is deaf.

—WALTER LIPPMAN

The Nature and Importance of Principles

T HE WORD "PRINCIPLE" OFTEN GETS THROWN AROUND IN THE MARTIAL ARTS community and so before proceeding, we need a clear definition at least with respect to how I will use it in this text? The dictionary defines a "principle" as follows:

1. A fundamental law or truth upon which other techniques and actions are based;
2. The natural way a thing [such as the human body] operates; and
3. A philosophical or moral tenet.

Considering *principle*[1], the words "fundamental" and "truth" delineate the essential distinction between principles and non-principles, namely that *principles are universal to all martial arts*. For us to consider it a principle, it must apply equally to all styles, irrespective of national origin and whether they are "hard," "soft," "internal," "external," "long ranged," "short ranged," "striking-based," "grappling-based," etc.

For the purposes of this book, were an instructor to say, "one of the principles of *my* style is . . ." then he or would not correctly use the term, "principle." A "principle" that exists in one style but not another, or in some styles but not all, cannot be a true principle as we define it here. *It still might be a valuable technique or method*, it just does not fit our definition of "principle."

On the other hand, consider Newton's Third Law of Motion: "For every action there is an equal and opposite reaction." That truth applies to all martial arts, regardless of their nationality, combative objective, range(s) of combat, or the nature of their techniques. Thus, we can safely call it a "principle."

Yet that Newton's Third Law applies to all arts equally and without exception does not mean it does so in the same regard. Throwing a kick poses different complications with respect to Newton's Third Law than does throwing a person. Hence, a Karateka and a Judoka must contend with Newton's Third Law equally but differently. In short, no art can escape that law, and its inescapability makes it a *principle*[1] for our purposes.

The same holds equally true for *principle*[2] in that all martial arts involve the movements of the human body, and the nature of the human body does not vary from *karate* to *kung fu* to *pentjak silat*, etc. While we do see minor variations in the particular body types—tall, short, thin, muscular, etc.—the nature of human anatomy does not change.

Principle[2] applies equally to *psychology*, as well. While we do see variations in our personalities, the nature of the human mind itself remains effectively the same from style to style. In other words, we might fear different things, but the nature of fear in and of itself remains the same; it only manifests differently from person to person, just as Newton's Third Law manifests differently when kicking vs. executing a takedown.

Principle[3] works much the same way. Philosophy, the conceptual mindset through which we approach martial arts, applies universally. While some artists dismiss philosophical premises as lofty ideas apart from the reality of combat, philosophy plays no lesser a role in our effectiveness than anything else, especially once we realize that the argument that philosophy does not matter is itself a *philosophy*. Therefore, we must respect philosophical principles, especially as they apply to martial technique.

Morality, though no less universal, certainly becomes infinitely more complicated. While there probably are universal truths with respect to morality; I for one lack the wisdom to see them with certainty, and so I will tread upon them lightly.

Yet all three types of principle hold certain things in common. First, *while a principle might manifest itself differently depending on the martial art in question, the principle itself applies to all arts equally and without exception.*

Second, *principles will affect techniques positively when understood and applied or negatively when overlooked or ignored.* For example, consider Newton's Third Law in the context of a punch. Given that Newton's Third Law is, in fact, a principle, it *will* manifest in some manner, meaning that *there will be an equal and opposite reaction to the action (of punching), period.* It is unavoidable and inescapable.

Yet if we did not know about Newton's Third Law, we might not know to look for it. We might miss "reactions" that weaken the technique. For example, suppose that our shoulder recoils when our fist hits the target. If we did not understand Newton's Third Law, we might not think to look for that recoil or recognize that every bit of recoil in our own shoulder represents less impact—"opposite reaction"—in the opponent. Yet in understanding and *applying* Newton's Third Law, we recognize that we want one-hundred percent of the "equal and opposite reaction" to occur in the opponent rather than in our own body.

Unfortunately, we often try to dismiss repercussions such as recoil as unavoidable. We tell ourselves that "there's always going to be *some* shoulder recoil." In fact, I have encountered instructors who when asked why a certain technique produces a certain result (or lack thereof), answer that "it just does." Yet nothing happens without explanation.

Which brings us to the third rule for principles: *All elements and results of all techniques can be broken down into and explained by principles.* In other words, everything happens (or fails to happen) for a *reason*(s). Nothing happens randomly.

Not only that, but a*ll principles interrelate yet never conflict.* Thus, if we return to the "opposite reaction" problem of shoulder recoil, we might need to look beyond Newton's Third Law to understand how the mechanics of the technique are causing the shoulder to react backwards. In other words, we cannot excuse any shoulder recoil on the ground that "there's always going to be some." That might be true were Newton's Third Law the only principle at work, but other principles equally impact the outcome. *Spinal Alignment, Indirect Pressure, Triangular Guard, Posture, Breath, Axis, Heaviness, and every principle listed in this text* (and others) affect Newton's Third Law, just as Newton's Third Law affects them. For that reason, many people find it very difficult to fix or improve particular elements of their technique in that any *one* overlooked or ill-applied principle will decrease the efficacy of other principles, as well as every technique we perform.

Granted, it often appears as though principles conflict. But that's illusion. If we examine two vague but important principles—the need to be *Defensively Sound* and the need to be *Offensively Powerful*—we might see them at odds with one another. Many traditional stylists, for example, learn to develop power by chambering the fist at the hip, thus connecting it to hip movement and affording it distance to develop momentum. Yet while possibly useful for developing *Offensive Power*, chambering the fist at the hip violates the need to be *Defensively Sound* it leaves the torso exposed. A far more *Defensively Sound* position involves keeping the hands up high, protecting the face and body, yet that would seem to undermine the *Offensive Power* of hip chambering.

However, as many experienced martial artists will agree, rather than being a problem of conflicting principles, this problem comes from a lack of proficiency. Experienced martial artists can cultivate as much (if not more) *Offensive Power* with their hands held in *Defensively Sound* positions as they can with their hands chambered at their hips. Therefore, the two principles do not really conflict, though it might seem that way to less experienced practitioners.[3]

Thus, principles not only will explain everything that happens in the martial arts, they also will explain how to accomplish everything we want to happen. As if that were not reason enough to study them, they offer other critical advantages: First, *studying a finite number of principles explains an infinite number of techniques*. While wrist lock number one differs from wrist lock two, three, four, five . . . twenty-three . . . etc., and all of them differ from shoulder throw one through twenty-seven, the number of principles remains constant.

Consider that a typical student might learn a block one day, a wrist lock the next day, a shoulder the day after, and so on. Learning so many *different techniques* can prove challenging, especially if the student sees no relationship between them. But what if those innumerable and different techniques could be viewed as a relative handful of principles? Under such a circumstance, the student would practice the same thing when blocking as when striking as when doing a shoulder throw as when doing a hip throw, ad infinitum. The context would change. The technique would change. The principles would not change.

In fact, once versed in principles, the student could look at *any* martial art and (to varying degrees) understand it because the student would see the same forces at work that are at work in his or her own style. The student would not instantly become proficient in other arts, but he or she could understand them and, most likely, learn them much more quickly.

In addition to explaining all martial arts, the study of principles offers us a common language. Rather than talking about what one art does differently from another art, we can talk about the same principles, albeit in different contexts. We can discuss and understand how *tai chi* and *karate* are governed by the same immutable, invariable forces. We can understand and appreciate our similarities.

That said, one hope I have for this book is that it will foster dialogue within the martial arts community. I am always saddened by discussions of which style is the best, especially when considering that we are all doing the same thing. We're all governed by the same principles. We all express the same principles. The rest is superficial. In fact, there's an old Chinese saying, "Bai Liu Ha Yi." It means, "A hundred styles flow into one." That does not advocate an "ultimate" style. It only means that we all practice "martial arts."

We all do the same thing differently.

---

3. I have no desire to advocate nor denigrate the use of hip chamber at this time. I use it only as an example. As with *all* examples in this text, understand the *principle* and do not worry about the particular application.

SECTION I
PRINCIPLES OF THEORY

"PRINCIPLES OF THEORY" REFERS TO THOSE CONSTANTS THAT GOVERN AND define the *idea* of martial arts. They define what we hope to achieve and *why*. I hope it obvious that we cannot proceed into the martial arts without first securing a concrete understanding of what a fighting system should achieve, why it must achieve that, and in what framework it must do so.

In short, knowing what we must accomplish dictates our choice of tools and the methodology of their employment. For example, challenged with transporting a pile of heavy stones fifty yards down a flat road, someone given a wheel and some lumber would be wise to construct a rudimentary wheelbarrow, one of the most significant and efficient tools of the pre-industrial era. Yet that same person would be foolish to build a wheelbarrow if the objective were to heave the stones to the top of a high, vertical platform. In such a case, a wise person probably would use the wheel and the lumber to construct a pulley system.

Thus, the nature of our objective governs the selection of tools and their use. Yet I have encountered many instructors who could not articulate a more specific martial goal for their art than that it "makes you fight well" or is "effective self-defense." While worthwhile goals to be sure, such answers strike me as vague. We need to ask what it means to "fight well." We need specific means through which to filter our selection of practices and techniques, and that is to what this section speaks.

Therefore, *Principles of Theory* seems like the logical starting place for a book on martial principles. Unfortunately, beginning with the theoretical as opposed to the physical delays discussion of the concrete and therefore could make the discussion of theory seem abstract, intangible, and impractical. Thus, I fear that it could prompt readers to object to what follows on the grounds that "it's all well and good in theory but reality is another matter." Such might be a reasonable response given the abstract nature of this section. However, reality and principles, even principles of theory, are never at odds. Any theory devoid of application serves no function. Therefore, *the principles in this section not only will help readers conceptualize the martial objective of the arts, it also will inform the nature of technique.* Therefore, I believe readers will recognize *Principles of Theory* as they actually are—perfectly pragmatic, if not outright essential. If not, the sections to follow will articulate how and why *Principles of Theory* are no less pragmatic than principles of punching.

1

The Principle
of Principles

*T*HE PRINCIPLE OF PRINCIPLES IS SIMPLE ENOUGH: *WE MUST EXERCISE all principles at all times to our highest understanding and without exception.* In other words, we must approach martial arts from the perspective of principles, and we must do so uncompromisingly. This proves itself true because, as the previous chapter demonstrated, if we are not acting with principles, principles still will act on us! One way or another, principles do not merely have *some* effect on technique, *principles govern everything that happens.* We can harness their power or be at their mercy.

By contrast, consider again the story I relayed in the introduction: My instructor, John Doe, plainly stated his belief that blocking and striking simultaneously worked more effectively than blocking and striking sequentially. While we ultimately may debate the value of simultaneity, we cannot debate John Doe's self-contradiction. He at once professed the value of the principle and then summarily disregarded it. Like John Doe, any time we dismiss, ignore, or fail to implement principles we find valuable, we degrade our technique.

Yet *The Principle of Principles* carries two exceptions: First, newer students might begin training with less-than-optimal versions of techniques. As with teaching students to generate power by chambering punches at the hip, the sacrifice of certain principles often proves *temporarily* permissible, if not useful, to facilitate coordination and student growth *provided that students do not habituate poor habits.* While less-than-optimally-principled motions might be acceptable for beginners, we must never employ *un*principled or *counter*-principled teachings.

The second exception concerns depth of understanding. I, for one, conceptualized many principles long before being able to integrate them into my practice of the arts. In fact, I still conceptualize many principles better than I apply them, and I suspect I always will. Yet I continue to integrate principles whenever and wherever possible, thus avoiding the same hypocrisy of which John Doe was guilty.

In other words, recognizing a principle's value binds us to it. In fact, recognizing a principle relegates us to a certain line of reasoning, one that mandates a veritable plunge into deeper and deeper applications of that principle. Consider, for example, the principle of *Economical Motion*—smaller, more efficient motions are better than larger, less efficient ones. Once we accept *Economical Motion* as valuable, it becomes a sink hole. As moving economically is superior to moving uneconomically, moving more economically must be superior to moving less economically, and so moving extremely economically must be superior to moving moderately economically, and so forth. Through such reasoning we have no choice but to conclude that *any motion less economical than it could be subsequently requires refinement.*

That, by the way, brings to light an imperfect but useful test for whether or not something is a principle. As with *Economical Motion*, most principles become recognizable not only by arguments supporting them but also, if not more importantly, because we cannot argue against them. Proficiency aside, I do not think that we can rightfully argue against *Economical Motion*. There appears to be possible rationale for devising, practicing, and applying *less* economical techniques. Who could construct a sensible argument for making techniques as *in*efficient as possible, or for making them at least a little less efficient whenever the opportunity presents itself? I cannot even envision such arguments.

The same cannot be said with respect to debates about styles and technique, which seem all too possible. We can argue for striking over grappling because it might damage someone faster and keep the opponent at a distance. We could argue for grappling over striking because it offers more control and because of our instinct to grab. Each one can counter the other on certain levels, just as every kind of *technique* has its own pros and cons. But while we can debate striking vs. grappling, we find no reasonable debate between being economical vs. uneconomical.

Consequently, we must make a healthy obsession of *Economical Motion*, as well as of every other principle, which means that we refine every technique, and every part of every technique, in the context of every known principle.

Thus, we do not measure principles by relative standards such as whether or not they work against a given opponent, within a given technique, in a given context, etc. Instead, we measure our exercise of principles by their ideal—perfectly *Economical* motion. While we will never attain perfection in any principle, to aspire to anything short of that seems foolhardy at best.

Yet we must follow all principles at all times. If we sacrifice *Power* so as to achieve *Economical Motion* then we failed to uphold the principle of

Power. Thus, *The Principle of Principles* means that we must follow *each and every* principle to its ultimate end with unrelenting dedication.

As James Webb said, "Where principle is involved, be deaf to expediency," and so could we equally say that *where principle is involved, be deaf to what is easy. The Principle of Principles* mandates that we do not succumb to what is easy or expedient, or even what is "good enough to get the job done." Thus, the fact that it might take time to understand and reconcile principles must not thwart our alliance with them.

There is, however, a lure to do just that, to give in to "expediency" and ease, to maintain the status quo. It is not easy to admit the need for change or modification in techniques we have practiced for years, if not tens of years, if not techniques with hundreds of years in lineage. Yet following *The Principle of Principles* means that we must at every given moment be willing to modify, if not completely re-envision, our techniques and training methods, even if that means disregarding years of previous practice and/or breaking from tradition. (In truth, I find modification far more common than radical transformation, but many minor modifications ultimately can lead to an entirely new product in the end.)

If change seems daunting, remember that *in studying principles we are studying the forces already at work in our techniques*. They will remain with us whether or not we respect them, so why not respect them? Therefore, we should not think of adapting techniques to principles as a matter of changing the techniques but rather as increasing our understanding of them, of their original intention, of their anatomical imperatives.

In conclusion, *The Principle of Principles* has four elements:

1. We must avoid the hypocrisy of disregarding or diminishing principles we acknowledge as valid.
2. We must pursue each principle not until we understand or express it "good enough" or satisfactorily, but rather tirelessly and infinitely towards perfection.
3. We must pursue all principles simultaneously as any sacrifice of any one principle violates number two above.
4. We must be "deaf to expediency" and ease.

2

Universality

To see a world in a grain of sand
And a heaven in a wild flower,
Hold infinity in the palm of your hand
And eternity in an hour.
—SIR WILLIAM BLAKE

A S PREVIOUSLY NOTED, WE CANNOT FOLLOW CERTAIN PRINCIPLES AND IGNORE others. While adopting any a lone principle probably will produce positive results, its true power will remain elusive until we implement all principles.

Fortunately, that does not pose too much of a problem because *Universality* tells us that all principles are omnipresent. Permitting for exceptions, every single martial arts technique involves every principle in some form. I say "in some form" because a given principle can appear radically different as the context varies.

This poses quite a challenge, forcing us to seek out the manner in which every single principle operates in every single technique. Despite its appearance, however, that task is not too daunting. Once we begin to view martial arts as an expression of principles rather than as a conglomeration of different techniques, the principles start to stand out and the techniques fade into the background.

At the same time, however, it reveals the truly magnificent truth that *the entire world of martial arts resides in any one technique.* A practitioner able to break down any one technique into all of its principles subsequently will be able to break down any and every technique into the same principles. By the same reasoning, a practitioner able to apply all the principles of any one given technique should be able to manifest those same principles (though differently) in every other technique. Thus, the theoretical mastery of (the principles within) a single technique would amount to mastery of all martial arts.

Putting aside the elusive goal of "mastery," principles constitute the language of martial arts. Understanding language leads to understanding all subjects. In other words, understanding English permits us to understand any topic written about in English, such as gardening, history, football, quantum physics, and martial arts. Similarly, understanding the language of martial arts—principles—permits us to understand any subject within martial arts—*Shorin-Ryu Karate, Daito-Ryu Aikijujitsu, Hung Gar Kung Fu, Escrima, Mongolian Wrestling*, etc.

3

The Pure Objective

I F WE APPLY THE SECOND ELEMENT OF *THE PRINCIPLE OF PRINCIPLES*—WE must pursue all principles towards perfection—to the combative goal of martial arts, we find it unsatisfactory to merely fight well enough to achieve victory. Winning alone becomes unsatisfying. While we obviously must prefer winning to losing, mere victory does not uphold the theoretical goal of our practice for two reasons: First, winning/losing represents an inconsistent if not arbitrary means to evaluate our technique because it depends on the relative skill of our opponent, and we do not measure principles by relative or inconsistent standards. Second, once we prefer fighting well to fighting poorly, we also must prefer fighting exceptionally well to fighting moderately well, and so forth. If followed to its end, such reasoning leads to an inescapable, two-part goal that I refer to as "The Pure Objective" because it speaks to such a simple, clean goal for martial combat:

1. Victory must be *instantaneous*.
2. Victory must be *effortless*.

As in the case of *Economical Motion*, the easiest way to argue for this entails pointing out the futility of arguments to the contrary. We find no way to advocate that martial arts *should* take a long time and involve a lot of work. Lengthy, exhausting techniques offer little appeal as a *goal*, and so we must resign ourselves to seek the opposite.

Despite how it might seem, however, *The Pure Objective* does not necessarily represent a lofty, unreachable goal. Were we to defeat a bear hug by grabbing our assailant's testicles, that would be a relatively instantaneous and effortless victory. While we can debate the merits of that particular technique, it serves to demonstrate the pragmatic nature of *The Pure Objective*. Still, perhaps some greater consideration would prove valuable.

With respect to part one—"Victory must be *instantaneous*"—I think it evident that we must prefer faster victory to slower victory, and therefore must prefer immediate victory to all else. In fact, we must recognize the danger in techniques that interfere with instantaneous victory. To illustrate this, I return to the simple example of blocking first and punching second, a tactic we find at some level and in some form in virtually every martial art. (If "block" does not meet your style, replace it with parry, pass, dodge, etc. I have no wish to fixate on any one particular technique but rather the concept behind it.)

The block itself, though defending the immediate attack, typically fails to end the conflict. While I do not deny that a basic block ultimately can contribute to victory, by creating an opening for counterattack, for example, we nevertheless must find it contrary to the goal of *instantaneous* victory, or at least not as well suited to it as other techniques are. Thus, we cannot be satisfied with techniques that merely *contribute* to a victory. *If we seek instantaneous victory then any technique that cannot deliver victory only interferes with our goal.*

Initially, this might appear too stringent a standard. Blocking, after all, serves us much better than getting hit. But our objective extends beyond "not getting hit"; our objective involves *instantaneous* victory. To that end, *the block only consumes an opportunity to execute a technique that could fulfill the Pure Objective.* In short, in that moment in which we are executing a block, which *for the sake of this argument* cannot end the fight in and of itself, we are not executing a strike or lock that could end the confrontation. In this sense, any technique not forwarding the ultimate aim is interfering with it.

Thus, we must judge techniques relative to our ultimate goal. For example, if we compare blocking first and striking second against simultaneous blocking and striking, we find the latter better suited to *The Pure Objective*. Thus, once we recognize the value of simultaneous defenses and counters, we must execute them whenever and wherever possible and practical, and whenever our proficiency will permit. To do any less violates *The Principle of Principles* and *The Pure Objective*.

Consider this same idea through the rock-moving metaphor. If we desire to move the rocks as quickly and efficiently as possible, we could make an excellent argument for building a sled. Given that the sled will permit one person to transport more rocks with less effort than carrying one stone at a time, it seems like a good choice. Relative to carrying each stone by hand, it *is* a good choice, but not so when contrasted against an even more efficient tool: the wheelbarrow. The sled is not bad; it's just not optimal. Thus, the point is not that blocking is bad; the point is that blocking is less optimal than other options.

To recap, because we cannot see an argument for wanting our victory to be prolonged, we must seek faster victories over longer victories, which ultimately leads to seeking instantaneous victories. Any technique that does not offer the *potential* for instantaneous victory—any technique that cannot in itself end the fight—consequently becomes inferior to one that can and, to varying degrees, contrary to *The Pure Objective.*

We use the same logic when examining the second part: "Victory should be *effortless.*" First, we obviously find no rationale for wanting techniques to require more effort. Given the choice between techniques that require intense struggle and techniques that more easily achieve comparable ends, we must seek the latter. It follows, therefore, that more-easily-applied techniques become preferred over less-easily-applied techniques, which eventually leads us to desiring techniques that require no effort at all. (Note that I am *not* discussing the *training* of a technique, which might and probably should be exceptionally difficult and to which we should devote untold amounts of effort. Rather, I am speaking to the nature of the technique as applied after it has been "learned.")

On a more physical level, we must work from the premise that attackers will be bigger or stronger, or bigger *and* stronger, than ourselves. After all, smaller, weaker people seldom attack bigger, stronger people. More to the point, we must presume a physical deficit if only because it is that eventuality for which we must be most prepared. We presume that big, strong people do not *need* martial arts to win against small, weak, untrained people. Therefore, it is smaller, weaker people who *need* martial arts if they are to win against physically superior opponents, and so we must train with physically superior attackers in mind.

To exemplify the point, consider this short cast of characters that I will use for the remainder of the book: Supposing equal proficiency, Joe, at 6'2" and 185 lbs, would have little to fear from Jane, who stands at 5'1" and weighs 110 lbs. Joe hardly would reasonably expect to be attacked by Jane, and Joe should not *need* martial arts ability to defeat an equally unskilled Jane. Therefore, a Joe would not take up martial arts on the premise of having to learn how to defeat a Jane, but a Jane would take up martial arts on the premise of having to defeat a Joe. Yet both Joe and Jane need be concerned with defeating the likes of "Gargantua," my nightmare opponent. At seven feet tall and 400 pounds of chiseled muscle, and in addition to being a trained fighter, Gargantua is not only high on PCP, he also operates under the misguided belief that I assaulted his dear old mother.

Therefore, "effortlessness" does not necessarily mean a complete lack of expenditure of energy, but must mean an utter lack of conflict of *strength* (note that I said "strength," not "power"). This conclusion seems inescapable because a Jane obviously will not be able to out-muscle a Joe, to say nothing of a Gargantua. In other words, both Joe and Gargantua can exert a far greater amount of physical strength than Jane. Jane's hope, therefore, *must* lie in martial techniques that enable her to defeat an opponent without having to overpower them through physical strength. (Note that this is *not* advocacy of "soft" styles over "hard" styles but rather a statement as to the nature of power.)

Furthermore, as we shall see later on, exertion can consume rather than generate force. I will discuss that in the *Percentage Principle* and *Relaxation* but for now suffice it to say that every percentage point of force held in our body equals one less percentage point of energy we can transfer to our opponent. Despite how it might seem, this again does *not* necessarily advocate "soft" or "internal" styles. Regardless of style, as techniques grow more anatomically sound and as we become more proficient at our techniques, our bodies require less physical tension to express them, even if only because the movements become more natural and less strained, and more ingrained in our neuromuscular system.

I should note that I have no interest in condemning strength, which can be a great ally when harmonized with technique. Yet strength and effort cannot be relied upon *as* technique because we inevitably must concern ourselves with larger, stronger opponents.

Ultimately, *The Pure Objective* requires us to filter every technique through the following two questions:

1. Given a reasonable level of proficiency, does the technique in question hold the *potential* for a smaller person to effortlessly apply it against the larger person?
2. Given a reasonable level of proficiency, does the technique in question hold the *potential* to instantaneously bring victory?

Obviously, "reasonable level of proficiency" becomes the operative phrase. When I was younger, for example, I found myself in schools where I was told that technique X could put an opponent down, but I did not see anyone, instructors and "masters" alike, who could do so. Thus, I remained unpersuaded that the technique held the *potential* its practitioners claimed.

Yet we need not dismiss every technique we do not see demonstrated. I personally cannot apply certain techniques well enough to fulfill *The Pure Objective*, but I can demonstrate that they hold the *potential* to do so. Any technique that does not hold such a potential is a technique I can do without, and as martial artists we must seek to refine our practice of the arts by a similar standard.

Having dealt with the purely combative elements of *The Pure Objective*, I will add a third:

3. Techniques should not harm the opponent.

Ultimately, proficiency in martial arts technique must contend with serious considerations of morality. Since the martial arts seek masterful expertise in combat, it stands to reason that true expertise must include the *option* to not-harm the opponent. Given the practitioner who *must* harm to win vs. the practitioner who equally may or may not harm, we must find the latter superior if only because he or she possesses more options—an increased freedom and ability to act—and thus more power. In other words, the practitioner who must harm is more limited, and therefore less masterful, than the practitioner who *may* harm. True mastery of martial arts, therefore, must include the option of compassion, an option we would hope to exercise whenever possible.

4

Control

IT TOOK ME YEARS TO REALIZE THIS BUT THE NOTION THAT MARTIAL ARTS IS about winning fights is not only erroneous, it actually distracts us from and even inhibits our acquisition of true power. That might sound contradictory to *The Pure Objective,* and it might sound as though I am going to begin a discussion of esoteric values—character development, enlightenment, peacefulness, etc. Yet while I affirm each and every one of those values, my point lies elsewhere. It lies in the seeming paradox that the more we attempt to win a fight, the more prone we become to losing one.

Here's why: Focusing on fighting well means focusing on how much our techniques affect the *opponent*, as in forcing the opponent down, crippling the opponent with our strikes, submitting the opponent through a joint locks, etc. Yet the opponent must be of little concern relative to integrity of our own actions. Put another way, focusing on affecting the opponent only leads us to compromise our own execution of martial arts.

Anyone who has witnessed sparring has seen this occur. In an effort to land a strike, martial artists all too often compromise their posture, overextend their techniques, leave rather noticeable openings in their defense, and commit an assortment of other indiscretions that end up doing more harm than good and that undermine their expression of their art. This same problem extends to all areas of martial arts, not just sparring. When we become single-minded about the *opponent*, we sacrifice some measure of technique.

I spent quite a few years caught in this trap. I focused on affecting my opponent, on making sure my techniques "worked," which I viewed as the ultimate goal of the arts. While we do need to affect the opponent if we are to fulfill *The Pure Objective,* the real objective involves keeping control of ourselves. Lacking control results in two potential outcomes: we'll either win but do so purely by chance or we will lose.

Yet while we *might* win a fight by chance when lacking control, *we cannot lose a fight when in control.* As long as we maintain complete control of ourselves, defeat remains impossible because what is "defeat" if not in some fashion being controlled by the opponent? Is that not the core of combat? Are not all techniques first and foremost about *controlling?* Punches, joint locks, throws, chokes, etc. all attempt to establish *Control* one way or another, to have our will (to knock down, knock out, injure, etc.) manifest in the opponent.

Thus, (1) the extent to which an opponent remains in control of his or her own self is the extent to which we must overcome that control, and (2) the extent to which we lack control of our own self is the extent to which we aid the opponent in controlling us. From this perspective, all martial arts training concerns gaining control over ourselves, as in controlling our response to attacks through the exercise of techniques. Therefore, the greater our *Control* over ourselves, which comes through principles and technique, the greater our *Control* over the situation/fight. And as we shall see later on, the fight and the opponent are one in the same.

Consequently, maintaining or re-establishing control becomes the primary impetus for martial training. On a physical level, that means *Controlling* our body and not permitting it to fall under someone else's control, as might happen when being hit, thrown, pushed, etc. We seek to maintain physical autonomy. We seek to prevent an aggressor from manipulating, even injuring, our physical selves.

In truth, such physical concerns stem from psychological roots. After all, what could put us in greater psychological chaos than the manipulation of our very bodies? Consider being pushed, something typically too mild to injure. It represents no real physical threat. The problem comes in feeling psychologically "pushed." It makes us feel out of control.

The same applies to injury and pain, which we rightfully try to avoid. Pain not only hurts, it also points out that we lack so much *Control* over our physical body that someone else can injure it. And because it hurts, it takes control of our minds by demanding our attention.

Yet we also train in martial arts to control our emotions, most notably fear. We want to walk home at night (go to a bar, walk the hallways of school, etc.) without having to worry. In fact, we not only want to diminish our fears but also diminish the fear of fear—the worry that we will be made to worry. In essence, we seek to prevent circumstances (or potential circumstances) from controlling us psychologically—fearing them—before we actually enter them.

Regardless of the particular motivation and no matter how we examine a fight scenario, *Control* becomes the dominant issue. For example, the jealous boyfriend who assaults us for unwittingly striking up a conversation with his girlfriend does so out of insecurity about his relationship with her. He assaults us to eliminate a theoretical threat to his relationship, i.e. to maintain *Control* over it. Were he secure in himself and his relationship then he certainly would not *fear* our approach.

Thus, because he cannot control the internal—his emotions, his faith in the relationship—he seeks to control the external. Instead of making the relationship sound he chooses to act upon those who might threaten it. Were it sound then no one could threaten it, and he would perceive no cause to act violently.

In fact, anyone who feels out of control in his or her life—disempowered— might seek to regain a temporary *sense* of control through controlling someone else. Such a person might feel better about his or her own circumstances by making someone else's circumstances even worse.

Yet while all of this rather abstract discussion of emotions and psychology might seem distant from martial technique, it isn't. Martial *technique* seeks to maintain or regain *Control* of a situation/person rather than have it/him/her control us. However, if we concern ourselves with affecting the opponent, presumably in response to an attack, then we commit the same error as the jealous boyfriend: *we attempt to control the external to compensate for a lack of control over the internal.* At its core, martial arts does not concern affecting the opponent through striking and grappling. That is the red herring. Martial arts involves *gaining/maintaining control over ourselves no matter how adverse the combative situation.* We train first to gain control over our own bodies and minds—coordination, self-discipline, confidence, etc. We then seek to maintain that control despite combative conflict, such as when grabbed, tackled, or hit.

That marks the critical conceptual difference between the aggressor and the defender. Because the aggressor (1) lacks a certain measure of control over his or her own life, emotions, relationship, etc., he or she (2) seeks to control the outside world to regain an internal feeling of control. The trained martial artist acts from the opposite motivation. Being (1) in control of his or her person and circumstance, he or she (2) chooses to prevent aggressors from taking away that control. In doing so, the defender acts on the aggressor, *but affecting the aggressor is not the objective. The objective is to maintain control of the self.*

This distinction effectively defines how we must approach technique. Since we foremost seek to *maintain* control of the self, we first must *possess* control of the self. We must establish control over our own body, *so much control over our own body that it cannot be controlled by another body—* a radically different mindset than concerning ourselves with establishing control over another person (so as to ameliorate a feeling of internal chaos).

In other words, we seek to have (1) more control over our own bodies than our opponents have over their own bodies and (2) more control over our own bodies than our opponents will have over us.

Unfortunately, those who approach martial arts as a means to control the *other* become prone to sacrificing self-control, which only defeats their initial objective. As I mentioned, this tendency might become manifest in sacrificing posture to execute a takedown, or leaving an opening while over-extending to land a punch, or some other sacrifice of integrity for the sake of controlling the opponent. Thus, we must *conceptualize* martial arts as an exercise of *Control*, and realize that control begins and ends with the self, which means that we must approach every single technique as a riddle of control: how can we best maintain control of ourselves in this situation? Only after successfully answering that question can we concern ourselves with how we might exploit our opponent's lack of control.

The aggressor, on the other hand, does not mind losing control of the self because he or she never possessed it. If our opponent possessed self-control then he or she would not feel compelled to attack. It follows, as well, that opponents will willingly sacrifice physical self-control to gain control over us, especially since controlling us provides them with the greater *sense* of control they seek. That serves our purposes well because if we have self-control then we can more easily exploit those who do not.

Therefore, we must practice only those techniques that cultivate self-control. It makes no sense to suggest that we can gain control over any situation by first *losing* control of ourselves.

5

Lengthening Our Line

TOO MANY MARTIAL ARTISTS ATTEMPT TO EXPLAIN AWAY THEIR DEFICIENCIES by placing the blame on the opponent, arguing that certain physical deficits will be insurmountable, e.g. that a Jane could not possibly be expected to apply a wrist lock to a Gargantua. Proficiency aside, we ultimately cannot hold the martial arts responsible for a lack of success.

After all, any martial art that fails to presume the presence of violence against us cannot be said to be a martial art at all. And any martial art failing to realize that such violence probably will come in the form of bigger, stronger attackers cannot be called an effective martial art. As I mentioned before, what possible need do we have for a martial art that only allows us to defeat physically inferior people? Therefore, the very premise of a martial art must be that we can defeat otherwise superior physical aggression.

Consequently, *because we can only call a martial art a "martial art" if it presumes and defeats physically superior aggression*, any failures on our parts to defeat aggression cannot be blamed on the martial arts. While I am not necessarily arguing that we should be able to dodge bullets, if we cannot defeat an opponent then our understanding and/or application of the martial arts must be the problem.

Looking at this same premise from the perspective of *Control*, the martial arts assumes (1) that people will try to exert control over us and (2) that our techniques permit us to remain in control despite that fact. Therefore, we cannot blame attackers for trying to control us because the martial arts presumes that we will remain in control of ourselves not only under normal circumstances—when anyone should be able to maintain control—but *when some outside force is attempting to exert physical control over us through violence.*

A simple wrist grab demonstrates the point. No matter what martial art we practice, any response to that wrist grab, such as a wrist escape, throw, joint lock, counterstrike, etc., seeks to regain control of our wrist, the situation, and ourselves. Thus, martial arts works on the very premise that we will in some manner be able to re-establish control over a combative situation.

Hence the daunting reality of personal responsibility: Because the premise of martial arts is that we can maintain control of self despite being attacked, we have no choice but to view loss of control as representative of our own deficiencies, be they in our art, our understanding of our art, our understanding of martial theory, etc. It probably is some combination of all those, but it certainly is *not the fault of the attacker or the attack.*

A non-martial artist enjoys greater liberty. Such a person justifiably could blame an attack or attacker for a loss of personal control because that person has not trained to neutralize aggression. However, if a martial artist blames an attacker for a loss of control of self then it amounts to nothing short of scapegoating.

Thus, a simple equation:

Martial arts has the potential to maintain control

\+ martial arts failed to achieve that control

\= some understanding and/or application of martial arts on

our part proved insufficient to the task.

Yet the logic follows to a deeper and even more daunting level. If we bear responsibility for failing to *regain* control of a situation, must not we equally bear responsibility for losing control of the situation in the first place? If Jane, Joe, Gargantua, or anyone else can *establish* a measure of control over us, it is because we are not centered enough, grounded enough, postured well enough, did not react well enough, etc. to begin with.

Put another way, were Jane *perfectly* centered, would even the likes of Gargantua be able to budge her? No. Thus, that Gargantua can establish *any* measure of control over Jane is Jane's "fault" as a martial artist, though obviously not so as an imperfect human being. Obviously, as a martial artist, Jane must pre-suppose the possibility of being grabbed by Gargantua and thus cannot blame Gargantua for putting her in a grab that she already envisioned. Such would be akin to a quarterback being surprised by the pass rush, or to bend Bruce Lee's analogy, a swimmer being surprised by the water.

Of course, none of us will achieve perfection. All martial artists have their limits, and we cannot but expect that we might encounter persons who can grab harder than our proficiency can counter. The question, however, is whether or not our art holds the *potential* to overcome grabs of any strength. The second question is whether or not we practice towards that aim.

(Perhaps it would be useful to note here that the phrase "strength and size do not matter in martial arts" strikes me as only partially accurate. A more accurate statement would be that "strength and size *ultimately* do not matter in martial arts," which means that they do play a role, albeit a surmountable one. Someone giving up 50lbs must achieve less centeredness to overcome his or her attacker than someone giving up 100lbs. The more important question concerns whether or not each deficit *can* be overcome through martial technique. Thus, size and strength matter in relative, temporary terms, but martial arts can overcome them.)

All of this points to personal responsibility as *critical* to martial training, an idea no one captured more poignantly than Joe Hyams in his classic, *Zen in the Martial Arts*. Hyams recounts an exchange with Kenpo pioneer, Ed Parker. Parker drew a line and asked Hyams how to make it shorter. Hyams proposed various methods until Parker finally drew a second line beside the first, the new one being notably longer than the first.

"How does the first line look now?" Parker asked.

"Shorter," replied Hyams.

I read that story a long time ago but did not understand its importance until more recently. I realized that much of my martial arts practice had been focused on making the attacker's line shorter, when it should have been on making my own line longer. The contrast seems small but it might be the single most important conceptual lesson I have learned.

If we return to our wrist grab and consider a simple defense, such as prying out of it, we find that there are two fundamental ways to approach the situation. The first potential line of response would be to kick, punch, pinch, etc. so as to weaken the attacker's grip and thus shorten the attacker's line, which means diminishing the general quality the grab itself. At first, this seems perfectly in accord with *The Pure Objective* and the general goals of the martial arts. Upon closer inspection, however, and when viewed in terms of lengths of lines and issues of *Control*, we find that it neither improves ourselves nor our technique. Why? Because it hinges *on diminishing the quality of the attack rather than improving the quality of the defense*. It makes the opponent less powerful *instead* of making us more powerful.

If we can pry out of a grab only when there is not much of a grab at all then our technique is obviously lacking. Doing so concedes from the outset that a wrist grab *can* control us. It works from the premise that attackers have more power than we do. In fact, it suggests that we cannot make our own line longer than the given attack. Such a defense presumes that the attacker can, or must, have control of our wrist, that we have no choice but to be at a disadvantage.

Now let us approach the same scenario from the converse perspective. What if, instead of distracting the attacker and diminishing the quality of the attack, we instead examine our own deficiencies to understand why the attacker can have any control at all. That the attacker might be in possession of our wrist should not *necessarily* dictate that the attacker has gained any control over our person. Since we know that if we were perfectly centered the attacker would not exert control, we must look at the elements of our own self—centeredness, posture, anatomy, etc.—that permit the attacker some control over us. Thus, we approach technique not from the perspective of diminishing the attack—shortening the attacker's line—but from the perspective of improving ourselves relative to the attack—lengthening the lines so as to make the attacker's line "shorter" by contrast. In addition, we not only examine ourselves but our technique, or more importantly, the principles expressed through that technique. After all, a *wrist escape that cannot escape a wrist grab is not a wrist escape at all.*

What we find is that the martial arts do offer the *potential* for us to maintain control no matter how powerful the attack and/or attacker. Yet note that this discussion concerns the inherent potential of martial arts, not our proficiency. Therefore, were I to find myself in an actual conflict and grabbed in such a way that I did not feel I could escape without first shortening the opponent's line, I most certainly would do so. Thus, I believe such tactics are worth knowing and worth practicing. *However*, I find that exercising them as the mainstay of martial training only limits my understanding and proficiency because it excuses me from having to gain enough insight into techniques to make them work against longer lines. Thus, I typically train against the strongest grab I can manage, or perhaps a little stronger than I can manage, and practice escapes that do not require distractions and strikes so that I learn to lengthen my line and eventually discover technique that counters even the strongest grip.

Thus, techniques always should possess the inherent power to defeat the anticipated attack, no matter how powerful it might be, period. At the same time, any technique in which we do not find the *potential* to defeat stronger attacks must be questioned. Either we must deepen our understanding of its principles and make it applicable or we must discard it. Obviously, that seems like a rather hard-lined stance on the matter, but I see no rationale for betting my very life on techniques devoid of the inherent capacity to achieve the necessary aims.

6

Efficiency

WHEREAS *ECONOMY OF MOTION,* WHICH WILL BE DISCUSSED LATER ON, refers specifically to physical motion, *Efficiency* concerns how we conceive of and practice martial arts, including its curriculum, its pedagogical method, its approach to combat, etc.

Efficiency challenges us to streamline our arts. We should exclude any technique that does not have the realistic potential to fulfill *The Pure Objective*. As I noted in the previous chapter, martial arts concern a life and death struggle. It is not play. It affords no room for dilly-dallying, no room for error. Therefore, we have no choice but to view any technique insufficient to our needs as an obstacle in several regards:

First, it consumes training time that otherwise could have been devoted to more fulfilling techniques. Every minute we devote to a technique that might manifest some nice combative elements but ultimately does not offer the outcome we require is a minute we could have spent on a more valuable technique.

Second, practicing less-than-optimal techniques also habituates us to them, developing *Reflexive Action* and other tendencies we might need to unlearn, or at the very least modify, when we do eventually turn our time toward more optimal expressions of *The Pure Objective*.

Third, practicing inefficient techniques produces the perception effect of progress despite the fact that we might be moving in a wrong direction. We *feel* as though we are becoming more proficient, and in certain respects we obviously are, but we are not necessarily moving any closer to our final goal—*The Pure Objective*.

Fourth, and perhaps most importantly, any technique that does not defeat the opponent, and "defeat" does not necessarily mean harm, provides the opponent with more time to act against us, and with more time comes more opportunity to succeed. I will discuss this further when I speak to the *Offensive Advantage/Defensive Disadvantage*, but for now it will suffice to say that every additional opportunity we offer the opponent to attack results in yet one more attack we need to defend. What could be less efficient than offering the attacker additional opportunities to continue attacking?

Thus, *every technique should in and of itself hold the potential to end a confrontation instantaneously and effortlessly*, and that should hold equally true for parts of combinations of techniques. If we were to examine a block, punch, kick, throw combination, we optimally should find that the block, the punch, the kick, *and* the throw *each* hold the potential to end the confrontation.

Remember that I am speaking to a systemic objective—the goal of martial arts. I am not necessarily suggesting that every martial art immediately present the solution to the *Efficiency* conundrum. For example, I cannot say that every technique I teach has the potential to fulfill *The Pure Objective*. There are some that do not yet, some for which I am seeking superior replacements. Perhaps your style already fulfills the objective in every movement. Perhaps not. The dominant question, however, asks whether or not *Efficiency* and *The Pure Objective* are dealt with seriously.

We can examine *Efficiency* from a slightly different perspective, as well. We first might examine techniques in groups: Does combination X—such as cross block, counter punch, leg sweep—offer the potential to fulfill *The Pure Objective*? Do all combinations we practice offer such potential? From that point, we could begin to break the combinations down: If taken individually, which techniques in the combination could end the confrontation in and of themselves? Could we form new combinations using just those parts? Would that be a more efficient way to train? A more efficient use of our time?

We must ask such questions if serious about our martial arts training. Once again it comes down to finding no opposing argument of merit. I simply cannot see an argument for devoting time, habituation, and even our potential safety to techniques that ultimately cannot achieve what the final analysis requires.

7

The Percentage Principle

*T*HE PERCENTAGE PRINCIPLE LOOKS REMARKABLY SIMPLE IN CONCEPT, AND yet it might be the principle that unvaryingly poses us the greatest challenge. From a certain perspective, and as with many other principles, this entire text could be brought under the umbrella of this one principle.

Simply, *The Percentage Principle* states a basic truth: *any one body can generate only a finite amount of force at any given moment.* Of course, the quantity of that force will vary depending on the body in question and its training, nor can we measure the total amount of force a particular person can generate at a particular time. Even if we measure the power of a punch in pounds per square inch, that only accounts for the amount of power generated against the pad, not the *total power expended by that person when punching*, which usually includes exertion in other parts of the body. Hence, we cannot measure the total amount of power that a person generates.

Therefore, *The Percentage Principle* does not reference the amount of power in a punch. And that's the problem. If we all converted the full percentage of our body's power expenditure into a given technique then we would fulfill *The Percentage Principle.* Unfortunately, *The Percentage Principle* holds importance because we almost invariably *fail* to punch with the full percentage of our body's output. In other words, while our goal entails acting with 100% of our body's energy output, we typically use only a fraction of that percentage towards any given technique. Some percentage of the force we generate ends up consumed by unnecessary muscle tension, inefficient technique, a lack of proper intent, etc. Many of the chapters to follow speak specifically to the ways we fail to employ the full measure of the power we generate. For now, however, I content myself with describing the principle itself, and making it clear that we must strive to employ the full percentage of the power we generate in any given moment.

Honestly though, I do not think I've seen any martial artist use a full 100% of his or her power, but I have seen some rare individuals come close. By contrast, I find that most novice martial artists use only a small percentage of their power in their techniques, perhaps as little as ten- or twenty percent, though that figure obviously varies depending on the individual.

Beginners and black belts alike, many martial artists fail to use high percentages of their power because they do not approach technique with this principle in mind. While they deeply, if not obsessively, concern themselves with expending a lot of effort, they often overlook an issue of greater importance: the percentage of their generated force that actually makes it into the technique. If our strike represents only 25% of the power our body generated then it is not how hard we hit that needs work, per se. What needs work is getting a higher percentage of our force to the target.

We can analogize this to a bow and arrow. In archery, it would be erroneous to merely concern ourselves with the power of the bow. True, a 100-pound test bow ultimately can generate greater power than a 50-pound test bow. But the art of archery involves a great deal more than the draw power of the bow. For example, it involves the relative cleanliness of the release. Someone using a 100-pound bow with a poor release will realize only a fraction of the bow's raw power-potential. In addition to the finger release itself, the final power actually communicated to the target also will depend on the how smoothly the arrow passes the shaft of the bow, how straight the feathers keep the flight, the quality of the tip, and an assortment of other issues that expert archers balance.

The same holds true for martial arts. We invariably concern ourselves with how much power we're *generating*, i.e. the pull of our bow. Yet that accounts for only a fraction of the power communicating through technique. Granted, we can never communicate more power than we generate, but we can strive to communicate the full sum of it. Thus, if we work from the premise that Gargantua can generate far more power than Jane, which does not necessarily hold true, he nevertheless might strike with less force. If he is unduly tense, if his physical structure proves faulty, if his motions waste energy, etc. then he communicates only a small fraction of his overall power. Jane, on the other hand, if well trained and highly conscious of *The Percentage Principle* might generate far less power but strike more powerfully nonetheless.

As always, we must remember that it is not Gargantua against whom Jane must measure herself. Jane, like all of us, Gargantua included, must measure ourselves against the principle itself. Whether Jane can communicate more power than Gargantua might matter if they actually fight, but as a martial artist Jane simply must strive to communicate 100% of her power.

8

A Standard of
Infinite Measure

*He who is fixed to a star does not
change his mind.*

—LEONARDO DA VINCI

HOW DO WE KNOW WHAT MAKES FOR EFFECTIVE TECHNIQUE? IT SEEMS LIKE such a simple question, and yet against what standard are we to measure our practice of the arts? We cannot simply measure them by their popularity or their heritage. That many people practice a technique does not make it sound. That it is an old or new technique does not make it sound.

Yet martial arts offer an obvious standard of measure for determining the effectiveness of a given technique. It's a simple question: Does it work? First, does it function in the context for which it is designed? Sport techniques, for example, might not be suited for street fighting, but do sport techniques work in the context of sport fighting? As this book emphasizes self-defense, does a technique work in a given self-defense scenario, against a skilled opponent who will resist at every available opportunity and in every conceivable manner?

Bruce Lee deserves considerable credit for advancing the "whatever works" philosophy. His process was simple—he put techniques to the test. If he could apply it against a resisting opponent then it worked, and if he could not then it did not, and there was no adherence to technique except for that measure. On the whole, this seems like a valid, if not essential process of examination for all techniques. After all, if the martial arts truly concern self-defense, we cannot afford to stake our well being on untested techniques. Similarly, we certainly would be foolish to apply the "whatever doesn't work" philosophy, as that sounds a tad less logical. Thus, while allotting for level of skill, I am a firm proponent of asking the "does it work" question. I cannot see a way around its value.

At the same time, however, we must acknowledge that "does it work?" is an inconsistent, if not outright arbitrary standard of measure because what "works" against one person might not work against another. It might work against a Joe but not against a Gargantua. It might work against a slower opponent but not against a faster opponent, or a shorter opponent but not a taller one, or a right handed opponent but not a left handed one, or . . . Thus, the "does it work?" measure varies greatly.

Yet in *addition* to the "does it work" measure, we have *principles*. Perfect *Efficiency* as an ideal does not waver. It does not fluctuate from person to person or situation to situation. It is a constant. It is a constant we will never reach but it is a constant nonetheless. All principles are equally constant. Thus, they permit us no complacency. We may indulge no luxury in having defeated any given opponent or even all opponents for such victories do not bring us any closer to the ideal of fulfilling principle.

It is like William Faulkner wrote: "Don't bother just to be better than your contemporaries or predecessors. Try to be better than yourself." It shall come as no surprise to my readers that we always can improve on ourselves. There is no revelation in that. But what does it mean to "improve"? As Faulkner pointed out, it is not "just" a matter of using those around us as a measure of our own improvement ("does it work?"). Rather, it means evaluating ourselves between two points, between where we are and the ideal.

Paradoxically, we are forever and ever in point a, never to escape it. And though we improve every day, we'll never reach point b. But we can measure our growth by point b. We might not be able to determine our precise proximity to it, but we can know if it grows nearer.

9

The Power Paradox

*T*HE *POWER PARADOX* DEFINES THE VERY NATURE OF POWER ITSELF:

1. True power feels, and actually should be, effortless.
2. That which feels like powerful exertion is not.

The nature of power—true power—*must* be as described. There is no alternative.

If we define power as a ratio between the amounts of effort relative to the degree of effect, then the greater the effort required to produce a given effect, the less powerful we must be. The less effort required, the more powerful we must be. Thus, because Joe and Jane each would expend greater effort than Gargantua in lifting a barbell, regardless of its weight, Joe and Jane are less powerful than Gargantua *in that regard*.

Yet in lifting barbells everyone would expend at least some effort, even Gargantua! He might find it *relatively* effortless but probably not actually effortless in the purest sense. Actualized effortlessness, however, constitutes our goal in martial technique (see *The Pure Objective*). Thus, when I work with other martial artists, I often ask how a technique feels. If their response indicates that it "feels powerful" or that they feel powerful while doing it then that's a sign that it needs work. Why? Because a technique that feels powerful cannot actually be powerful, and it cannot actually be powerful because the feeling of power emerges from the sensation of exertion, and greater exertion means less power.

Consider punching a heavy bag. If we strike the bag and feel only a little bit of impact in our fist, it could be correct to conclude that we have not hit bag very hard. Determined to hit harder the next time, we summon up all our force, increase our effort and really give the bag a good hit. Still not satisfied, we reside ourselves to really giving the bag a good shot and sum-

mon all the effort possible, feeling a great deal of impact on our fist and seeing a greater effect in the bag itself. We have hit harder, yes, *but not more
powerfully.*

You see, many people confuse "harder" with "more powerful." If we
strike with greater impact through an increase of effort then *the ratio
between effort and effect has not changed,* and if the effort vs. effect ratio
does not change than our *power* remains unchanged. Thus, if we only
achieve a greater effect through greater effort, we have not become more
powerful, we only have worked harder. (Thus, a simple motto: "You can't
work harder for power.") Only when we produce a greater effect through
equal effort, an equal effect through less effort, or a greater effect through
less effort can we be said to have increased our power. Thus, *The Power
Paradox* manifests itself: If we hit "harder" through a greater expenditure
of effort, then we have not hit more "powerfully."

Many people find this counterintuitive. I think we all possess at least
some natural inclination to associate a greater effect with greater effort. In
fact, it actually *feels* more powerful when we expend more effort. We want
to feel "strong" or like we're working hard. Yet who is more powerful, Joe,
who puts Gargantua down through a wrist lock by expending a great deal
of effort, or Jane, who puts Gargantua down effortlessly through the same
technique?

Or consider this example: if we strike the bag and feel a great impact
on our fist, we associate that sensation of impact with power. If *feels* like
we hit hard, and we intuitively associate that feeling with power. Yet a hard
impact actually represents little power. Were we to punch into a big block
of gelatin, we would not feel a significant impact because the force of our
strike would be so far superior to the structural integrity of gelatin that it
would penetrate easily. The fist simply would not encounter enough resistance to induce the sensation of a hard impact.

Thus, the reason we sense impact when striking a heavy bag emerges
from the *resistance* we encounter upon meeting it. "Resistance," after all,
denotes the capacity of the bag to work *against* us—to *resist* us. Thus, the
extent to which it can resist us is the extent to which we do not overpower
it. Were we truly powerful in striking, we would overwhelm the bag with
power and thus encounter no resistance, effectively feeling virtually no
impact whatsoever, just like punching gelatin.

Of course, all of this remains contingent on effect. If we strike and feel
virtually no impact but create virtually no effect, we have accomplished
nothing. Instead, we seek to create an equal or greater effect with lesser and
lesser effort.

As I said, however, true power proves counterintuitive for most people, even for many martial artists. When I work with martial artists on a
technique, many often approach it through the effort-equals-effect method.

Yet once they align the principles of the technique properly, the technique happens with *relative* effortlessness, and they usually start chuckling in disbelief.

"But I didn't do anything," they say.

To which I respond, "That is why it worked." For that is the nature of real power.

Yet I do not mean to make this sound magical. Rather, the explanation for *The Power Paradox* really could not be simpler. If in executing technique we properly align all those principles that make us powerful while simultaneously exploiting the ways in which our opponent has failed to align his or her principles, we then cannot help but to encounter no effectual resistance. By acting in a way in which he or she is most powerful and by acting against the ways the opponent is least powerful, even the smallest person should experience little difficulty in defeating the largest person.

Regardless, the principle of *The Power Paradox* now should be clear. True power should be effortless and feel effortless.

10

Ratio

I TOUCHED ON THIS EARLIER WITH RESPECT TO *THE PURE OBJECTIVE* BUT IT warrants considerably more discussion. The *Ratio* principle concerns the relationship between energy and effect as manifested five different ways:

> *Ratio*[1]: Effort vs. Yield
> *Ratio*[2]: Power vs. Yield
> *Ratio*[3]: Movement vs. Yield
> *Ratio*[4]: Time vs. Yield
> *Ratio*[5]: Space vs. Yield

Dealing first with *Ratio*[1]: as martial artists we want a *positive ratio* of effort vs. yield, with "effort" referring to the energy we exert in executing a technique (which ultimately should be relatively nothing) and "yield" referring to how much we affect our opponent. A *positive* effort to yield *Ratio* means that our technique produces a greater effect on the opponent than the effort we expended in its execution.

Unfortunately, so many martial artists suffer from *negative ratios*. We see them exerting a great deal of effort into a punch only to see little result on the target. Given the amount of effort expended, we should expect to see extraordinary repercussions in what they hit. If a 150 pound person exerts all possible effort into a wrist throw against another 150 pound person and fails to execute that throw, the *Ratio* must be deficient by definition. If the same 150 person executes the throw with satisfactory success then that constitutes an equal *Ratio* between effort and effect. Yet if that that 150 pound person throws a 300 pound person with rousing success then we find a favorable *Ratio* between effort and effect.

As I discussed earlier, however, the real goal involves expending less and less effort while achieving greater and greater results, especially since *effort eats power*, which will be discussed in *Relaxation*. Therefore, we not only want to produce the same effect through less and less effort, we also want to produce a greater effect through less and less effort.

Yet effort is not the only issue. *Ratio*^{2} concerns the amount of *power* in a technique vs. the amount of effect. At first it probably seems impossible to produce anything but an equal ratio between power and effect. After all, if two punches contain an identical amount of power, how can one punch produce a greater effect than the other? The answer comes in *how* that power gets delivered to the target. Different striking techniques will communicate the same quantity of power to different results.

Consider pool: The cue stick strikes the cue ball and fills it with inertia. As the cue ball strikes against the eight ball, the eight ball, identical in mass to the cue ball, receives all the cue ball's energy and inertia. Consequently, the cue ball stops in its tracks and propels the eight ball forward. Supposing there was no loss of energy when they hit and no gravity at work, the eight ball would move away from the cue ball at the same speed at which the cue ball struck it. This would be an equal ratio between power (inertia) and effect.

Yet good pool players can make the cue ball strike the eight ball in different ways. Although striking with the same amount of force each time, the eight ball may move at different rates and in different ways depending on the manner in which contact occurred.

We see the same phenomenon in martial arts. Despite containing the same amount of overall power, even the amount of inertia, different striking techniques will produce different results in the opponent. Sometimes this means that the opponent receives less force than the punch contained—a negative power to effect *Ratio*—something that results from improper mechanics.

Of course, as martial artists we actually want *more* yield than power. This seems impossible. It seems as though I am suggesting that we want the eight ball to move *faster* than the cue ball that struck it. Yet I am not suggesting that at all. Nor am I suggesting that there can be more total energy delivered to the opponent than held in the technique itself (though we can learn to turn the opponent's energy back on the opponent). I am, however, suggesting that energy can be delivered in different ways, that it can produce lesser or greater effects depending on how it is managed. As a rudimentary example, because the human body is more susceptible to spiraling energy than straight energy, we can produce a yield greater than power if we use spiraling strike rather than a flat one. More on this in the chapter on *Complex Force*.

Of course, if we lose fifty-percent of our power through poor mechanics and gain only ten-percent greater reaction in the opponent through spiraling, we still face a forty-percent deficit. Therefore, all principles must align at all times.

Ratio^3—movement vs. yield—concerns how much we move vs. how much we make the opponent move. Obviously, we want a positive movement to yield *Ratio*, meaning that we want to move less and less while causing the opponent to move more and more.

Consider, for example, a cardboard circle with a straw poked through its center. If the circumference of the circle is six inches and the circumference of the straw is half-an-inch, then we would have to rotate the cardboard six inches (one full rotation) to create half-an-inch of rotation in the straw. Six inches of movement that produces half-an-inch of movement constitutes considerable negative *Ratio*. On the other hand, if we rotated the straw just one rotation—half-an-inch of movement—we would produce a full six inches of rotational movement in the cardboard, a considerably positive *Ratio*.

Ratio^4 states that *power is relative to Time*. Imagine getting hit by a given amount of force, as in a single punch, even a remarkably hard one, over a period of ten seconds. Each second would deliver only 1/10th of the force, and each tenth of one second would only deliver 1/100th, or one percent, of that force. However, take the same amount of force and condense its impact to one second—still a long time for a punch—and the punch will hit with ten times the impact as before. Condense it from one second to half a second and you have doubled the power again. The more we condense, the more powerful the punch becomes. It follows, therefore, that the *same amount of power delivered in half the time equates to twice as much power*.

Yet increasing the speed of the impact does not necessarily decrease the *duration* of the impact. I often see martial artists strike fast only to spend a great deal of time with their hand on the target, with "great deal of time" obviously being a relative term. Moving quickly to the target accomplishes little if we still spread the impact over a long duration. Therefore, we must not only focus on the speed at which we reach the target, but also on shortening the length of time it takes to impact the target.

Yet just as *Ratio*^{4} suggests that the same force delivered over less time results in more power, so does *Ratio*^{5} mean that the same force concentrated into a smaller area results in greater power. Reduce the surface area by half and increase the power by two. For example, if we dispersed all of the force of a given punch over the entire surface area of a person's body, the recipient would hardly notice the punch, if at all. In contrast, concentrating the same force into a single fingertip strike would amplify its effect. Therefore, we must explore ways to focus our energy on smaller and smaller surface areas.

Yet *Ratio*^{5} seems even more apparent in issues of locking and throwing. When applying a wrist lock, for example, many martial artists will wrench the entire joint, dispersing their force throughout it. Typically, however, the same lock can be delivered by focusing force on just one point within the larger joint. This produces the same effect as the larger lock, but does so more painfully. Unfortunately, the distinctions between such applications prove far too subtle to illustrate here. They must be experienced to be appreciated and learned.

In martial arts, we must not use large motions to produce small ones in our opponents. If we take one step back to receive a punch and then two steps forward to execute a wrist throw then we have moved three steps to the opponent's one. Clearly, that's a deficient *Ratio*. Conversely, if the opponent strikes at us and we move half-a-step to produce several feet of motion in the opponent, we then construct a positive *Ratio*. If applied to footwork, the same idea would mean taking smaller steps than the opponent, or better yet, taking small steps that force the opponent to take large steps.

Ultimately, we do not want just *one* ratio working in our favor; we want all ratios working in our favor. Every technique should offer a *positive effort to yield ratio, power to yield ratio, movement to yield ratio, time to yield ratio, and space to yield ratio.*

11

Simplicity

Simplify! Simplify! Simplify!
—HENRY DAVID THOREAU

A S THE WORD, "SIMPLE," CARRIES MANY DIFFERENT DEFINITIONS AND connotations, *Simplicity* actually comprises one of the more complex principles. Yet at first glance, *Simplicity* does not seem notably complicated. As a general rule, we should move towards reduction. Less is more. Fewer movements with less to memorize and fewer "moving parts" result in easier techniques than multi-faceted combinations of physically challenging movements that compound each other in their difficulty. As in anything else, Murphy's Law applies to martial arts: anything that can go wrong, will go wrong. Thus, the less that can go wrong, the better. And the simpler we keep the conflict, the less that can go wrong.

However, *Simplicity* can be defined in two very different ways and to two opposite understandings of the intricacy of technique. The first understanding emerges from the fact that a fight will be fast and furious. Complicated, pre-planned combinations of techniques will be difficult to pull off if only because of the speed, ferocity, and chaotic nature of the clash, to say nothing of its sheer unpredictability. Who knows in what ways our opponent will wriggle and squirm to avoid defeat?

This perspective typically recognizes the "adrenaline response" that will occur during real face-to-face combat. The sheer power of our own fight or flight response and its accompanying autonomic reactions might make us forget most or all of the techniques we trained for hours in our local martial arts studio. If we experience the adrenaline response, only gross motor motions will remain intact; the subtler techniques of our art will slip away.

In light of that very real possibility, we can equate simplicity with the practice of grosser, more general techniques, techniques that closely mirror, or at least emerge from, the adrenaline induced state we might find ourselves in during a true fight or flight situation. With that in mind, we would avoid the study of "fancy" techniques and keep to a few strikes, a few simple takedowns, a few finishing holds, etc. We see this method and its effectiveness clearly demonstrated in IMPACT-style rape defense courses, where women learn to use just a few tools at full force against a padded attacker during high-stress attack simulations. The self-defense value of such training is undeniable. It has been proven again and again, and it is something I do with people who want to learn effective self-defense training.

Yet while the above approach to *Simplicity* holds great merit, I do not necessarily think it represents the only valid interpretation of the concept. In fact, while I find exceptional value in the method above, it remains incongruent with some of the other core principles in this text, such as *The Power Paradox* and *The Pure Objective*. Near-instinctive techniques can be exceptionally effective for self-defense but they are not necessarily equitable with higher forms of combat.

Toward that end, a different interpretation of *Simplicity* must be used. In such a case, *Simplicity* pertains to the *application* of a learned technique, but not necessarily to the complexity of the technique itself. While all techniques must remain simple in their application, meaning that they must not have too many "moving parts," good techniques might be quite intricate and difficult to learn. They might involve subtle muscle movements, minute muscular control, the ability to maintain centeredness, finesse, and the multitude of principles in this text. Thus, *learning* these techniques might be anything but *simple*, but once learned, the techniques are simple in their application.

Of course, the adrenal "fight or flight" response remains an obstacle that must be overcome. If we lose centeredness and succumb to fear then we will "forget" true martial technique and revert to grosser motor movements. That is not bad in itself but such gross techniques will not bring us to the *Pure Objective*. In short, Jane will encounter considerable difficulty in facing Gargantua with gross movements—we must presume that Gargantua gets those too—but would dispense him with ease if expressing all martial principles well.

Thus, we need not *necessarily* equate simplicity with "basic" technique. *Simplicity* must refer to keeping technique straightforward and of minimal moving parts, but such categorization could apply both to (1) techniques that involve gross motor movements or (2) techniques that are difficult to learn but are straightforward in their application. In my personal experience, techniques in category one, though important to learn, do not uphold all the principles in this text. Techniques in the second category do uphold such principles, but they require considerably more time to learn and master.

Put another way, techniques that will fulfill the *Pure Objective* against the likes of a Gargantua will require considerable skill and practice. They will require not just refined technique but equally a refinement of ourselves.

12

Natural Action

W E CAN DEFINE THE PRINCIPLE OF *NATURAL ACTION* IN TWO DIFFERENT ways:

1. Movements that are instinctive and/or "come naturally," or
2. Movements that conform to the body's way of movement.

At first, *Natural Action*[1] seems appealing. There's undoubtedly certain logic to building on the body's natural instincts for defense. I already spoke of this under *Simplicity* when referencing styles that work with gross motor movements, movements that occur relatively naturally as we enter the "fight or flight" adrenaline induced state.

Yet we need not be in an adrenaline induced state in order to exercise movements that "come naturally." Some systems attempt to build on our instinctive reactions by constructing techniques from similar motions. For example, if unexpectedly seeing someone striking at their face, many people will throw their hands up with their palms out and their fingers extended. Typically, they also will lean back and turn their head away from the threat.

In light of such tendencies, some styles build their blocks and counters, and in some cases their offensive techniques, around the raising of the hands in this manner. They work from the premise that since such reactions are "natural" and instinctive; techniques built on them will be easy to learn and equally easy—natural—to execute. Such tactics carry a certain logic. Our bodies possess natural instincts for self-preservation and we should tap into that power for the sake of self-defense.

However, while such an interpretation of "Natural Action" proves valuable to a certain extent, as martial artists we *ultimately* must strive to act in ways that most people would *not*. We ultimately do not train for hours upon hours so that we can fight as if untrained. This in no way den-igrates instinct-based techniques. For the development of quick and effec-tive self-defense skills, they are immeasurably valuable.

Yet as martial artists, we ultimately strive to move far beyond the instinctive motions to which most people remain constrained. This takes time—lots and lots of time. It requires that we practice until we re-train our instincts.

Thus, *Natural Action*[1] proves useful to a certain extent, and yet while we always must respect the power of instinctive tactics, we ultimately might strive for something different. This brings me to *Natural Action*[2], which concerns the idea that all techniques must closely adhere to the finer work-ings of the human being. As martial artists, we must concern ourselves with *exercising the intrinsic power of the body, mind, and spirit*—the "natural."

Yet "intrinsic power" does not refer to what is common; it refers to the ways in which the human being is anatomically, mentally, and spiritually powerful. In short, we must seek the "natural action" of the human being not in terms of the most common action or the initial action, but the deep-est inherent connection to power.

13

The Michelangelo Principle

"I saw the angel in the marble and
carved until I set him free."
—MICHELANGELO

MICHELANGELO'S ARTFUL WORDS SUGGEST THAT THE "ANGEL" EXISTED IN
the marble prior to his carving, or that he did not carve the form of
the angel but rather chipped away everything that was not the angel waiting to be "freed" from the marble. At least in this sense, martial arts and
sculpting are alike.

When applied to martial arts, Michelangelo's words suggest that we
must not accumulate techniques but rather "chip away" all the things we do
that fail to conform to martial principles in their purity. In that sense, our
pursuit of martial excellence becomes a process of reduction rather than one
of accumulation. Put another way, the "angel" already exists in all of us.

Of course, I fully recognize the differences between human beings and
blocks of marble, and I no less recognize the differences between sculpting
and martial arts. Yet in this one particular sense, sculpting and martial arts
could not be more alike. If we examine Michelangelo's statement more
closely, his point rests on the premise that the initial size, shape, and grain
of a block of marble ultimately determine what should be be carved from
it. The marble contains an inherent shape for which it is best suited, and it
is up to the artist to bring that shape forth. In essence, the sculpture pre-
cedes the sculptor.

Hardly a radical concept, we find it manifested in other forms of art.
Gem cutters, for example, will examine the quality, size, clarity, and flaws
of a stone before determining how to cut it. They look to see the inherent
type of cut—round, oval, square, etc.—that pre-exists their cutting, hidden

LONDON PUBLIC LIBRARY
20 EAST FIRST STREET
LONDON OHIO 43140

deep within the rough, unfinished stone awaiting the touch of their tools. Sometimes a large, uncut stone will yield multiple smaller finished cuts, and other times it might yield just one large cut. Regardless, about 50% of the initial stone gets "chipped away" in the cutting process.

Regardless of the particular yield, it makes sense that a given stone will be pre-disposed to certain shapes over others, and probably to one best final cut overall. Yet while a block of marble and a diamond each exist as tangible objects, martial arts seems to be something far more ephemeral. As such, how can we approach martial arts with the same reductionist philosophy used by Michelangelo?

The answer is simple: while the martial arts lack solidity, martial *artists* do not. And martial artists of the past did not create the martial arts out of thin air. They discovered the martial arts, finding them in the "block" that is the human being. They discovered that human anatomy generates more power one way than it does another, that it bends certain ways and breaks in others, that it is vulnerable in certain respects and strong in others, etc. The strengths and weaknesses of the total human being pre-existed the emergence of martial arts and martial artists. It waited in the "block" of humanity for martial artists to "set it free."

Ironically, I find this notion of the pre-existence of martial arts more troubling than rewarding. Its implication strikes me absolutely daunting: the true power of martial arts already exists in us. It's there now. It is in you now. It is in me now. Waiting. Dormant. We are angels within big, rough, unpolished blocks of humanity.

Thus, if true martial power already exists in us—our body's capacity for incredible speed, power, and technique pre-exists our understanding of it and our opponent's weakness pre-exist our ability to exploit them—then *martial arts cannot be about accumulating practices that empower us but rather ceasing all practices that disempower us!* This drives me quietly mad. We do not have to start doing the right things but rather stop doing all of the things that interfere with the "angel" of a martial artist within.

Which brings me to Miles Dewey Davis Jr., the trumpeter. Said Davis, "Sometimes you have to play for a long time before you can play like yourself." In other words, it takes a long time to chip away the marble. Yet it must be recognized, and Davis' words point right to it, that while we see a definitive distinction between the marble block and the sculptor, the distinction between the martial art and the martial artist is fuzzier at best. As martial artists, we are both the marble block and its sculptor.

14

Reciprocity

BY DEFINITION, *RECIPROCITY* SPEAKS TO THE STATE OF MUTUAL DEPENDENCE, often of opposites. *Yin* and *Yang* reciprocate one another. Or if we return to Newton's Third Law of Motion, an "equal and opposite reaction" is the reciprocal of "action."

In martial arts, the concept works similarly. While we could distill martial arts down to maximizing the ways we are powerful (*yang*) while exploiting the ways our opponent is weak (*yin*), that does not really address the notion of *Reciprocity*. More specifically, reciprocity in martial arts means that *the way in which we are strong is the opposite of the way in which we are weak*.

As a brief demonstration, I offer the notion of the missing legs. Human beings are, in effect, two legged tables, and a table with only two legs is obviously a problematic one.

If standing in figure Rec1, a two-legged table with one leg in each of the white dots would invariably fall towards either of the black dots. Conversely, were the two-legged table's legs placed in either of the black dots, it invariably would fall towards either of the white dots.

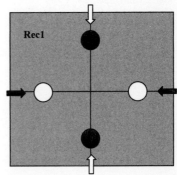

The same applies to human beings, who are essentially two-legged tables. Despite our ability to balance, we are invariably strong in two directions and weak in the *Reciprocal* directions. Were we to stand with one foot in each of the white dots—as in a horse stance—we would be strong against pressure from either of the black arrows. However, we would be weak in the *Reciprocal* directions, meaning that we would easily succumb to pressure from either of the white arrows and towards either of the black dots. Were we to reverse our stance by placing one foot on each of the black dots, as in a rather narrow forward or front stance, then we would be strong against pressure from the white arrows but weak against pressure from the black arrows.

Therefore, strength *Reciprocates* weakness. With limited exception, if the human body is strong in one regard, it will be weak in the opposite regard. I will demonstrate this further, and in more specificity, in parts of the book that follow.

However, *Reciprocity* actually means something deeper, as well. I will discuss this as it arises but from a certain perspective, the ways in which we are strong actually are the ways in which we are weak! We will see that weakness in one context is strength in another, and vice versa.

15

Opponents Are
Illusions

I N ONE SENSE, I ALREADY TOUCHED ON THIS TOPIC WHEN SPEAKING ABOUT "Lengthening Your Line." From a certain perspective, any need to concern ourselves with opponents is purely fictitious because once we accept the premise that martial arts can defeat any given opponent then the caliber of that opponent becomes irrelevant, if not distracting. We need not and should not focus on what we do to our opponent but rather on our proficiency in technique, or more pointedly, our proficiency in principles. If we do that well, the presence of an opponent, as well as that opponent's relative size and strength, becomes meaningless.

Therefore, opponents are mere illusions. Yet *illusions have power if we believe in them*. If we give life to the concept of "opponents" by worrying about what they might do to us and what we can or cannot do to them then we risk compromising techniques in order to produce certain results. In this way, *giving credence to the notion that the opponent holds power actually gives power to the opponent*!

Case in point, let's says we square off against a menacing opponent, someone big, mean-looking, and aggressive. In response, we become frightened consequently forget our techniques, lose our *Centeredness*, and resort to uneconomical motions, and so on. In reacting as we did, we fed the opponent power. Being initially fearful of the opponent, whom we might have defeated through proper technique, we compromised our ability to execute our art, which then becomes an authentic point of concern, hence a vicious cycle. In other words, buying into the notion that the opponent was powerful only made the opponent more powerful.

The same holds true in our daily lives. As an educator, I often see this in the classroom. Students who consider themselves shy fear contributing to discussions in class. In never speaking aloud during class they never become comfortable speaking aloud during class, and the longer they go without speaking the more fearful they become of it. Yet that there is really something to fear about speaking aloud during class is only an illusion. Those who do not feed the illusion with their fear of speaking find that the illusion loses all of its power and dissipates. Those who do feed the illusion only find the illusion more and more powerful.

In martial arts, we see this on a far more physical level, as well. If when grabbed at the wrist we *believe* that the opponent controls our wrist, we will tend to resist at the wrist. As we presume a stronger opponent, resisting at the wrist only helps our opponent because that is the focus of the opponent's strength.

On the other hand, if we do not resist at the wrist and do not buy into the opponent's grab, we discover that the opponent lacks power. Later I will discuss *Indirect Pressure*—moving the body from a location other than the place of contact with the opponent. (If you just said, "But there is no opponent," you understand this chapter well.) In this case, that could entail flexing the triceps rather than the muscles surrounding the wrist. As a result, the elbow moves, which moves the "wrist" quite easily. Yet that only works if we do not buy into the wrist grab.

In short, believing the opponent has power gives the opponent that power. Disregarding the opponent, provided we execute principled technique, dispels the illusion of power. As always, proficiency applies.

Yet we must learn to disregard, or at least stop blaming, our opponents. As martial technique itself already presumes physical conflict, *we* need not worry about that conflict itself, only about understanding and applying martial arts. Put another way, you do not have to worry about the opponent; the art will do that for you. You need only worry about expressing the art.[4]

---

4. I will note that this mode of thinking is in itself a kind of *Indirect Pressure*. We do not concern ourselves with the opponent directly. We do so indirectly through our concern with martial arts. As always, principles are holistic. If *Indirect Pressure* works physically, so too can it serve us mentally.

16

Reflexive Action

I T SHOULD GO WITHOUT SAYING THAT MARTIAL ART TECHNIQUES MUST BE practiced until instinctive. The fraction of a second it takes for the opponent to attack leaves no time for any cognitive thought. While we always want to remain in control of ourselves and our actions, techniques must "happen," *almost* whether we want them to or not.

For better or worse, the only way to develop *Reflexive Action* in any technique involves repetition, lots and lots of repetition. Practicing a technique repeatedly not only makes us more proficient, it also literally trains our neuromuscular system to act in accordance with our practice.

It does that most dramatically when we practice to the point of physical and mental exhaustion because doing so forces the mind and body to work together better. Furthermore, the *Body-Mind* learns to streamline its movements down to the absolutely essential elements of the technique. When it returns to that same technique the next practice session, it remembers which muscles it absolutely needs to use and which it does not, and therefore continues to work more efficiently and effectively.

The same thing happens with the mind. As it grows weary, it stops thinking cognitively. It stops thinking *about* doing the technique, e.g. "Am I in the right position?" or "Be sure to move from the hips," and starts making the body just *do* it. Consequently, the technique seeps into the subconscious mind—the only place that will generate *Reflexive Action*. In fact, it seeps into the *Body-Mind*.

Consequently, we must exercise stringent care in choosing the techniques we drill into reflex because the golden rule of *Reflexive Action* states that *unlearning a reflex takes at least twice as long as learning one*. Those of you who have been driving for any number of years can understand this easily enough. If when driving we see an urgent need to stop, our foot reflexively flies from the gas pedal on the right to the break pedal left. Yet what would happen if the next car you drove reversed the two pedal positions? How long would it take to unlearn the reflex? I for one would get in many accidents before I finally learned the lesson.

Contextual to level of proficiency, we must practice only those techniques that work towards the *Reflexive Action* we ultimately desire. That, by the way, can be one of the pitfalls of permitting beginning students to spar. Untrained in technique, they might develop *Reflexive Actions* they will need to later unlearn.

Regardless of how we acquire them, *Reflexive* techniques invariably occur faster and more powerfully than non-reflective techniques of the same ilk and by the same practitioner. Teach a beginning student a rising block and he or she will perform it with contrived speed and power; the student *consciously* will try to make it fast and hard. Yet surprise that same student by reaching a hand at his or her face and the student will perform a faster "block" than before. When moving reflexively, the mind and body act as one, using the most refined motion possible, thus making *Reflexive Action* superior to contrived action. This does not argue for exercising untrained motions, only for training carefully thought-out motions deep into our reflexive memory.

17

Training Truth

WE MUST TRAIN THE WAY WE WANT TO FIGHT[5] OR WE WILL NOT FIGHT THAT way at all. Of course, how we fight depends on our objective. Sport oriented styles must train according to the practices and rules of their competition. Combat oriented styles must train according to the true nature of combat.

Yet we see styles of martial arts that practice one set of techniques during training and then apply a different set of techniques when sparring or practicing combat. To be fair, sparring, though an excellent drill, is *not* the same as real combat for many reasons. Yet if we exercise one block when training and a different block when sparring, or if the "same" block looks different in the two contexts, then are we *Training Truth*? If we do not exercise the technique we practice *in the way we practice it* then why should we practice it that way?

Some contemporary martial artists fault traditional martial arts for lacking combative applicability and over all "realism." From a certain perspective, they have a point. The techniques we see in some traditional arts sometimes fail to make the transition to sparring or street combat. Yet we must not view this as an indictment of traditional arts, per se, many of which prove themselves quite applicable to modern contexts. After all, the anatomical dynamics of two humans clashing in unarmed combat has not changed much since . . . well, since there were humans. Do we really think a bar fight was much different in feudal Japan than it is today?

The difficulties we sometimes see in transitioning techniques to combat, be they traditional or otherwise, concern how we bridge them from prac-

---

5. I use "fight" for lack of a better term. As this book asserts, we never should actually be "fighting" anything because "fighting" denotes resistance and effort. We always should avoid conflict. Should it happen, it should happen effortlessly.

tice to application. We must use effective drills to *transition* techniques from abstraction to application.

Also, the original meanings of some arts have been lost or changed over generations, especially in the modern age. Yet the potential for worthwhile applicability remains. It only needs to be unleashed.

Of course, I'd also suggest that the proper understanding and application of martial principles is required if that functionality is to be unleashed, but I suppose I'm biased.

As I mentioned, sparring, though an essential exercise, constitutes something different from real combat. As both parties recognize that they are engaging in a drill, sparring involves a different kind of *Intent* and emotional content than real fighting. Each party knows that the other will fight, and both parties often possess a general sense of the techniques their opponent will use. Finally, each party plays an equal role in their willingness to participate.

Combat, on the other hand, holds different characteristics. In combat, one person launches aggression at someone who may not want to fight. The aggressor's intent is not to "win," per se, but to hurt. And the aggressor typically does not possess foreknowledge of the defender's skills. In a real fight, the combatants typically do not spend time feeling each other out, either. In fact, combat usually lasts *considerably* less time than a sparring match.

Thus, techniques that work in real combat might not be as applicable during sparring, and vice versa. This does not necessarily invalidate the *essential* nature of sparring as a tool.

Yet *Training Truth* remains imperative. If we cannot translate the techniques we practice into the actual context in which they must be applied, we must question (1) the technique itself, (2) the training method, and (3) the nature of the context.

18

Imperception and Deception

S PEAKING OF THIS PRINCIPLE MIGHT APPEAR TO CONTRADICT THE *LENGTHEN Your Line* principle, so I want to be careful to make the distinction. *I&D* suggest that we execute martial arts most effectively when we do so beyond our opponent's perception. In short, if our opponent (consciously or unconsciously) does not know what we are doing then the opponent cannot counter it. I am not talking about understanding. Most opponents will not understand the dynamics of a wrist lock but that has nothing to do with *I&D*. Rather, if the opponent does not perceive force against the wrist and/or an effort to take him/her down then it becomes easy to apply that wrist lock. Or more simply, the easiest strike to land is the one the opponent never sees coming.

The distinction between the two particular ways of keeping the opponent in the dark are as follows: *Imperception* refers to acting in ways that the opponent cannot perceive. Later in the book, for example, I talk about the *Body-Mind* principle and explain that the mind will locate itself where there is bodily tension. Coupling that with *Indirect Pressure*—moving from a place other than where the opponent is focused—we can move relatively *Imperceptibly*. In other words, if the opponent grabs our wrist then the opponent's mind becomes fixated on our wrist. If we move from our wrist directly against the opponent's grip, the opponent will perceive and resist that action because it occurs exactly where the opponent is paying the most attention. In contrast, if we move from our elbow, our wrist might move as a result of the elbow movement but the wrist will not directly resist the opponent's grip. Hence, we can move more freely because we move where the opponent's mind is not. This is effectual *Imperceptibility*.

Deception works similarly but functions by misdirecting the opponent's mind away from our actions. We see this frequently enough in martial arts in the form of distractions. If grabbed at the wrist, for example, we might kick to the shin to draw the opponent's attention away from grabbing our wrist and to the pain in the leg, thus weakening the grip and allowing ourselves to more easily escape the wrist grab.

Deception also manifests itself in other ways, such as in feints that draw the opponent to block a false technique, thus creating an opening through which we can hit. Many *kung fu* and *silat* styles invoke a tactic whereby the practitioner creates an *intentional* opening in his or her defenses, thus inviting the opponent to strike to a particular location that appears unprotected. Of course, it's a trap and when the opponent strikes he or she typically ends up defeated. Even knowing that this tactic was being employed, I found myself surprised at how powerful the urge is to strike wide open targets when sparring. Whereas the conscious level of my brain recognized that I was being set up, it could not communicate that fact to my body fast enough to stop myself from instinctively striking open target areas.

As I stated before, however, one problem with *I&D* is that martial artists over-rely on it. *We must not use I&D in place of otherwise sound technique.* We only should use *I&D* in addition to sound technique, which is one of the reasons why I typically teach techniques without *I&D* elements first, and then add *I&D* only after those techniques are functional. This is why it should not violate the *Lengthen Your Line* principle: a wrist escape must be able to counter a powerful wrist grab without *I&D*, but it ultimately is foolish not to invoke *I&D* for more effective technique—*Efficiency*.

SECTION I
PHYSIOKINETIC
PRINCIPLES

ALSO REFERRED TO AS *BIO-MECHANICS, PHYSIO-MECHANICS, KINETICS,* AND *applied physiology, Physiokinetics (PK)* encompasses the study of the mechanistic working of the human body.

Regardless of the specific term, this entire book could be said to deal with this subject. Martial combat, after all, comes down to two *homo sapien* body structures acting on each other. Therefore, the stronger our understanding of *PK* and its relationship with martial technique, the faster, more powerfully, more efficiently, and more effortlessly we will act. It not only teaches us to maximize the effectiveness of our own body motions, it simultaneously instructs how to exploit *Physiokinetic* flaws in the opponent. That alone seems to go a long way to defining martial arts—maximizing our own anatomical movements while exploiting anatomical weakness in the opponent.

Going back to Joe and Jane vs. Gargantua, we must presume that Jane will enjoy little hope of defeating her opponent if both manifest equally sound *Physiokinetics*. In other words, as long as Gargantua remains as *Physiokinetically* sound as Joe or Jane then Joe or Jane will succumb to Gargantua's relative size and strength. Thus, Joe and Jane must exercise one of three options:

1. Improve their own *physiokinetics* to the point where their anatomical structure can compensate for Gargantua's advantage in size, strength, and range.
2. Exploit the *physiokinetic* weaknesses in Gargantua, which we can do only when *expressing sound PK ourselves*.
3. Both.

Fortunately, and as I noted before, *all* martial arts include some understanding of *PK*. Virtually every martial art will make its practitioners more *physiokinetically* sound than the layperson. Yet *some* understanding of *PK* does not suffice. Once again, we simply find no argument for seeking weaker *Physiokinetics* than possible. Thus we must use *PK* as a tool, a tool that deciphers the *how's* and *why's* of our techniques. It explains why when punching, for example, we stand a certain way, position our feet a certain way, use our fist a certain way, etc. It explains everything from the focus of our eyes to the tension in our toes. In short, *PK* potentially unlocks all the mysteries and answers all the questions, and we subsequently must exercise that knowledge in becoming more effective martial artists.

Remember, martial technique does not emerge randomly. Techniques do not, or at least should not, emerge from "just because" rationales. If a given style or instructor cannot sufficiently explain a given art, we would be wise to question our dedication to that art, to say the least. Yet in credible martial arts, *technique emerges from and is limited by how the body works, and how one physiology best works against another*. Therefore, we must surpass our devotion to technique and delve instead into the *PK* that makes technique functional.

Ultimately, *PK* becomes our master. Once we keep *The Principle of Principles* in mind, and once we accept that martial technique must not in any way contradict *best* understandings of physiology (how can we trust techniques we believe to be anatomically unsound?), we then possess no choice but to modify techniques in accordance with our best understandings of *Physiokinetics*. Thus, our understanding of *PK* begins to dictate our techniques.[6]

There's good news and bad news about *PK's* dictatorial role in martial arts: The good news is that *PK* does not dictate *style*, per se. Because each and every style already derives its techniques from human physiology, the study *Physiokinetics* does not demand that we give up style X and take up style Y in its place. We must realize that there can be more than one anatomically sound method of accomplishing the same end.

The bad news, however, is that exploring *PK* requires us to permit technique to evolve. While this does not change the fact that we strike, lock, throw, etc., it does change *how* we strike, lock, throw, etc. Such changes might be subtle, if not nearly imperceptible to the unpracticed eye, but the changes can be dramatic nonetheless. Such changes might include rotating an arm a few degrees more or less, positioning it a few centimeters differently, using certain muscle groups in the arm instead of others, or any number of other subtle modifications. Or they might be far more radical. Yet we should not alter technique for change's sake. Only adherence to principle matters.

---

6. Of course, I reserve this comment more for instructors and advanced students than for inexperienced martial artists, which is to say that there could well be anatomical rationales to techniques that escape the inexperienced eye. At the same time, however, we reasonably should expect every instructor to be able to explain every technique from an anatomical perspective.

That changes might be subtle does not diminish their importance. *Physiokinetics* functions as the doorway to *The Pure Objective*. Any time we do not exercise *PK* to its potential, we consequently fail to exercise maximum *Efficiency*, and therefore consume more time and expend more effort than we would desire. To put it more specifically, (1) any time we do not maximize our own *PK*, we *must* use strength to compensate for our lack of sound mechanics, and as we must presume our opponent to be bigger and stronger than ourselves, we consequently must presume that our strength will prove inadequate. (2) Any time we fail to exploit Gargantua's *physiokinetics*, we enable him to exercise his strength and size on us. Given our supposed deficits in those areas, we must presume our own defeat. If, however, we exploit his *PK* then his size and strength ultimately become irrelevant, as a building without a sound foundation. The strongest building in the world will topple if its foundation fails.

A small, physiokinetically sound person who exploits the Physiokinetic flaws of a larger opponent (instead of confronting his size and strength) will emerge victorious. I do not mean to make that sound easy or simplistic. It should be so if done "right," but doing it right, to say nothing of first determining what is right, can prove challenging, to say the least.

As I said, virtually all of this book could be placed under the umbrella of *physiokinetics* because every martial art distills down to the conflict of two human structures. If nothing else, we must recognize that martial arts techniques exist within the confinement of what the human body can do. Fortunately, we have yet to determine the precise limits of the human body's potential, and so the "confinement" remains only theoretical.

19

Breathing

HAVING BEEN IN MARTIAL ARTS FOR TWENTY-ONE YEARS, I AM ONLY *BEGINNING* to understand breath's true connection to power, an understanding that will develop for the rest of my life. What I have come to understand, however, is that how we breathe *ultimately*, at the most advanced levels, determines the quality of our techniques, and I mean that in very mechanistic/anatomical ways with respect to body structure, and also in more esoteric ways with respect to energy flow—*ki, chi, Prana, internal energy*, etc. (You may not be persuaded of the existence of internal energy, and that is fine. This book does not rely on such acceptances. I, however, am persuaded of it, though I understand it only in infantile ways, and so I will limit my discussion to breath's more mechanistic functions.)

It may seem odd to list breathing so early on since it is the *last* principle any martial artist will come to understand. Yet full mastery of breath will produce *Relaxation, Centeredness,* and other advantages that potentially supercede the need for other principles, or will at the very least manifest them naturally and without conscious effort. Therefore, I begin with breathing for two reasons: (1) It will take the most time to understand and thus should be practiced from the outset, and (2) it is integral to all the other principles.

With respect to number two, proper breathing begets posture, and without proper posture all *Physiokinetics* suffer, and if *Physiokinetics* suffer then we enjoy no hope of defeating Gargantua. Thus, proper breathing literally sits as the foundation of sound martial arts technique.

Proper breathing means inhaling and exhaling from the *hara, dan tien,* or, as we call it in the West, the "center"—the spot located two-to-three inches below the belly button and half-way in towards the spine. Such "diaphragmatic breathing" or "abdominal breathing," embodies the natural way to breathe, the way we do so when born and, typically, when we sleep.

Proper breathing exercises all of our lungs. Unfortunately, most people exercise only the top half of their lungs, something that requires a considerable amount of effort. When we breath from the top half of our lungs, we must contract the muscles at the small of our back and around our waistline in order to lift our chest with the muscles in our upper torso, including the shoulders and the neck, which is why so many people experience lower back pain, neck tension, and tension headaches.

By contrast, we should breathe by allowing our torso to fill with air from the bottom, expanding not just from the "stomach" but from all sides equally. I liken this to breathing like a water balloon, which fills from the bottom to the top, as opposed to a balloon filled with air, which expands in all directions at once. Similarly, we should fill our lungs from the bottom, thus allowing them to expand outwards first and upwards second. Only properly deep breaths will expand the chest naturally and effortlessly.

Depending on the authority, we should breathe in through the nose and out through the mouth or in through the nose and out through the nose. Few authorities advocate breathing in through the mouth as this encourages tension in the chest and upper back. There is also "reverse breathing," which is breathing specifically for power, but its specific uses are not important for this discussion.[7]

Improper breathing radically alters our practice of martial arts. If we breathe improperly and consequently raise our chests, contract our midsection, and foster unnatural tension in our upper bodies, we inevitably restrict and stiffen our movements. In fact, a number of ramifications occur:

1. We raise our center of gravity, thereby diminishing our balance, and thereby forcing us to invoke more muscle use so as to remain upright.
2. We create tension that inhibits speed of motion in striking and other techniques.
3. We inhibit the relaxation response that naturally should occur with each exhalation.
4. We decrease the amount of oxygen in our bloodstream, thus decreasing our stamina.
5. We consume through muscular tension a greater percentage of our mind's attention, which consequently inhibits both tactile and visual perception, as well as reaction time.

This is but a partial list of the many potential negative effects of improper breathing.

---

7. As there is a wealth of information available about the positive mental and anatomical effects of abdominal breathing, to say nothing of instruction as to how to go about it, I will not delve into such discussions at this time. Other authors have covered them at much greater length and depth.

20

Posture

THE PREVIOUS CHAPTER'S DISCUSSION OF *BREATHING* INEVITABLY LEADS TO the subject of posture. I cannot believe how long I spent ignoring this topic, ignorant of its eminent importance. While I always believed good posture important, I did not realize just *how* deeply it impacts martial arts.

Before discussing *Posture* further, consider the power of simply being able to stand without tension: If we do not need to devote part of our energy to the mere act of standing upright then we can use all of our power in the application of techniques. (See the *Percentage Principle*) Unfortunately, I work with many martial artists who lose significant percentages of their power because they do not create proper alignment in their own bodies.

Consider it this way: As the human form is meant to stand a certain way, doesn't it make sense that improper alignment will degrade the quality of martial technique? Structural integrity not only facilitates power, it also facilitates speed because we need not (1) release tension from some part of our body in order to move it, and/or (2) fight against tension in one body part in the process of moving another. Not only that, we also will enjoy a greater range of motion as a relaxed musculature is a more flexible one.

Moving on, proper *Posture* permits tremendous increases in the speed of our footwork, especially when we understand the true nature of walking, which for most people consists of falling forward and catching themselves in a controlled fashion. We see a rudimentary and exaggerated version of this in Boris Karloff's classic portrayal of Frankenstein's monster in the 1931 film of the same name (figure P1). Karloff's body tilts and falls forward before being caught by the leg that steps. If we could draw a vertical line through Karloff's body, we would see that it tilts forward, returns to a more upright position, and then tilts forward again, thus restarting the cycle.

P1

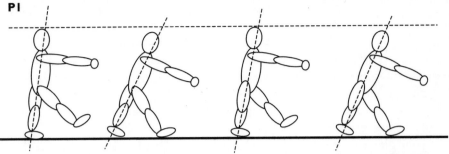

Toddlers walk in much the same manner. Most toddlers actually fall forward and then hurry their legs to keep up, which is why many of them gain speed with the more steps they take, eventually moving too fast for their little legs to catch them, and thus falling down. Their pace quickens because they have not yet learned just how much they can "fall" and still catch themselves.

Toddlers teach us something else, as well. Though exaggerated, they demonstrate that most people do not walk in a smooth, horizontal process. If you watch a toddler learn to walk, you see that they essentially hop from foot to foot. They nearly bounce. While most people do not actually bounce as they move, they do bob up and down. Returning to P1, we see that the figure does not move forward evenly. Rather, its head raises and lowers as it tilts, catches itself, uprights itself, and tilts again.

Obviously, we move forward best when *only* moving forward and not up and down. Failure to breath properly from the lower abdomen only raises the center of gravity to the chest and creates artificial tension in the torso, making us all too much like Frankenstein.

Instead, walking should be about moving from the *Center*. If we can establish proper posture, we can move the entire upper body—everything above the center—all at once, without having to bob up and down, and thus with greater *Efficiency*. Notice that in P2, the head remains level as the body walks forward.

Consider it this way: If we had to move a stack of ten wooden blocks, the easiest and fastest way to do it would be to maintain their stacked struc-

P2

ture. If we tilt the blocks forward, the stack will collapse. It is not much different with the human skeletal structure. While it is not precisely a stack—the spine actually curves—it moves best as an intact unit, which means upright. When the "stack" of bones tilts forward, the body has to exert muscular force to stop it from collapsing, which not only wastes energy but also proves inefficient for fighting.

To get a sense of the power of *Posture*, I suggest two basic exercises. First, practice walking without bobbing up and down. Walk by pressing your center forward on a horizontal plane, allowing your feet to graze the floor. You soon will find yourself gliding across the floor faster yet with less energy expenditure. This more efficient means of lateral motion works because you will not disperse energy unnecessarily by tilting or dropping your weight forward. Many people become amazed at how fast they walk when converting all their effort to lateral motion, and many martial artists become amazed at their sudden acquisition of speed in footwork.

The second exercise consists of having someone stand behind you on top of a chair, thus raising their hips roughly to the height of your shoulders. Establish what you believe to be proper posture, which should manifest from proper *Breathing*, and have them push *straight down* on you. It is essential that they do not push forward, backward, or to a side. If you have proper posture, you will be able to remain perfectly upright without feeling any strain at all no matter how hard they push. However, improper posture will cause you to feel tension, and perhaps discomfort, in any part not properly aligned. Obviously, pressure should be applied gradually and this drill should never be done if it becomes painful.

This exercise provides an exaggerated example of what happens in every martial technique. In some fashion, a force presses on us, even if that force comes from an "equal and opposite reaction" to our *own* technique. Thus, in performing a wrist throw, some fraction of the energy we direct into the opponent's wrist also presses back on us. The more deficient our posture/structure, the more energy—muscle tension—our body must expend to maintain itself, and thus the less energy we can devote to the technique itself. Furthermore, the more inefficient my posture, the more the "equal and opposite reaction" will manifest in my own body rather than in the opponent's.

Of course, when we work with smaller partners, this might not *seem* like a factor because the repercussions against our own body remain minimal. Unfortunately, we must concern ourselves not with those who are smaller but with Gargantua. In applying a wrist lock to a mass greater than our own, our structural inadequacies become all too apparent. Typically, our body yields instead of compromising the opponent, and the technique consequently fails.

If we examine P3, we find both Joe and Gargantua manifesting improper posture. Focusing on Joe alone, we find that those parts of his body left of the dotted line are unsupported by his legs/base. This produces several ill consequences: (1) His center of gravity moves up and forward. (2) He must exercise excess muscle tension in his back and forward leg in order to maintain his position. (3) He also might be leaning on Gargantua's hand for support, albeit unconsciously.

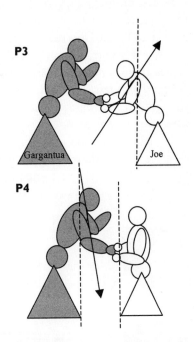

As a result, Joe no longer can use his entire body in application of the wrist lock. He cannot properly drop his weight into the technique. Effectively speaking, only those portions left of the line become involved in the technique, meaning that Gargantua does not need to fight all of Joe's body, only Joe's arms and shoulders, and Joe's arms and shoulders are not powerful enough to combat the likes of Gargantua.

Worse, because of his body's misalignment, Joe cannot connect force to his legs. Instead, it will work against Joe, following the path of the arrow and consequently lifting Joe's shoulders, if not raising his entire body. I have seen people nearly lift themselves off the floor trying to force larger opponents down (note the word, "force").

Yet the most dangerous consequence of Joe's posture concerns how he puts himself at risk of being pulled to the floor by Gargantua. As Joe lacks structural integrity, Gargantua needs only drop his arm to drop his opponent, making Joe an unwitting victim of his own attempt at a wrist lock.

P4, in contrast, illustrates what Joe should do in order to exploit Gargantua's posture. Because his entire upper body rests vertically on his base, Joes's body acts in structural unity. Therefore, any resistance to his wristlock acts not against just his arms and shoulders but rather against his entire body. At the same time, as Joe need not expend any notable energy to maintain his own posture, all his force converts into the wrist throw. By contrast, Gargantua has to use some of his own muscularity to maintain his own poor posture—supporting those points right of his dotted line. Meanwhile, Joe can direct his wrist lock towards the space on the ground right of Gargantua's dotted line, thus directing it where Gargantua lacks foundation. What's more, Joe can do so using the weight of his whole body— *Heaviness*—rather than the strength of his arms.

Obviously, skill level in technique, not to mention the application of other principles herein, will determine the final outcome of Joe's wrist lock.

I do not mean to suggest that Joe *definitely* will defeat Gargantua given these factors alone. I certainly do suggest, however, that given the choice between P3 and P4, I do not see how we can opt for P3.

When properly employing *Posture,* our structure can support the force we exert and simultaneously *exploit structural weaknesses in the opponent. Without proper Structure, we must rely on strength, which only attacks strength. When there is proper poster, we can rely on structure, which in turn attacks structure.*

Consider another technique, this one being a punch. In P5, the figure is concave in the chest, and its back becomes rounded, off its *Center,* and

P5

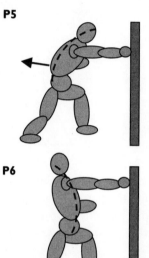

P6

unaligned with its legs. When the P5 figure exerts force forward, it vents force through its lower back and hips.[8] Conversely, a convex chest will vent force through the upper back and shoulders, thus making the figure in P6 lean back more. Yet proper posture eliminates all of the above problems, *Rooting* force in the solid floor and communicating all of it to the target.

All said, some arts might require different postures to be successful. Wrestling, for instance, involves such low, full body grappling attacks that practitioners must adopt more tilted positions to wedge the opponent's force to the earth. Judo must do the same, though I should note that footage of Judo's founder, Jigoro Kano, shows him nearly upright in his later years, possibly because he learned to *Root* energy without tilting, which is entirely possible.

On a slightly less anatomical level, posture impacts the visual and psychological power of presence. Martial arts history offers countless examples of persons able to dissuade attackers simply by looking powerful, by carrying themselves in such a way that any onlooker discerns their training. Such will occur only when we present the appearance of a unified being. Someone who moves in uncoordinated fragments cannot possibly look powerful. In fact, once we become accustomed to embodying proper *Posture* and to working with people who do so as well, people with problematic *Posture* will begin looking weak, fragmented, and even uncoordinated. This results in a wonderful increase in confidence because when people do not appear strong, even larger people, we tend to fear them less, if at all.

---

8. That we might sometimes be striking flimsy targets seems no argument to disregard proper structure. First of all, we expect that many opponents will be heavier, bigger, and stronger, and thus present targets that are quite solid. But opponents aside, the question is one of how good the technique itself is.

21

The Triangle Guard

G IVEN THAT SO MUCH OF MARTIAL ARTS INVOLVES THE USE OF THE ARMS, IT stands to reason that the particular positioning and structuring of them holds considerable importance. As with many other anatomical concerns, the difference between structural integrity and structural inadequacy comes down to a matter of inches, if not fractions of an inch. A few degrees of rotation or angling can make untold differences in the power we generate and the efficacy of our techniques. Such subtleties often surprise martial artists. They learn that many of their techniques can become remarkably more potent through subtle changes in body structure. Often, the untrained eye cannot distinguish between the more and less functional structures, but that does not diminish their power.

Which brings me to the *Triangle Guard* (not to be confused with the *Triangulation Point*), which represents an essential anatomical structure for our arms. To manifest it, comfortably extend your hands, thumbs up, and touch your finger-tips together directly in front of you. Notice how a kind of triangle forms, its apex being at the tips of your fingers, your arms forming each of its sides, and the width of your back creating the base. (TG1)

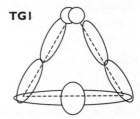

Merely forming a roughly triangular geometry will not tap the body's power. The *Triangle Guard* becomes structurally sound only when our elbows face downward rather than facing out to our sides. They also *must* remain within the width of the torso. Under such circumstances, the body can generate and receive force with great efficiency because the triangle constitutes one of the most structurally sound geometric shapes.

Notice, by contrast, that allowing the elbows to drift outwards changes

TG2

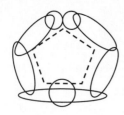

the structure from triangular to pentagonal, the latter being a structurally *unsound* geometric shape (Fig. TG2). A quick examination of the two geometries reveals what should be a clear conclusion: If each of the shapes were to receive force at their apex—the point farthest from the body—the triangular structure will be more powerful because the torso serves as a solid foundation. The shoulders stabilize the arms, the spine stabilizes the shoulders, and the legs stabilize the spine, and the legs get their stability from the planet itself. By contrast, the force against the pentagon cannot reach the shoulders because the elbows receive no support. Consequently, the pentagon can withstand only as much force as there is strength in the arms.

To do a rudimentary test of this theory, comfortably extend both arms directly in front of you with each of your palms facing directly away from you, and with the palm of one hand pressing against the back of the other. Adopt a forward stance—one foot comfortably in front of the other—and insure that you manifest good posture. "Square" your shoulders and hips, making each equidistant to your hands. Ask a partner to push straight forward on your hands, applying pressure in slow increments.

Do this twice. The first time, allow your elbows to rotate outwards so that you construct the pentagon. Note how much pressure you can absorb. The second time, comfortably rotate your elbows so that they face downwards. Again note how much pressure you can absorb. If you manifest proper posture and structure, you'll absorb far more pressure in the second version because you will have constructed the triangle.

While some readers might rightfully note that most arts do not use immobile, extended arms, the principle nevertheless remains valid. A punch from the body can pass through a triangular structure or a pentagonal one, and the difference in power will change accordingly.

Therefore, we find the *Triangle Guard* a critical principle, one that obviously moves us toward fulfilling the *Percentage Principle* and *Efficiency*, and one that utilizes the implicit structure of the body.

Yet the *Triangle Guard* also serves an immediately combative function. It establishes a kind of "Cone of Protection." The farther our arms extend from our body while maintaining *Centerline*, the more we decrease the number of angles through which our opponent can land an attack. As I will speak to later on, this also helps us dominate the *Primary Gate*.

Consider the difference between TG3a, with arms tight to the body, and TG3b, with arms partially extended. Imagine attacking TG3a and note where you would strike and how you would attack those points. On the other hand, consider how you would attack TG3b, a stance that not only

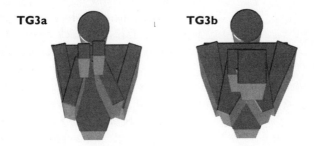

TG3a   **TG3b**

diminishes potential angles of attack, but simultaneously discourages potential attacks *because our attacker typically would need to bring his or her face closer to our hands in order to circumvent our guard.* In other words, where could you attack TG3b without bringing your face close to the defending hands?

I must note that both TG3a and TG3b represent slight exaggerations and that recognizing the power of the *Triangle Guard* does not *necessarily* mean that TG3b must become a fighting stance in and of itself.

Interestingly, closer examination of the *"Triangle" Guard* reveals it to be a collection of triangles that actually form a pyramid, and pyramids take the geometric strength of one triangle and multiply it by four. Where are the four triangles? The first was depicted in TG1, which gazes from above. The second and third become apparent from the side view (Fig. TG4), which can be viewed from the left and from the right. The fourth is roughly the shape of the torso, to which the bases of the other three triangles connect (Fig. TG5). The grand sum of all the triangles produces the pyramid as seen in figure TG6.

Note once again the importance of properly aligned elbows. When turned down and under instead of out, any pressure placed on them transfers downward into the legs and ground instead of out beyond the structural sides of the body. In effect, the elbows enjoy no support when outside the torso, as in the pentagon. However, when the elbows are underneath, the pressure transfers first into the body, which more specifically means into the spine, provided there is good posture, and

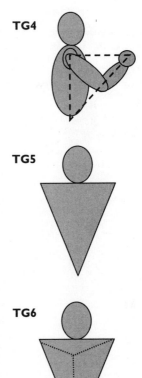

TG4

TG5

TG6

TG7

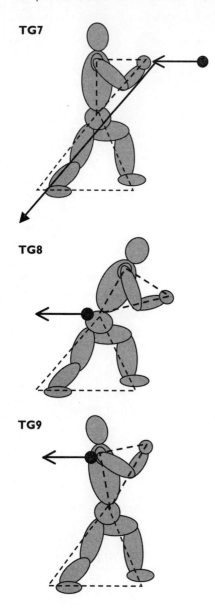

TG8

TG9

then into the legs (TG7). The legs, consequently, provide a powerful foundation for the pressure. Furthermore, if the legs are relaxed properly, the force ultimately will *Root* into the floor.

If, as in TG8, we manifest even a slight bend at the hips, the upper triangle will not align with the lower one, thus venting force out at the lower back. On the other hand, if the spine leans back, the force tilts the body backward, lifting it off its base as in figure TG9.

Therefore, we see how the triangle and the pyramid rely on *Posture,* and how all three interact. More importantly, when a geometrically sound structure clashes with a geometrically unsound structure, the sound structure wins. And when our structure falters, we must exercise strength to compensate, which leads to defeat because we assume an opponent stronger than ourselves.

Let's look at it more pragmatically, purely in terms of geometric structure, imagining what it would be like to see a triangle in combat with a pentagon. If a triangle clashes with a pentagon then the pentagon will fold at the "elbows" and the triangle will penetrate (Figs. TG10a and TG10b). This must happen

TG10a

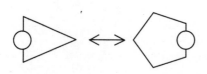

TG10b

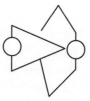

because a pentagon cannot structurally withstand as much force on its point as can a triangle.

Similarly, if a triangle comes up against a non-triangle, an opened "triangle," or opened "pentagon," it will penetrate with equal ease (Fig. TG11a and TG11b).

TG11a   **TG11b**

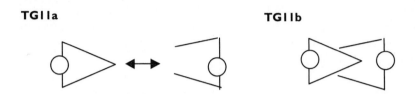

Of course, the geometric battle occurs equally on the vertical plane. As noted, a proper triangular structure will channel force downward, redirecting the force of the incoming attack and neutralizing it downward. (Fig. TG12a and TG12b).

TG12a   **TG12b**

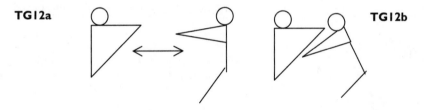

Or the sound triangular structure in TG13a will collapse the unsound structure in TG13b, forcing TG13b's arms back into its chest and ultimately tilting TG13b's entire body backward.

TG13a   **TG13b**

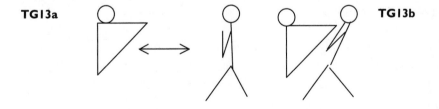

No matter how we look at it, a sound anatomical tri-   **TG14**
angle will defeat other structurally unsound physiologies.
In fact, its superiority works with equal effectiveness
against circular strikes. Against such assaults, the *Triangle*
Guard works through forward extension; it penetrates the
empty space created within the circular attack (Fig. TG14).

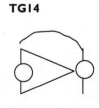

Of course, the structure does not work alone; we must advance quickly enough so as not to get hit in the head, and the proper use of sidestepping typically does not hurt.

While it seems as though a plausible alternative would involve opening the triangle to block the incoming circular attack with one arm, that creates two potential problems (TG15): (1) If we bend the arm we use to block and/or move it outside our torso, we construct the pentagon, which fails to receive force with the body, and requires us to use arm strength alone. (2) Because the force hits the side of the triangle, where it is weaker, rather than apex, it can cause us to rotate away from the opponent, which obviously leaves us compromised.

TG15

TG16

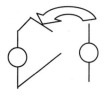

TG17

In light of this structural problem, a more geometrically sound approach to the problem involves angling the triangle to point into the oncoming force.[9] This could intercept the oncoming force at any point in its journey and at any point along the attacker's arm, and it would do so with structural/triangular integrity (TG16). Rather than blocking, an alternate approach would simply involve angling away from the attack and striking the opponent directly (TG17). Of course, these all illustrate gross motions and equally gross concepts. Techniques typically are much smaller and more subtle, though should express the same principles nonetheless.

Let's examine this same idea in the context of an actual technique, say a cross block, or any defensive technique that starts from the outer edge of the body structure and moves inward. Some styles call this an "inside block" or "inside parry." Virtually every style, soft or hard, has some version of this.

In TG18a-c, Jane executes a cross block against Gargantua's punch. Notice that her arm moves from outside her body inward.

---

9. Obviously, proper *Distancing* would be crucial so as not to defend a right punch by walking into the left. I note this because of its importance but once again I must emphasize that I am not talking about techniques in the proper sense.

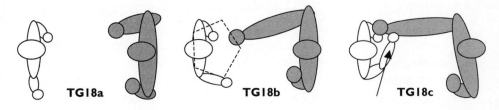

TG18a   TG18b   TG18c

In this example, Jane's block essentially moves through the structure of a pentagon. Aside from this being an obviously uneconomical path to the punch, it also results in two significant structural weaknesses: First, as her arm moves from its position in TG18b to that of TG18c, it does so without the support of her body structure. The arrow depicts the path through which she delivers force. Yet the base of the arrow has absolutely no structural support. Consequently, she will possess little ability to change the course of Gargantua's massive arm and its inertia.

The second weakness TG18 exposes concerns the final placement of her blocking arm relative to her body. Her arms ends up left of *Centerline*, thereby effectively collapsing her *Triangle Guard* and negating *Spinal Alignment* (TG18d). Were Gargantua to push on her right arm, she would possess little ability to stop it from collapsing against her body. Unfortunately, that is *exactly* what Gargantua does by punching at her.[10]

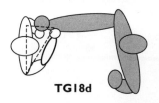

TG18d

TG19a   TG19b   TG19c

Yet Jane need not block in such fashion. Instead, she can block as we see in TG19a-c, turning her body slightly towards Gargantua's punch and delivering her block from shoulder forward along the path of the *Triangle Guard*, thereby supporting its impact with the shoulder, torso and legs. Of course, this represents just one example of many possible applications that all could manifest sound structure while still being different techniques."

---

10. Some readers also may have noted that TG18 also demonstrates how Jane has exposed herself to a counter from Gargantua's left punch. As both of her hands are on the left side of her body, she is ill-positioned to launch a quick and powerful defense.

In truth, particular attack-defense scenarios hold little importance. The essential point concerns the imperative to exercise the *Triangle Guard* in concordance with *Breathing* and *Posture* so as to gain the advantage of structurally deficient opponents. When we view this from the *Michelangelo Principle*, we understand that defeating such opponents becomes less a matter of "doing" something than of (1) eliminating our own structural deficiencies and (2) naturally exploiting the structural failings in our opponents.

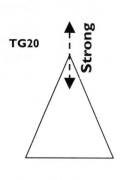

Yet no explication of the *Triangle Guard* would be complete without discussion of its *Reciprocal* forces. As stated, the *Triangle Guard* is structurally sound when force is applied between the point and the base (Figure TG20). By the law of *Reciprocity*, however, it *must* be weak in the opposite directions, as in when pressure comes from the sides (TG21). In such cases, the tendency will be for the triangle to turn from isosceles to scalene, as in TG22a&b. The result? Attempts to apply force, as in a block, in the directions of TG21 or TG22a&b invariably will be weaker than force applied along the TG20 path, which not only is strong when force is applied directly to the apex but also when force is applied along each "arm" of the triangle.

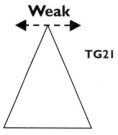

Fortunately, as TG19 demonstrates, conforming to the triangular structure poses us no actual difficulties. All techniques can be applied within that construct provided we exercise proper movement of the body. This applies to everything from hard style blocking to the soft parrying we might see in T'ai Chi Ch'uan.

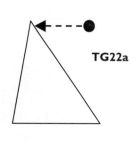

Aside from the *Reciprocity* found in the counter-directions above, the *Triangle Guard* also contains a fascinating, if not outright ironic, element. Just as the *Triangle Guard* receives force well, so does it *release* force well. Put another way, the *Triangle Guard* excels at receiving force towards its base *and* releasing force away from its base. In essence, the body *wants* to release force through the triangular path, meaning that we will have an easier time "forcing" our opponents arms along the triangular path than along other paths. (A second major reason for this involves the *Triangulation Point* principle, discussed later.)

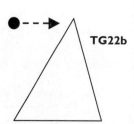

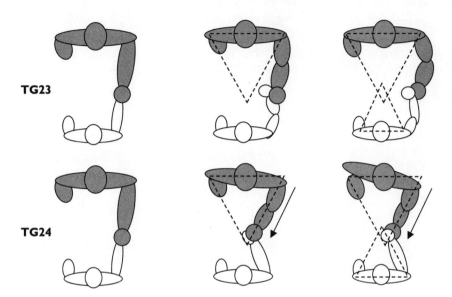

TG23

TG24

How does this manifest itself? If we consider a simple counter to Gargantua's wrist grab, it will be easier to release from that grab if we move his arm through his triangular path (TG24) than not (TG23). However, that applies only to a release that moves his arm away from him, not one that penetrates towards him, in which case TG23 will be easy and TG24 will be difficult.

Note that it is not only Gargantua's *Triangle Guard* that becomes a factor. Joe's *TG* equally comes into play. He must maintain the integrity of his own triangle, which Gargantua might be opposing. To accomplish this, Joe might need to exercise footwork.

Yet the *Triangle Guard* presents yet another element of *Reciprocity*, namely that of *negative triangles*. Looking at TG25a&b—a modification of TG1—we see the three essential negative triangles, shown in gray. Hence, the arms—solid matter—represent the positive triangle, while the triangular spaces where there is not solid matter represent the negative triangles.

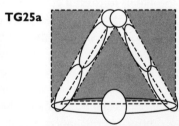

TG25a

The outer negative triangles represent those areas best exploited when entering against a wrist grab or off a punch, for example. If combating a wrist grab using the technique depicted in TG26, we want to move into one outside negative triangle. If we approach the technique as in TG27, we move their solid body mass into

TG25b

TG26

TG27

TG28

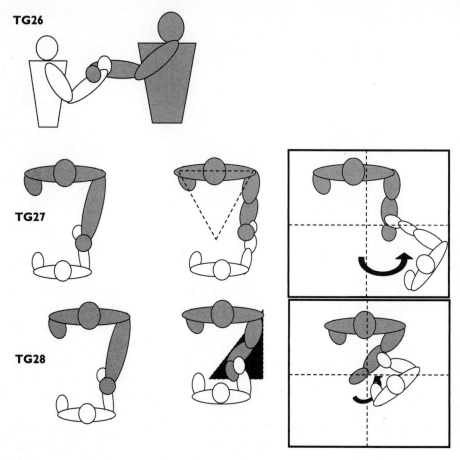

the open space of the negative triangle, thus eliminating that void and forcing us to cover a great deal of distance, which not only takes up time but also permits our opponent considerable opportunity to resist. Yet entering as in TG28, we slip into the existing void of the negative triangle and decrease the amount of movement, allowing us to apply the *Void* principle—"fighting" the opponent where the opponent lacks the physical presence to resist us.

I also want to note that the inner negative triangle can be used just as well as the outer ones. The applications become a bit more subtle but the principle remains constant.

This chapter fails to offer a complete account of the *Triangle Guard*, which probably would require a short book of its own, but it delves into its key elements and establishes a foundation for the principles that follow. Nevertheless, readers should have ample ideas to test and practice. We need to explore all the ways that all of our techniques can exercise the power of the triangle.

22

Centerline

T O BE SURE, THE ART THAT POPULARIZED THIS PRINCIPLE IS *WING CHUN*, which does a wonderful job of expressing its value in close range or "trapping" range combat. Yet while *Wing Chun* offers a great arena for demonstrating the principle's value, it manifests equally in all arts, a point too often overlooked by those who do not play the trapping game.

The *Centerline* principle works on two premises: Premise 1: As most vital targets are along the centerline of the body, we must protect our *Centerline* while controlling the opponent's. Premise 2: Control the centerline, control the confrontation. However, we need not fight head on in order to reap the benefits of this principle.

Returning to the first premise, we see in Cen1 that preferred targets sit along the centerline of the body. In fact, as we move away from the centerline we see the number of viable targets diminish (pressure points excluded).[11] Interestingly, most centerline targets only become useful when struck head on. The solar plexus, throat, eyes, and groin can be hurt only by forward-directed force. Otherwise, attacks against them simply run into bone and/or muscle. Why are such targets so well protected? Because their vulnerable nature would leave us all crippled if they were not. This, of course, explains why some styles adopt "side-facing" stances, ones where the *Centerline* faces away from the opponent.

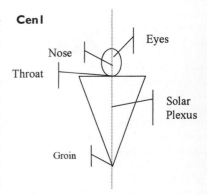

Cen1

Eyes

Nose

Throat

Solar Plexus

Groin

---

11. I do not advocate striking such harmful and/or dangerous targets unless the situation offers no other ethical alternative.

Whatever the stance, understanding centerline targets proves essential, but not as essential as understanding the importance of *controlling* the centerline itself. If we can access the opponent's centerline but the opponent cannot access ours then we should win the confrontation. Illustration Cen2a and Cen2b demonstrate this from a front-facing context. In Cen2a, both opponents square off equally. But in Cen2b, the person on the left captures the centerline, "boxing out" attacks from the figure on the right. Because the shortest distance between two points is a straight line, and because the person on the right will have to launch curved attacks that cannot strike centerline targets, the person on the left gains the advantage. Or perhaps Cen3, though a slight exaggeration, illustrates the point better.

Cen2a

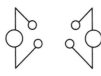

Cen3

Cen2b

Cen4

And so the question becomes one of where you would prefer to be standing, on the left or on the right? If you are standing on the right then nothing stands between you and your opponent's fist. Yet if you are on the left, your hands sit directly in front of you, and thus protect your centerline targets, and nothing obscures you to the opponent's primary targets. Thus, and this is crucial, the value of controlling centerline does not stop at facilitating access to vital targets, rather it more pointedly concerns dominating the fight itself. Whether or not we intend to strike centerline targets, we have established a *Position* of dominance, a position equally useful for striking, grappling, and trapping.

I suspect that many of my readers already will have noted the remarkable similarity between Cen2b and TG11b & TG14. Obviously, this is because, as I noted, the *Triangle Guard* concept overlays the *Centerline* theory, as is represented in illustration Cen4. I must note, however, that the two are not interchangeable terms or concepts. Whereas *Triangle* theory primarily concerns anatomical structure, *Centerline* theory concerns controlling primary target lines and the most efficient routes to them. Nevertheless, we cannot not easily discuss one without the other.

Towards that end, we already have seen three ways in which we may get control of the centerline: (1) By "boxing out" the opponents arms as in Cen2, Cen3, TG11 and TG14; (2) by forcing their arms and posture down as in TG10, and (3) by forcing their arms up and back as in TG13. Those constitute three possible results of what happens when *Triangle Guards* clash, and in each case one person maintains control of the centerline.

Yet we can access the *Centerline* through proper *Angling*, as well. If, as in Cen5, two triangles meet head on but each is *just slightly off line from the other*, meaning that their tips do not directly hit, then each turns off to the side in equal measure to the other (supposing two parties of equal size).

Cen5

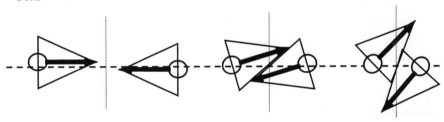

However, *that only occurs because neither one focused on the other's Centerline from the start.* (This actually initiates discussion of *Spinal Alignment*, which I will hold off until the next chapter.) Consequently, we can see how the above scenario will play out differently if one *Triangle Guard* faces the centerline and the other does not. Notice that in Cen6 the right figure does not begin with its centerline facing the left figure's centerline. Consequently, the right figure does not engage force at its tip but rather with its side. As a result, the right figure spins off against the left figure, turning away. The left figure, however, always points its *Triangle/Centerline*, and thus its weapons, directly at the centerline of the right figure, even as the right figure turns away. Consequently, the left figure becomes positioned to strike targets the right figure cannot defend.

Cen6

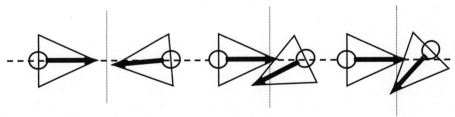

Cen7

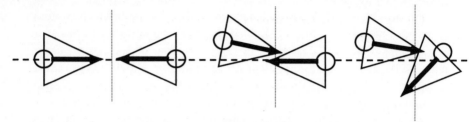

Of course, supposing that attackers will not begin in misalignment, we can create the same scenario through slight *Angling* and footwork. As in Cen7, we see the left figure seize the advantage by shifting slightly off the line of attack *while keeping fixed on the right figure's centerline*. The right figure, on the other hand, continues its attack straight forward along the initial line. As a consequence, the right figure, no longer pointed towards the opponent's *Centerline*, must yield. Hence, the left figure gains the advantage.

Therefore, the *Triangle Guard* maintains structural integrity as long as it meets force straight on with its point. A triangle that meets force with its side possesses no more strength than a line, especially when given the human anatomical imperative that force needs to be grounded through the spine, which I discuss in the chapter to follow.

For now, however, note that the *Centerline* applies no less to grappling arts and other ranges of combat. While listing all such examples would be impractical, I will offer two. First, in kicking, establishing *Centerline* presence becomes no less valuable, not only for reasons that have to do with power and *Spinal Alignment* but also for defensive considerations.

I encounter many martial artists who execute a front kick as depicted in Cen8. While it might look relatively sound, the kick overlooks *Centerline* theory. The right leg kick never quite takes control of the centerline, which produces three ill effects: 1. It leaves the groin and lower extremities unprotected. 2. The power of the kick cannot connect to the spine and then root

Cen8

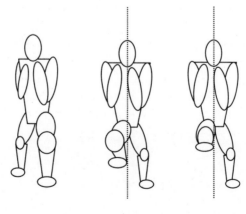

into the rear leg. 3. The kick takes longer because it does not follow the most efficient path.

On the other hand, Cen9 depicts a different execution of the technique. Note that the right knee moves to chamber by crossing slightly in front of the body until it aligns with the *Centerline*. Consider how much more difficult it would be to attack that figure's groin or rear leg. As the technique completes, note how the foot aligns with the spine and, to a lesser degree, the rear foot. While these distinctions might seem subtle at first, their effect is not. Those more accustomed to kicking in the Cen8 method typically become amazed at the sudden increase in the speed of their kick when switching to Cen9. Initially, they usually state that it does not "feel" as powerful because it relies less on musculature (also see *The Power Paradox*) but they soon agree that it transfers more power to the target.

Moving on to grappling; while the *Centerline* need not be seen, it certainly can be felt. In ground fighting, for example, as when one person sits on top of another, sensing the *Centerline* permits the grappler to understand the opponent's weight distribution, a key factor in selecting the next appropriate technique. Furthermore, grapplers often will attempt to gain control of the *Centerline* by getting their hands to it rather than grabbing at the opponent's shoulders or elbows.

Cen9

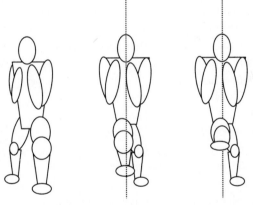

Though I'll touch on this more in the *Spinal Alignment* chapter, a final word about the *Centerline* principle concerns its psychological impact, or rather how impact affects our psychology. Even without being hit on certain vital targets, being hit along the *Centerline* proves far more disturbing than being struck in other areas, just as it is more disturbing to be grabbed there than at the shoulder. Essentially, and at the risk of becoming to abstract, a greater percentage of our "being" resides in our torso than in our extremities. Thus, attacking the *Centerline* attacks our "core," which is why we must seek it in our opponents while simultaneously protecting ours from them.

23

The Primary Gate

(Zero Point, Apex, Main Gate or Center Gate)

A S I'LL DISCUSS IN A CHAPTER TO FOLLOW, COMBAT CAN BE VIEWED AS A simple battle for a control of space, meaning that if we *Control* how our opponent accesses (or does not access) our own space while simultaneously controlling how we access his or her space, we win. When viewed from the perspective of the entire spatial mass of two human forms and the distance between them, the control of space can be daunting. Fortunately, we can distill much of combat, especially that within arms reach, down to a battle for dominance over a relatively small area, what I call the *Primary Gate*.

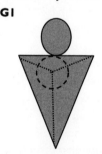

The *Primary Gate* principle directly emerges **PG1** from *Triangle Guard* theory. Consider, after all, the location of the *Primary Gate*, which sits roughly in front of the solar plexus or between the solar plexus and the chin. (It actually floats up or down slightly depending on the height of our opponent.) Referring back to the *Triangle Guard*, we see the *Primary Gate* as a floating circle where all of the triangles converge (PG1).

First and foremost, consider how many martial arts techniques function on protecting that zone. If we consider traditional karate-style blocking as an example, virtually all of the blocks pass through that zone of the body. A right handed downward block might start at the left shoulder and end near the right hip. A right cross or inside block might start by the right shoulder and end near the left. A rising block starts near the solar plexus and raises up. And so on. Most traditional blocking techniques (karate or otherwise) concern defending the *Primary Gate*, and that is no accident.

It emerges from a very real anatomical premise that I mentioned in the

Triangle Guard chapter. If we consider the natural arc of our arms, we find that we enjoy the greatest range when they stretch out horizontally from our shoulder and parallel to the ground. As in PG2, that range diminishes as our arms arc upwards or downwards. The distance from the shoulder to the hand always remains the same, of course, but the ability to reach our opponent diminishes as the arms swing up or down.

Consider what happens when two figures face off against each other, as in PG3. Though equidistant from each other, were the gray figure striking to the high or low position then the white figure acquires the tactical advantage by maintaining control of the horizontal path, i.e. the *Primary Gate*.

To compensate for a deficiency in range, the gray figure might make a tactical error, namely one of leaning forward or twisting, or both, so as to extend the range of the attack. Consider PG4. Gargantua, in an effort to extend his range and circumvent Joe's *Primary Gate*, leans forward to reach lower targets, thus bringing his own face right into Joe's hands!

Or imagine what it would feel like to be the figure on the right in PG5. You cannot strike through the *Primary Gate* but your opponent can, which not only means that you have to go around that center path in order to strike, it also means that *any and all movements around the Primary Gate will leave your face and chest undefended.*

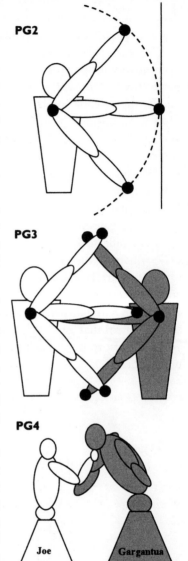

PG2

PG3

PG4

Joe   Gargantua

PG5

When first exposed to the *Primary Gate* idea, many martial artists think it a good idea to try to make the gate as large as possible, to cover as much territory with their blocks and strikes as possible. In theory, the opponent would be forced to use larger and larger angles of attack. Yet that actually causes a problem. The larger our *Primary Gate*, the more our own limbs move off the most efficient and direct line of attack.

Therefore, as we want to keep our movements as *Efficient* as possible, we then want to *decrease* the size of the *Primary Gate* until it is no larger than a pea. If the opponent does not protect that pathway, we strike through it.

Try a simple drill: Square off with a partner and place your fists directly in front of your partner's fist, both in the *Primary Gate* position. Let each partner take turns with casually launching strikes around the *Primary Gate*, and let the defender practice striking straight through the *Primary Gate* as soon as an opening presents itself. This can be done at a variety of ranges and to varying degrees of competitiveness, but it should be noted that this is *more* a conceptual drill than a functional training method.

Of course, while the *Primary Gate* concerns the arms, a lower gate concerns the legs. We find it at hip level, where the legs enjoy the greatest range. In close quarter combat, where we get too close to kick at the hip or higher targets, the gate floats down to knee level.

Returning to kicking range, consider the difference between PG6 and PG7, which are the same as Cen8 and Cen9. Then try a simple drill. Square off with a partner and have your partner throw a left leg snap kick or round kick without first capturing the *Centerline* and the hip level gate (PG6). Each time your partner kicks, execute a front kick as depicted in PG7. In short, control that gate! While the distinction may be subtle, with practice you can learn to seize that gate whenever you see your opponent leaving it undefended.

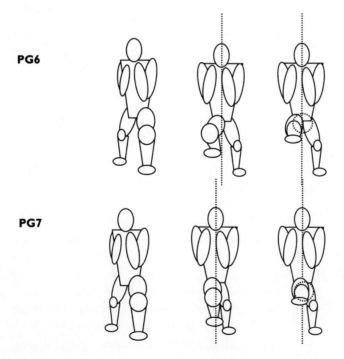

PG6

PG7

Note that controlling the kicking gate does not necessarily mean kicking to the groin. Once you establish control of the gate, you can strike surrounding targets while maintaining the advantage, just as controlling the *Primary Gate* does not mean having to strike to the solar plexus.

I have seen martial artists so effective at controlling the *Primary* and *Kicking Gates* that they nearly could fight without moving. They needed only to wait for their opponents to leave those lines of attack unprotected, which usually did not take long, and then strike through them.

24

Spinal Alignment

ARGUABLY, THIS IS THE SINGLE MOST OVERLOOKED PRINCIPLE OF MARTIAL arts. When it comes to generating power and applying technique, I see considerable discussion about using the hips, the structure of the arm, the depth of *Extension and Penetration,* etc. but very little discussion concerning how to properly align techniques with the spine.

Ultimately, *all* power must be grounded, generated, and conducted through the spine. Part of this discussion will have to hold off until I discuss *Heaviness* and *Wave Energy,* but part of it can be discussed now.

First, I must back reference P5 and P6, which demonstrate what hap-

P5

P6

pens to the anatomy when the spine is misaligned when striking. If concave, the body's "equal and opposite reaction" will be to leak power through the rounded back and hips (P5). If convex, the "equal and opposite reaction" to the strike will be to leak power by leaning back (P6). Either way, the misalignment of the spine prevents the legs from stabilizing the body and offering a solid foundation from which to exercise the power of the punch.

The thin air behind the figures in P5 and P6 cannot stabilize the punch. Instead, the *spine must function like a post.* Metaphorically speaking, we should envision our spine extending straight down into the ground deep enough to withstand all the force we could press against it (Fig.

Sp1). Imagine the stability you would feel if a straight post ran through your spine and deep into the ground. Consider how such stability would prevent any power leakages.

While the spine itself does not literally extend into the ground, it effectually does by branching off into the legs, which in turn reach "into" the ground (Sp2). Of course, the spine must be in proper alignment if the legs are to become functional. If misaligned—P5 and P6—the spine will fail to direct energy into the legs, and consequently diminish or nullify the value of proper foot stance.

Some argue that the upper body can lean forward up to 22½ degrees (Sp3), or perhaps to the point where shoulders do not pass the vertical plane of the knees, *provided that the spine does not become convex or concave*, which means that it *must tilt from the hip alone*. Any other violation of its structure will bleed energy upwards or backwards. At 22½ degrees, however, the force can still ground into the legs through the spine.

Another school of thought permits us to bend to the point where our shoulders align vertically with our toes, *but*

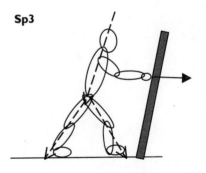

never beyond. Depending on style, this can work as well but *proper posture must be upheld*, which means the torso much tilt as a unit from the hip. At such times, proper alignment of the solar plexus becomes critical. I should note, however, that I am increasingly less persuaded of the permissibility of tilting the spine as it poses challenges for *Wave Energy* and other principles that follow.

To be fully understood, however, *Spinal Alignment* must be understood from another angle, and this returns us to our *Centerline* discussion. In order for our exertions of force to root through the spine, they must align with it, which *when front facing* means they must occur along the *Centerline*. What is *critical* to understand is that they must not only *end* on the centerline but also begin along it, or at least close to it.

Sp4

Sp5

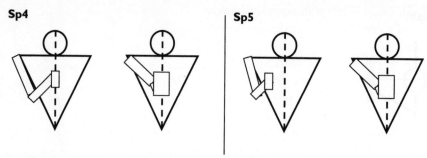

In the purest sense, this would look like figure Sp4, but again, depending on your school of thought, some leeway might be permissible. Once again, the degree of angle must not exceed 22½ degrees. In which case, it could look like figure Sp5, where the punch begins just off the centerline.

We can see how punching in such a fashion both protects *Centerline* targets and aligns power with the spine so that it can be supported by the legs. *Spinal Alignment* therefore dictates that the spine must act as a solid, unyielding post. Every degree it turns amounts to a degree it effectively *yields*—succumbing to "opposite reaction" rather than generating force—and thus a degree of power lost or misdirected. In fact, if the spine acts as a pivot instead of stalwart post then our *Triangle Guard* will be deflected off target.

Sp6

Sp7

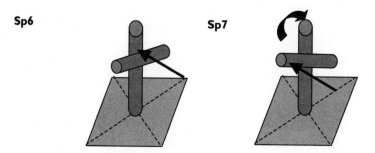

In this sense, consider the spine to function like a big lower case "t." If *Rooted*, we can apply pressure *directly forward* onto the vertical post without it yielding or spinning (Sp6). However, if we apply force to either "arm" of the horizontal T-bar then the vertical post will pivot one way or the other (Sp7).

Precisely the same thing happens to the human body when it exerts force from the shoulders rather than aligning force with the spine. The spine fails to function as a solid, stable post and instead acts as a weak, turning pivot, which ultimately results in a loss of power. If, as in Sp8, the punch fails to meet the centerline, the shoulder becomes susceptible to recoiling in direct opposition to the direction of the punch. If, as in Sp9, the punch crosses over centerline, the body becomes susceptible to pivoting the other

Sp8   **Sp9**

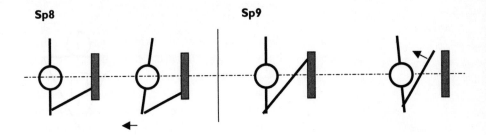

direction, or the arm simply collapses toward the body with the shoulder acting as the hinge.

Depending on whom you ask, the shoulders either do or do not have to be square—equidistant—to the target for the spine to align properly. I have heard people say they must and I have heard people say that it is unnecessary. Certainly, the *Triangle Guard* brings to light the importance of at least a certain amount of squaring in the shoulders, but the great equalizing factor in this particular matter always seems to come down to landing the strike directly between the shoulder lines so that the energy still grounds back to the spine. Figure Sp10 demonstrates the incorrect application of this idea, whereas figure Sp11 demonstrates the effective application of this idea.

Sp10   **Sp11**

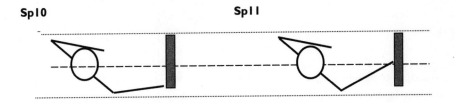

Notice that Sp10 will incur the same problems as Sp8. Sp11, on the other hand, could ground the force back into the spine, using it as a post instead of as a pivot. However, *much of that would depend on the trajectory.* If Sp9 extended the punch from the shoulder—the bottom dotted line—instead of from the centerline then the force would recoil against the shoulder and pivot the body. However, if the punch extended from the middle line, along the *Centerline*, the tilted position of the shoulders would at least be less detrimental, if detrimental at all. I should note, however, that I am less persuaded by the ability of the body to tilt in delivering power because doing so seems to impact the alignment of other principles.

The importance of understanding *Spinal Alignment* goes deeper still. As with all principles, we want to exercise it properly so as to maximize our own power and simultaneously use it to exploit our opponent's anatomy. It follows, therefore, that just as the spine connects the body to power, so does it receive power into the body. Thus, if applying a wristlock like the gray

Sp12

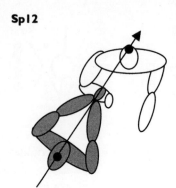

figure is in Sp12, we must apply force directly :toward the opponent's spine. Doing so immediately seizes control of the opponent's entire body because all parts of the body connect through the spine. *This does not just seize the arm or wrist, it seizes the body in totality,* thus forcing the opponent to succumb not merely through pain compliance but rather through holistic *Physiokinetics.*

If we misalign by even a few degrees, it will permit or even encourage the opponent's spine to act as a pivot rather than a post, and

Sp13a   **Sp13b**

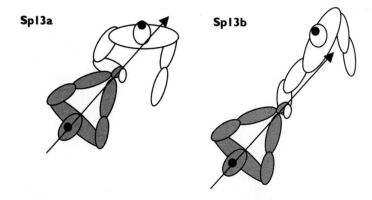

the opponent will escape the lock by rotating. We see this in Sp13a&b. The lighter figure pivots using its spine as an axis, thus conforming to the line of the force. While we must recognize that this nevertheless could produce an opportunity for a different lock, we must also remember that said secondary lock will encounter the same problem as the first until the line of attack strikes the spine directly.

Sp14a   **Sp14b**

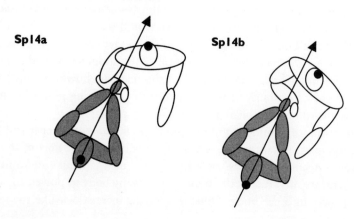

Converse to Sp13, if the line of attack misses in the other direction then the opponent not only once again enjoys the opportunity to evade the true direction of the force but also may pivot inwards so as to land a counter attack. (Sp14a & b)

Of course, if we *want* the opponent's body to turn, then we exercise the principle of *Spinal Alignment* by intentionally missing the spine with our force, thereby forcing it to act like a pivot.

When examining this principle, I originally wondered if there was a contradiction in directing force toward where the opponent derives his or her power. And so this must be precisely clear: exercising proper *Spinal Alignment* does not mean physically moving force into the spine itself, e.g. forcing an opponent's wrist to his or her chest. As the name suggests, this principle merely concerns *aligning* force between our spine and our opponent's on a vertical plane.

25

Axis

O UR "*AXIS*" REFERS TO THE INVISIBLE LINE RUNNING DOWN THE CENTER OF the body, roughly between the centerline and the spine. Thus, if we view it from above (AX2), where the dotted line represents the *Centerline* and "S" represents the spine (which does not actually extend to the top of the head), the black dot represents the *Axis*. (Ultimate, the *Axis* can move depending on the positioning of the legs but such changes matter little).

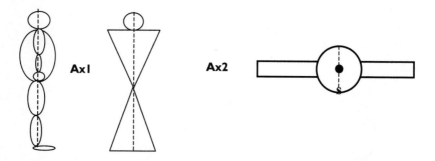

Nevertheless, the *Axis* constitutes the center of full-body rotation. The *Axis* principle dictates that we must maintain a vertical *Axis* and seek the tightest possible rotation when turning. With that in mind, we must respect two rules: (1) rotation becomes slower as our *Axis* grows thicker, and (2) rotation becomes slower as our *Axis* tilts. Perhaps figure skaters offer the clearest example of this. When spinning, they leave their arms away from their bodies to spin slowly, thus creating a large *Axis,* and draw their arms back into themselves to increase the speed of their rotation. The smaller the cylinder, the faster it will spin.

Which figure in Ax3 could rotate faster, the great big cylinder or the thin one? Obviously, the thinner cylinder would revolve more times more quickly because of its smaller circumference.

As martial artists, we need to exercise the smallest *Axis* possible, one ultimately no thicker than a thread. It probably comes as no surprise that this relies on sound *Posture*. Figure Ax4 demonstrates the width of the cylinder when we have good posture, whereas Ax5 demonstrates what happens when our poster falters. Ax5 can be read two different ways, either as a right facing figure with a plumed chest and protruding buttocks, or as a left facing figure with a belly and rounded back. Either way, the incorrect posture widens the cylinder.

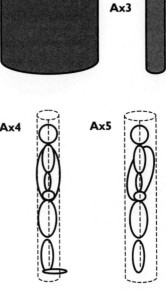

Notice that in Ax5 the body maintains equilibrium—the *Axis* runs down the center of the body, effectively splitting it in two. Much as a balance scale, the human body always will seek to maintain such balance—the weight must be equal on both sides or the body will tip. (Actually, as previously noted, muscular exertion can compensate for extra weight on one side or the other, but this once again returns us to the problem of the *Percentage Principle*.)

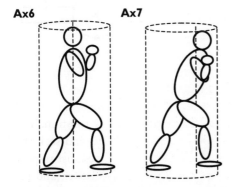

As Ax6 and Ax7 demonstrate, we also can widen the cylinder by foot placement and body tilt, which means that we must seek small footwork and upright *Posture*.

Yet not only does leaning forward widen the cylinder, it actually changes the cylinder from round to oblong and/or de-centers the *Axis*. Either way, rotation slows. While we find the cylinder in Ax7 no wider than in Ax6 (provided that the head/body does not lean past the feet), we also find that *the axis no longer splits the body in half*. The *weight* remains equally distributed but the *mass* of the body becomes lopsided. Consequently, the mass, as we see in the rear leg, extends farther from one side of the axis than it does from the other.

In result, the body will no longer spin like a top. It will wobble around

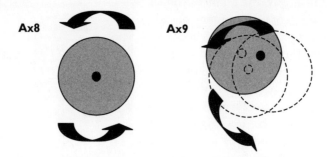

its off-center axis. Looking at the cylinder from above, Ax8 represents equal mass distribution and a circular rotation. But Ax9 demonstrates what happens when we lean forward, which causes lopsided rotation.

Ax10 and Ax11 offer the same problem with human examples, both seen from directly above. In Ax10 the axis remains centered in the mass even though the legs are split. In Ax10, where the figure leans forward, the axis moves, effectively turning the cylinder into something more like an oval.

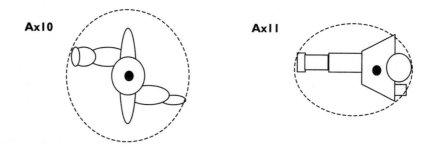

The centralization of our axis and the speed at which we rotate obviously impacts techniques, perhaps most obviously with respect to evading oncoming force. Ax12 obviously enjoys a far better circumstance with respect to rotating off an attack than does Ax13, whose rotation actually moves its head across the path of the attack. To be sure, in the case of a *Centerline* attack, both figures would need to "step" offline regardless of their rotations, but Ax12 would need to step notably less.

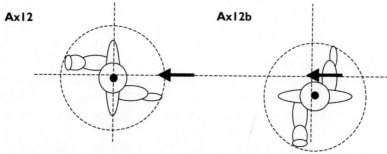

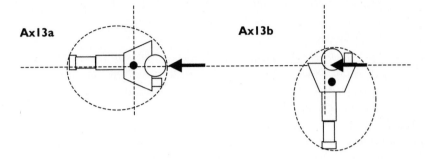

Ax13a　　　　　　　**Ax13b**

As we see, if we move the axis in Ax13b the same distance offline as Ax12b, Ax13b fails to evade the oncoming attack. In fact, its head passes directly through the line of that attack. This is because the upper body in 13b must lean forward so as to counterbalance the lower body's rotation as it spins away from the line of attack.

Furthermore, AX13's lengthy, oblong shape will make it rotate slower than AX12, just as its improper *Posture* will compromise foot speed. Thus, given the same amount of time, Ax13 would *not* complete the full 90 degree rotation that Ax12 completed.

I must note, however, that I have encountered some systems, mostly Filipino and Indonesian ones, that use the body tilt to their advantage in evading attacks to the lower body. If we revisit Ax13b and envision the arrow as an attack to the midsection, it would miss the midsection. I am neither advocating or denigrating such a technique. I am merely noting exceptions where I have seen them.

The same problem we see in Ax13b occurs when striking, throwing, or applying a joint lock. We see this in the application of a *kote gaeshi* wrist throw, as seen in illustrations Ax14a&b. Purely from a rotational perspective, we see that the off-center nature of the rotation actually turns more mass and energy *away* from lock instead of into it. In other words, note how much of the body in 14b moves *away* from the place where the hands meet. Though not a fully accurate analogy, applying a lock in this fashion roughly equates to hitting a baseball with the *short* end of the bat instead of the longer end. By contrast, rotating the technique with a centered *Axis*

Ax14a　　　　　　　**Ax14b**

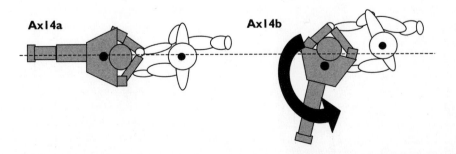

would impart at least as much power into the technique as turns away. (Other principles ultimately permit *all* power to surge into the technique, but that is a discussion for later on.)

Regardless of the technique in question, we must secure as small an *Axis* as possible so as to maximize our speed of motion, speed of rotation, and relative power to our opponent. At the same time, we must keep in mind how increasing the size of our rotation violates the *Percentage Principle* by requiring us to exercise more muscular force to swing greater and more distant parts of our bodies along longer rather than shorter paths.

Consider again a basic punch. If in order to punch we must execute some spin in our bodies, even if only through *Wave Energy*, then the slower rotation produced by a wider *Axis* will (1) increase the time it takes to launch the punch and (2) decrease the speed at which it travels. If we can punch using a smaller *Axis*, the punch will release sooner, travel faster, and also more easily align with our spine because its angle will be straighter. For this reason, one of the first exercises I engage in with those I'm training to strike is that of tightening their *Axis*.

The *Axis* principle essentially comes down to a simple premise: when rotating, we must make our rotations small and fast rather than big and slow. Nearly all techniques require at least some rotation of the body, and so if we can devote less time to rotation it frees up more time to take other actions.

26

Minor Axes

[Radical Principle]

H AVING DISCUSSED THE *AXIS* PRINCIPLE, IT SEEMS A FITTING TIME TO POINT out that the body contains *Minor Axes*, places where we can rotate limbs within tighter or wider circles. Genergally speaking, the same rules apply to all *Minor Axes* as to the major *Axis* of motion; rotations should be as small and tight as possible, thereby maximizing their speed and power.

Consider a corkscrew punch. If thrown as in the MA1 series, we see it traversing a rather large arc, with the black dot in MA1c representing the *Minor Axis* of that movement. Such a circular path not only takes longer than a straight one, it also disperses the force of the punch in multiple directions, *Centrifugally* releasing force at every part of the arc itself. This circularity happens when we fail to rotate the fist *within the circumference of the arm* itself.

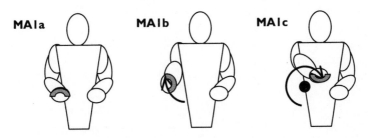

By contrast, the MA2 series throws the same punch with no less rotation but with a tighter *Minor Axis*. As the punch moves forward, all rotation occurs within the circumference of the arm itself. Whereas the MA1 punch will hit the opponent with some lateral motion and thus glance off to some degree, the MA2 punch will strike the target moving forward only,

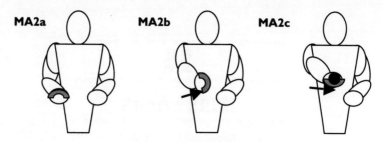

and with tighter rotational action. The straighter = shorter path of the punch also increases its speed.

Yet respecting *Minor Axes* does not necessarily mean avoiding all curvature in motion. It only means two things: (1) seeking the smaller axes possible in any given technique and (2) rotating within the circumference of the limb itself whenever possible. As we apply both elements to strikes, locks, throws, etc., we find that we can conserve our own force and equally deliver more concentrated power to the oponent.

27

Structure

FROM THIS POINT FORWARD, WHENEVER I USE THE WORD, "STRUCTURE," it will refer to proper *Breath, Spinal Alignment, Triangle Guard, Posture, and Axis.*

I also should note that sound anatomical *Structure* strikes me as perhaps the martial artist's greatest ally. While we typically will find ourselves at significant deficits in terms of size and strength, we easily can find ourselves at a significant advantage in terms of *Structure*. It does not take size, strength, or even much coordination to exercise sound anatomical *Structure* in technique, and when we begin to understand *Structure's* power we equally begin to understand how to exploit weak structure. Thus, a Joe or Jane, though at physical deficits when facing Gargantua, can compensate being structurally sound themselves while simultneously seizing upon Gargantua's structural flaws.

28

Heaviness[12]

LET'S START WITH A BRIEF EXERCISE. STAND WITH GOOD POSTURE AND TAKE some long, slow, proper breaths from your center. Each time you breath out, relax your body, releasing tension from your joints. Let them hang. As you do this, pay attention to the bottom of your feet (make sure they are relaxed too), and recognize how each step towards relaxation increases the pressure between your feet and the floor. This is you "getting heavy."

Applying the principle of *Heaviness* means exercising our anatomy in such a way that we not only maximize the use of our weight, we actually *apply* weight to techniques. *Heaviness* plays obvious roles in grappling arts such as *judo, jujitsu, shia shao,* etc.. The heavier we are in terms of actual points, and the more we exercise *Heaviness,* the more difficult it will be to throw us.

Heaviness, however, extends to other applications; every art benefits from it, if not requires it. To understand this, try a second exercise: Stand up and walk over to the nearest wall. Without leaning forward, and while keeping both feet about eighteen inches away from the base of the wall, go ahead and give the wall a push. Notice that the wall remains stable while your own body retreats. Then try leaning against the wall, seeing how much of your weight you can bring to bare against it. Notice that you can bring more force against the wall by leaning than you can by pushing. In fact, while only a few pounds of pressure will push us away from the wall, we can deliver a considerable amount of weight into the wall without repercussion.

Obviously, "for every action there is an equal and opposite reaction." In the case of pushing the wall, the reaction should be obvious—we move

---

12. To fully understand this chapter, it must be read in accordance with the following two: Relaxation and Wave Energy. It also must be understood in the context of Rooting.

away from the wall because we lack the power to move the wall away from us. In the case of leaning, however, we incur absolutely no "opposite reaction." *All our force transfers into the wall; none of it returns into us.* This reveals an absolutely *essential* point about *Heaviness:* For all intents and purposes, *dead weight does not and can not incur the reaction to its own action.* That is why it is "dead," and that is why *Heaviness* works so well.

When pushing against the wall, we can compensate for the "equal and opposite reaction" by leaning forward (H1). Doing so enables us to support our forward push by angling the body so as to use the rear leg as a brace. However, if in adopting that stance we relaxed our rear leg, we would push ourselves away from the wall, which "pushes" back in equal measure to how much we push against it. Thus, the more we push against it the more it "pushes" against us, or more accurately, the more we push oursleves away from it.

Therefore, H1 is an *unstable* position. Remove the wall and the figure will stumble forward, if not fall on its face— hardly the kind of controlled "technique" we seek in martial arts. Furthermore, H1 will encounter a multitude of problems with respect to its *Axis* and *Structure*. Therefore, we must find a way to exercise *Heaviness* without succumbing to self-defeating and unstable angles.

To do so, we first must recognize how our body works *against* us when we "push" with muscle rather than executing *Heaviness.* To that end, I offer two examples I encourage you to try. Though simplisitic, they demonstrate the point. First, as in H2, have someone *at least* as strong as you stretch his or her arm out stiffly. Stand at your partner's side and

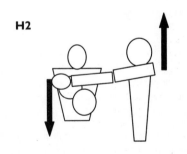

press down on his or her arm with your own arm, which must be fully extended. Notice, as you do, the reaction in your shoulder: it will raise up in compensation for your exertion of downward force. Depending on the strength of your partner, the shoulder movement will be slight or great.

Worse, the shoulder might not be the only part of your body to counterbalance the downward force exerted through your arm. Your entire body mass may lift up slightly. I've actually seen people lift themselves off their heels.

Unfortunately, the same anatomical effect occurs when punching. Without striking too hard, simply push your fist into someone's chest, a body shield, a heavy bag, or a wall, and notice the reaction in *your* body.

Depending on your *Posture* and punching method, you probably will feel repercussions in your shoulder, chest, or hips. You might not actually feel those parts move but, if properly attentive, you will feel them tense up to compensate for the forward force you exert. Either way, your body will in some fashion react to its own action, and as the *Percentage Principle* reminds us, every bit of reaction in our own bodies results in less reaction in the target.

The remedy involves replacing muscular power with weight in motion— *Heaviness*. Returning to H2, that means using only *weight* to drop our partner's arm, which means using the minimal tension required to extend our arm at all. Any and all additional tension in our own arm only decreases its *Heaviness* because tension results from muscles that "lift" the arm.

Thus, if we return to the H2 example, we should not exercise tension and should instead require our partner to hold up both our arms. Yet as this will not produce enough force to drop our partner's arm, we need to amplify our arm weight with our body weight. I will explain that more accurately in *Wave Energy*, but if we dropped in our knees while maintining the angle between our arm and our body, we will add weight to the exercise. This requires exerting just enough tension in our shoulder to keep our arm level, but once having done so we can drop our partner's arm down without having to *push* it down, and thus without the simultaneous consequence of pushing ourselves upwards.

Of course, that's a *bad example*. We do not want tension in our shoulder because it ultimately decreases our *Heaviness*. It has other ill effects, too, some of which will be discussed in the next chapter.

Nevertheless, we must understand the relative power of weight. If dealing with a stronger opponent and working from the premise that martial arts must overcome strength, then we must accept that a weaker person will never push a stronger person's arm down. In the H2 example, Joe and Jane will never push Gargantua's arm down. However, imagine if Gargantua were for some odd reason holding his arm outstretched and a 100 pound weight suddenly and unexpectedly materialized on his wrist. Unprepared for the sudden force, his arm would drop. Even if the weight were anticipated, the outstretched position of the arm would make *suddenly* supporting 100 pounds of dead weight difficult even for Gargantua, especially if he were structurally unsound. None of this yet considers the addition of momentum, such as if the weight fell from ten feet above.

Thus, weight can be difficult to contend with when added gradually but far more overpowering when added *suddenly*. Consequently, my discussion of *Heaviness* typically refers to sudden manifestations of weight that manifest our *Heaviness* faster than the opponent can compensate.

Before we can get there, however, we must understand how the exercise of weight intimately connects with *Structure*. As noted, improper *Posture*, e.g. leaning forward so that the upper body no longer sits on its spine, makes the body want to fall forward and down, which our body resists by tensing muscles in our back and stomach. Those muscles are then fighting *Gravity* and essentially lifting a portion of our weight. Thus, every muscle we use to keep ourselves upright is one that works against *Heaviness* by combating gravity and making us "lighter."

I must note the distinction between *Heaviness* and weight. Our weight does not change with posture, but our ability to *apply* that weight—*Heaviness*—does.

Let us consider a simple arm bar. The particulars of how we achieve this final position do not matter. What does matter is that it demonsrates the importance of *Heaviness* as connected with *Structure*. If your style does not include this technique, you've probably seen something similar. If not then take the *principle* from the example because that is all that matters anyway.

In H3a, we find the *uke* in a compromised position—bent forward with arm outstretched and nearing hyperextension. *Tori* (the person applying the arm bar) wants to drive *uke* (the recipient of the arm bar) to the ground and into a prostrate position, and wants to do this by applying pressure to the arm. As with all techniques, a myriad of factors and *principles* affect the outcome, but I will limit the discussion to those factors immediately relevant to *Heaviness*.

H3a

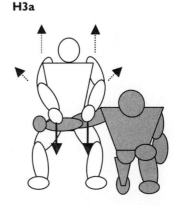

In H3a, Joe pushes Gargantua down using the strength in his arms, with the solid arrows representing action and the dotted arrows representing reaction. Much like in H2, we see Joe's elbows and shoulders yielding in "opposite reaction" to the force he exerts downward. Thus, the dotted arrows denote Joe lifting himself up rather than forcing Gargantua down. If Joe's strength cannot overcome Gargantua's, and it cannot, Joe will push himself upwards as if pushing down on a table.

Though in a compromised position, we must remember that a compromised Gargantua can be *stronger* than an uncompromised, or less compromised, Jane or Joe. Furthermore, even Joe ultimately can push Gargantua down, and the extent to which we must push represents the extent to which he will incur "opposite reaction." Thus, if Joe lifts 20% of his or her own weight up by pushing down then the armbar becomes 50% less effective!

Note as well that the pentagonal structure of Joe's arms also weakens his technique by requiring him to tense at his elbows to prevent his arms from collapsing. Were he in a more triangular structure, Joe could connect his arms to his body *(Spinal Alignment)* and deliver a higher percentage of his force to Gargantua.

H3b

Yet the positioning in H3b poses another problem. Because our weight always centers at our hips, our hips always want to go *straight* down, which happens by a release in tension at the knees. In H3b, if our hips went straight down then the majority of our weight would not help the technique. Instead of dropping into Gargantua's arm, it would drop onto the "x." Thus, we would not exercise *Heaviness.*

Supposing that Joe could accomplish the impossible task of dropping his weight evenly by lowering all parts equally and at the same time, his weight still would disperse over a large surface area rather than focusing on one spot Gargantua's arm *(Spatial Relativity).*

H3c

Yet to discover where his or her weight should be applied, Joe need only stiffen his arms and relax his hips. Figure H3c shows his hips swinging forward into Gargantua's arm where they will communicate the most weight. Yet H3c obviously does not represent sound tehcnique.

H3d

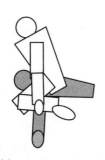

Figure H3d also does a good job of demonstrating *Heaviness* in *concept,* though it should be obvious that we do not literally want to jump onto the opponent's arm. Yet doing so would achieve the objective of suddenly placing all our weight into the technique while not producing any reaction—upwards lifting—in our own bodies. All our weight would be put to use and all our weight would drop on a small point rather than being dispersed over several square feet. Gargantua would not be prepared, nor structurally sound, for suddenly supporting *all* our weight with one outstretched arm, and most opponents could not support such weight even if prepared and stable. Yet while H3d demonstrates the *concept,* it obviously fails to be functional.

To use our weight more practically, we need only situate our center of gravity close to the arm *while exercising proper structure*, and then *drop* our weight *straight down (Gravity).* Hence, H4. From H4 we need only bend our knees *while maintaining good posture* so that our weight drops onto the arm, thus creating the same effect as H3d but while literally and figuratively "keeping our feet on the floor." But remember that in H4 we must not *push* down on the arm; we drop "onto" it by focusing our weight onto the arm itself. We must not *push* the arm down because pushing it down must to some degree equate to pushing ourselves up. Instead, we must apply the full dead weight of our body.

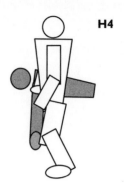

However, H4 also will demand some permissible compromise in posture. This happens because we can push Gargantua to the floor only if his arm clears the vertical plane of our knees, which requires us to lean forward slightly. In certain techniques, such as the one demonstrated here, a slight bend remains functional provided the shoulders do not tilt past the vertical plane of the knees. Yet as we see in H4a, our buttocks will protrude backwards, if only slightly, and our torso will lean forward. This compromise in posture will create some tension, which in turn will diminish weight, and thus must be minimized.

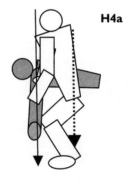

The best way I have found around this problem involves centering the weight on one leg instead of two, which encourages a straight spine, sound *Structure*, and a tight *Axis*. In doing so, we typically allow the unweighted foot to extend slightly forward and to be held just a few inches off the ground. If we drop exclusively from the supporting leg, the raised foot eventually touches the floor. We do not have to lower the raised foot per se; it just drops along with the rest of our body. This permits us to be *heavy* because our weight must go straight down on the supporting leg. See this in H5.

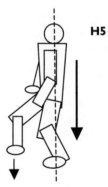

As an added bonus, H5 permits excellent *Posture* and the raised leg, because it does not support weight, actually adds to our total functional *Heaviness*. However, H5 does not represent a static position, meaning that we would not stand in it long. Done well, it takes no more time than any other footwork.

This should clarify the importance and functionality of *Heaviness*, which will be discussed further in the following chapters on *Relaxation*, *Wave Energy*, and *Grounding*, and also referred to in the chapter on the *Triangulation Point* (different from *Triangle Guard*).

29

Relaxation

MUCH OF *RELAXATION* HAS BEEN COVERED IN THE DISCUSSION OF *HEAVINESS*. In fact, when I tell people to relax I actually mean that they should "get heavy." But relaxation does have some of its own elements, and those warrant discussion here.

But before I speak on those I should note that valuing *Relaxation* does not necessarily mean favoring so-called "soft" or "internal" arts over "hard" or "external" arts. I refrain from categorizing my art as either one, preferring to call it a "heavy" art (if I am to call it anything at all). The distinction between the hard/external arts and the soft/internal arts blurs as we delve deeper into martial principles. I have met so-called "hard" stylists who are as relaxed and "heavy" as so called "soft" stylists. Sure, there are differences between styles, but relaxation supercedes being "hard" or "soft."

That said, we must *Relax* our bodies because tension both traps power and consumes it. With respect to its consumption of power, we must refer back to the *Percentage Principle*. The body can generate only a certain amount of force at a given moment. How much force varies with level of mastery, but any one body at any one time can generate only a finite amount of power. We must equally understand that tensing any muscle requires us to expend energy. It is impossible to tense a muscle without expending energy. Therefore, because we possess only a finite amount of energy, every tense muscle consumes part of that energy and *decreases* the amount of energy we channel into techniques.

Admittedly, this can seem paradoxical at first. After all, most people seem inclined to clench their fist tightly and stiffen their arm when they want to punch hard. For that matter, I do not mean to suggest that people who use muscle power cannot generate any force. Of course they can. If all other elements—size, skill, speed, etc.—are equal, the stronger person will win. I make no contentions otherwise.

However, if we examine a strike, *any* strike, we find that power comes from the places devoid of tension. Tense up your fist and throw a hard hay-maker. Note from where the power comes. None comes from the rigid fist and forearm. Some might come from the elbow as it flexes, but then it is the *movement* of the elbow—its flexing—that generates the power. More so, however, the shoulder and/or hip joints will generate the power through *movement*. The same holds true in any technique; power comes from move-ment in one or more joints.

Yet joints cannot move when tensed, and without motion there will be no power. As striking invokes movement in many joints, every bit of ten-sion surrounding those joints inhibits power. For that reason, improper *Structure* deminishes our power. An ill-structured body will need to tense various muscle groups to keep the body standing, and every bit of excess tension will limit the speed and range of motion in our joints. That said, I must note once again that, to a certain degree, *Structure* can be contextual to a style and its objectives.

Unfortunately, the problem of tension does not pertain to joint move-ments exclusively. Certain muscles extend our arm outward, such as the tri-cep, while other muscles, such as the bicep, contract. To reach maximum efficieny when extending, such as when punching, we want to exercise only the extenders and not the contractors. Unfortunately, if we tense up, we tend to tense up both groups of muscles, which makes the contractors resist the extenders. In short, the arm fights itself. The same phenomenon occurs in a variety of muscle groups throughout the body.

Another factor at work, though one remarkably difficult to discuss, concerns the movement of internal energy—*ki, chi, jing,* etc.—including its movement within the body and its transfer from one person to another. If we equate the energy moving through our body to water moving through a hose, then muscle tension, wherever it appears, acts as a knot or blockage in that hose. If any energy does manage to get through, it only trickles.

Why is this? It returns once again to the *Percentage Principle.* I have only so much *chi* with which to strike. That energy flows from my *hara* and moves through my body but is expended in certain places to make muscles tense.

We also can view this from the perspective of *Intent,* which I will dis-cuss at greater length later on. For now, I will state that striking begins with an effort of the mind, which wills the body to hit a given target. In a cer-tain sense, a strike is the *mind* moving to the target through the body. In order for any part of the body to become tense, the mind has to be at work because the body does not tense without the (conscious or subconscious) mind making it so. Thus, our bodies relax when we sleep because the mind sleeps. Yet when we wake up, our consciousness almost immediately translates into bodily movement as we will ourselves out of bed, into shower, off to work, etc. While most everyday movements do not require a moment's "thought," the mind drives them nonetheless, if only through biological electrical impulses.

Yet while I like to believe that the powers of the mind are potentially infinite, each one of us possesses only *finite* mental abilities at a given moment. Therefore, the *Percentage Principle* applies no less to the mind than to do the body. Since the mind wills us to strike, *any mental distraction only weakens and/or mitigates that will.* As tension emerges from the mind then it must serve to distract the body from the strike. In other words, if the mind wants to strike target X but muscle Y holds back then some fraction of the mind must be focusing on Y when it should focus only on X.

Thus, tension distracts and consumes mental power, and as mental power moves the body, which creates physical power, then every bit of mental power consumed translates into an equal amount of physical power consumed.

Viewed in this context, *Relaxation* becomes imperative not only for more efficient and powerful body motions, but also for keeping our mind uncluttered. A more relaxed body will permit the mind to expend more of its focus on perception and action, rather than on something silly like maintaining unwarranted muscle tension to maintain improper posture.

30

Wave Energy

(Hip Power, Striking from the Hip, Body Torque, Karate Drum)

"**W**AVE ENERGY," AS I CALL IT, RECEIVES CONSIDERABLE ATTENTION IN the martial arts. Virtually every martial art advocates using the legs and hips to generate power. Of course, not every art exercises that power the same way, but that does not matter for this discussion.

Wave Energy explains that that power begins in the legs and hips and moves up through the body until released through the arms. As a Tai Chi saying goes, "Power is rooted in the feet, generated in the hips, and expressed through the fingertips." Ideally, the body acts as a whip, with the lower portions of the body moving before the upper portions of the body. In fact, the lower portions of the body should generate the movement of the upper portions, meaning that the upper body should not move of its own volition.

WE1 and WE1a demonstrate how the body moves improperly, without *Wave Energy*. Notice that the shoulder and the hip rotate at the same time when moving from WE1 to WE1a. We see no whipping effect or wave; we see only the body turning.

WE1　　　　　　　　　　**WE2**

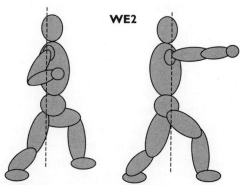

WE2a **WE2b** **WE2c** **WE2d** **WE2e** **WE2f**

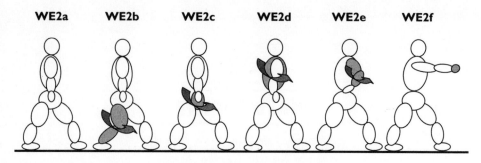

On the other hand, examine WE2a-f, which, although somewhat exaggerated, demonstrates how a wave of force should begin at the lower body and move upwards. While this does not demonstrate everything at work, it does demonstrate the point I want to note, however, that it is not a technique but rather simply an example of body movement.

We first see WE2a standing at rest. Then WE2b begins to generate wave power by swinging the right knee forward and inward. This must be done in a relatively sharp motion, but I will speak more to that later on. WE2c now becomes highly instructive. We see that the force generated by the right knee now turns the hip forward in the same fashion. Even more instructive, the knee that had twisted in WE2c returns to its original position, which demonstrates that *Wave Energy* moves one body part at a time rather than turning the entire body at once.

Moving on to WE2d, the wave now travels up the spine until manifesting itself in the arm in WE2e. Notice that the forearm, and even more so the hand, trails behind the elbow joint *because the wave has yet to travel that far*. Given how much this telegraphs our intention to strike, I must note once again that this is not a technique but rather an example of physiokinetic movement.

Finally, WE2f illustrates the wave reaching the hand.

Supposing that the fist remains relaxed enough so as not to consume the energy of the wave, there actually would be a WE2g that would illustrate how the energy of the wave leaves the body and travels into a target. Barring advanced *chi* work by people who can strike with energy alone, the *Wave Energy* does not project from the body—or at least does not do so with power—but can be transferred by contact. Much like other forms of energy, the wave must be conducted through a relatively solid medium to maintain its strength. That said, if the striker remains relaxed, the force of the wave can continue into the opponent's body in ways that exceed the mere momentum of the striking hand.

As WE2 demonstrates, *Wave Energy* spirals upwards from the lower body, with the upper body merely its conduit. A whip serves as a good analogy for this in that only the handle of the whip is manipulated, sending a ripple of force down the length of the whip until it "cracks" with tremendous speed and power. Furthermore, the *recoil* of the whip's handle contributes to that cracking power, just as the "recoil," or at least re-relaxation, of the lower body contributes to the power of the strike. Therefore, we can view the lower body as the "handle" of the "whip" and the upper body as the whip itself.

However, the human body differs from the whip in that its upper portions can also amplify the initial force, which typically means pushing from *behind* the wave by exercising *Indirect Pressure*. As previous discussions of the *Percentage Principle* and *Relaxation* point out, we must keep the upper body relaxed else tension will consume some or all of the force generated by the lower body. It follows, therefore, that general relaxation facilitates wave power.

In fact, tension present in any of the joints, even in individual vertebra, will prohibit force from freely moving from the hips to the hand. Why is this? Because wherever there is tension, *that* is where the force will locate itself, and thus *that is the part of the body that will move.*

We must think of the body as a cartoon firehose. I am certain most of my readers have seen cartoon images of water pumping through a hose, which shows large blobs of water moving down its length. The hose itself does not move, only the blobs of water do. Force travels up the body in the same way. One flick of the legs and hip creates a single burst of force that passes through the joints. Like the hose, a relaxed body will ripple slightly as the force passes through its different parts. We see flickers of motion in the spine and shoulder and elbow. But those parts do not actually move of their own volition, just as the hose does not pump the water running through it.

Yet if we tense a given part of the body, such as the shoulder, then that shoulder will be hit by the wave of energy generated by the lower body just as the knot in the firehose will receive the brunt force of the water. In short, the tension in the shoulder does not permit the force to move *through* it. Instead, it blocks the force, and that means that it effectively gets hit by the force. In fact, the force generated by the lower body always "hits" areas of tension in the upper body, especially tension in the fist.

When hit by the wave, a tense fist gets knocked outward twoards the target much in the way a bat knocks a ball forward. This certainly can be effective. However, I have found it problematic in two ways. If we are in a guard up position, the force hits the fist close to our own body rather than close to our opponent's body, which makes the punch most powerful when far from the target, i.e. when first struck by the wave. It will *lose* power as it moves towards target, much as a ball loses speed the farther it moves from the bat that hit it.

The second issue concerns how the force becomes mitigated. I mentioned this already with respect to relaxing the hand. If the fist consumes or blocks the force then the force *itself* does not hit the target. Instead, the force hits the fist and the fist hits the target, turning the force into an intermediary agent that prevents the primary force itself from being transferred. The opponent consequently receives only *inertia*—mass in motion—instead of the pure energy/force that generated the inertia.

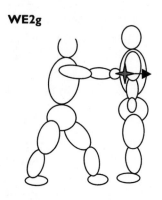

WE2g

Instead, better to allow the force to flow directly through a loose fist so that the force transfers directly into the opponent on contact. The force will "hit" whatever portion of the *opponent's* body they tense, and thus the force generated from our hip transfers more purely to the target (WE2g). In other words, as the force will cause reaction against *whatever* tension it encounters, we must prefer that tension to be in the opponent's body rather than in our own. I must note, however, that this is a more advanced application of the technique. Punching with a loose fist can be dangerous to the hand and the wrist until proper technique becomes internalized.

Regardless of such particulars, we see that the arm itself generates no power. It might *supplement* the power with some structure and motion—see *Indirect Pressure*—but it does not generate the power. Thus, the arm merely conveys lower body power to the target, much as the whip conveys the power of the flick of the wrist. The whip itself has no power.

We also must consider *Wave Energy* in the context of the *Percentage Principle*. As whipping motion generates only a finite amount of force, we must utilize that force at maximum *Efficiency*. In the case of striking, that translates to a small and sharp, though not necessarily hard or tense, motion. Consider taking hold of a whip and moving its handle with large, slow motions. Obviously, you will not provoke much of a result. To really crack the whip, you will need to flick it hard and fast. The smaller and more condensed your flick, the more powerful it will be. It is no different with the hip.

We equally must view this in terms of *Temporal and Spatial Relativity.* Large, big turning motions effectively spread out the finite percentage of force over a relatively long period of time and distance. The more we condense the motion, the more concentrated the impact. Once we understand this, striking with power becomes a matter of speed, of explosive bursts of power condensed into the shortest time posssible.

That realization brings us back to *Axis*. Improper *Structure* will prohibit the hip from moving freely and from moving on the tightest radius possible, both of which will result in its taking longer to complete its rotation, which will lengthen the unit of energy, slow down the strike, and thus diminish the power. A 25% fault in posture will incur *at least* a 25% loss of power and speed by this understanding.

Poor *Posture* creates yet another problem. As the wave of force moves through the spine, it locks the vertebrae like links in a chain. Lay a chain on a table and turn the first link over again and again. Eventually, the entire chain will turn. This is *roughly* what happens with the spine. In short, the force seeks to straighten the spine as it moves through it. (In reality, if the force condenses into a tight packet, all the vertebrae do not twist at once. Instead, only a few twist at any given moment. But the force still seeks a straight path.)

Imagine sending a ripple down a length of rope. If straight, the ripple moves down the length with relative ease. However, a rope with significant curvature will consume the force of the ripple because instead of traveling freely down the length, the force of the ripple will attempt to straighten the rope. In short, energy in motion does not want to turn. It will attempt to straighten the rope rather than following the sudden curve in that rope, and if there it lacks the requisite energy to straighten the rope then it will stop.

This analogy also serves to demonstrate the problem with tension. If we have a 10 foot length of heavy rope but make the last two feet stiff, as if tightly wrapped with tape, the energy it takes to move the last two feet as one lump consumes the energy of the wave, which until then has had to move only a little bit of rope at a time. This is what happens if the wave of force moving through the body hits a tense arm. Suddenly, it must move an entire limb instead of just a single joint, and both the change in direction and the weight of the limb consumes the wave of force.

Returning to improper *Structure*, as the wave travels up the spine it wants to move in a straight line and wants to move as few vertebrae as it can at any given moment. If the wave hits an unnatural curvature or tilt of the spine, one of two things will happen. Either *Wave Energy* will force the spine to straighten, in which case the spine consumes the quanity of force required to straighten it, or the force will not be able to straighten the spine, which means the spine

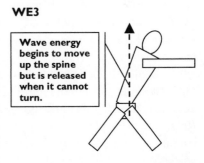

WE3

Wave energy begins to move up the spine but is released when it cannot turn.

will consume the force entirely. Illustration WE3 depicts this.

Bringing *Posture* into the discussion obviously leads us back to issues of *Heaviness*. As we saw, we want to be heavy when striking, bringing the weight of our bodies into the opponent. We want to "fall" into the opponent because dead weight effectually incurs no "equal reaction" in our own bodies. How do we "fall" forward without actually falling forward? *Wave Energy*. As our weight *Centers* at our hips—more on this in *Centeredness*—

we can strike our opponent with all of our weight by generating power from our *Center* provided that (1) we keep our body upright so that our weight sits on our hips, and (2) we *Relax*. In effect, the wave allows us to swing the *weight* of our entire body without actually swinging the body itself.

For those that consider the power of momentum to be important in martial arts striking, understanding *Wave Energy* becomes critical because we need not move our arm *any* distance in order to achieve momentum. As a strike properly begins at the knee and moves to finger tips, it covers a good six or more feet before the hand even moves.

Of course, punching is by no means the only context in which we find *Wave Energy* at work. It equally governs kicking, though it is more difficult to apply it in that circumstance, as well as joint manipulations, throws, blocking, and even in footwork. Using it in joint manipulations and throwing, however, can be dangerous because it will jerk joints rather than push them, so we should proceed with great caution into such applications.

As a word of caution, if we use *Wave Energy* we can be guilty of *Telegraphing* our techniques because our opponents will see our hips move before our hand moves. At more advanced levels, however, the hand actually can and should start moving *before* the hips explode and create the wave. If timed correctly, the blob of wave force will reach the hand just as the hand reaches the target, thus the perfect culmination of powers. This, however, requires considerable coordination and I do not recommend that my students worry about it until they first have become proficient with *Wave Energy* in other contexts.

Lastly, I should note that we must be very careful to avoid exaggerated hip motions in creating *Wave Energy*. While there's nothing wrong with teaching large hip motions to beginning students so that they can feel that power and learn to harness it, big rotations of the hip produce three problems: (1) They generate more sideways pressue than twisting pressure, meaning that they effectively throw power off to the side rather than sending it upwards through the spine. (2) They obstruct proper *Spinal Alignment* and *Structure* by turning the body sideways. (3) They clash with the *Relativity* principle in that large movements disperse power over greater lengths of time and distance rather than condensing it into shorter frameworks.

Therefore, the generation of *Wave Energy* should be imperceptibly *small* and refined, and should propel force from the spine forward without creating turning or spinning in the body. If used as such, it can accomplish remarkable feats with respect to generating power.

31

Convergence

I UNDERSTOOD *WAVE ENERGY* AND *HEAVINESS* FOR YEARS BEFORE SEEING the principle of *Convergence*, and then I could not have felt more foolish for not having seen it sooner.

Convergence reconciles the fact that two *opposing* forces produce any strike. The first force is *Wave Energy*. The second is *Heaviness*. Given that *Wave Energy* moves upwards and *Heaviness* drops downwards, the two forces might initially appear to oppose one another. They might, in fact, appear to cancel one another out, with the downward force of *Heaviness* squelching the upward force of the wave, and vice versa.

However, I then remembered something I learned about how waves form and break, namely that water rolls in from the ocean toward the shore and then collides with the undertow created by the previous wave sliding back into ocean. The resulting "clash" causes the water to curl over and crashes to shore, thus forming the classic wave.

I should note, however, that waves also are formed by the movement of the swell towards the increasingly shallow shore. We cannot perceive a 20 foot swell in 21 feet of water but will perceive half of it in 10 feet of water. However, the curling action of the wave nevertheless comes from the "clash" between the incoming swell and the receding water from the previous wave.

The same effect happens in our bodies when punching. The rising *Wave Energy* collides with the dropping of our weight, but the two opposing forces do not cancel each other out. Instead, they combine! As illustration Con1 demonstrates, they combine at the chest, releasing the energy outwards through a punch or other similar technique.

Con1

Con2

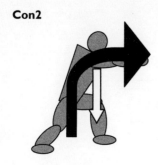

Con3

Of course, it only does so through correct *Posture*. If the body falls to one side or the other, if it tilts us forward or backward, then there will be no *Convergence* of forces. This not only affects the power of the punch but also the time it takes to deliver it. As Con2 demonstrates, a forward leaning body will result in *Heaviness* dropping in front of the upward moving wave. Consequently, the wave will not exit at the solar plexus but rather rise up through the shoulder, which not only represents a longer path but also tends to produce unnecessary shoulder tension. Conversely, if the body is tilted backwards, as in Con3, the dropping weight either will squelch the rising energy or draw it backwards, negating effective punching in either case.

Of course, *Convergence* applies no less to blocking or locking than to striking. As long as dropping force and rising force are harmonized, we can deliver considerable power to our opponents.

32

Centeredness

THERE'S SO MUCH TO SAY ABOUT *CENTEREDNESS* BUT SO LITTLE CAN BE expressed through words because, although somewhat distillable to physical properties, it really constitutes a state of being. That said, most of the preceding discussion of anatomical principles could be encapsulated under the heading of *Centeredness* because all of them seek to get the individual to act as a unified being—the very definition of being *Centered*.

Moving towards definition, your "center" refers to your physical center of gravity, located approximately two to three inches below your belly button and mid-way between your belly and your back. All movement originates from that singular point, which means we need only move it to move the entire body. Thus, to move forward we need not focus on stepping, per se, but rather on pressing our center of gravity forward on a level plane. Doing so increases our power because our movement ceases to be an amalgamation of different body parts and instead becomes a movement of a singular, unified being.

That leads into a discussion of true *Centeredness*, which differs from discussing the physical center of gravity. *Centeredness*, in its true sense, poses great challenges to explanation because it defines a state of holistic being centered in the physical center of gravity.

Let us first consider the connection between centeredness and *Heaviness*. As previously noted, *Heaviness* means using the weight of the body to accomplish effects on the opponent. This poses some applicational challenges. For example, if grabbed at the wrist, how do we transfer all of our *Heaviness* into our wrist so as to execute an escape, lock, or throw? One way to do this would be to jump into the air and land our bodies on top as our opponent's hand, which not only would be impractical but outright foolish. Another alternative involves true *Centeredness*.

Typically, the body acts as a large mass of different body parts, which means that the vast majority of our weight exists in places other than our wrist. On the other hand, imagine a kid's glass marble that weighs as much as you weigh, and then imagine the power of a 100lb or 150lb or 250lb marble! *Consider the power of condensing weight into that marble rather than distributing it over a large surface area.*

Such is our goal with respect to *Centeredness.* We want to take our body's entire weight and condense it into a marble located at our physical center of gravity. Imagine how it would feel to have that marble sitting in you. Imagine how immovable, *Heavy,* and focused you would feel. That is the notion of *Centeredness.*

Applying *Centeredness* means thinking of the entire body as *only* that little marble with the rest of the body being apparatus that contains no inherent power or function save that generated by the motion and weight of the marble itself. Illustration Centered1 depicts weight distributed over the entire body mass, as represented by the gray color. In Centered2, that gray weight becomes condensed into a dense, black marble.

Centered 1   **Centered 2**

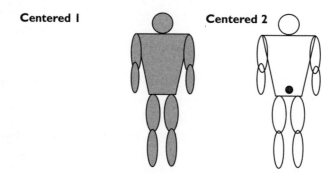

Instead of having a little weight in lots of different places, Centered2 depicts a lot of weight in one place, with that one place being the root of our power, mobility, and the literal center of our gravity. Thus, when defending a wrist grab, we need only drop the marble to drop the totality of our *Heaviness* upon the opponent's hand.

Furthermore, this constructs a positive movement vs. yield *Ratio.* Referring back to the example I used in that chapter, the marble becomes the pencil centered in the cardboard circle. Any slight motion in the marble generates far larger, more powerful motions in the surrounding unified body.

The challenge for us becomes how to condense our weight into the marble, and then how to connect the body to it. Not surprisingly, every principle facilitates *Centeredness,* but nothing substitutes for feeling the center of gravity itself. Feeling the center of gravity will allow us to feel *Centered* and consequently be *Centered.* One way to feel *Centered* involves simple abdominal breathing from the *Center* that relaxes weight into the *Center* with every exhalation.

Doing this, it will not take long to feel at least somewhat *Centered* and to exercise that *Centeredness*, especially when manifesting proper *Structure*. Next, when performing techniques, we should practice moving the marble alone—turning it, dropping it up or down. By "moving the marble" I do not mean moving it within the body. But I do mean "forgetting" about moving limbs independently of motions in the marble itself. If it turns, the body turns. If it drops, the body drops. If it moves forward, the entire body moves forward. Etc. As a result, we incur no risk of having some fraction of our weight/force move contrarily to technique.

Also consider as well how being *Centered* would affect state of mind. True *Centeredness* extends into our psychology, if not our entire perception of "self" because when unified weight and mass equally result in a focused consciousness. In fact, our consciousness—attention—becomes located at our physical *Center*, thus unifying the *Body-Mind*.

Furthermore, as our consciousness becomes unified in our body, we stop dispersing our consciousness over multiple "thoughts" and "events" at one time. Consciousness becomes unfragmented, and thus produces a single, clear, vivid experience. Aside from the general and humanistic value of such a state of mind, such clarity could not be more essential to martial arts, as will be discussed later in the chapter on *Zanshin*.

Returning to *Centeredness* in its totality, consider again a simple wrist grab. If we feel fragmented and our weight feels dispersed then when someone grabs hold of our wrist we will feel as though they control part of us. And they *do* control *part* of us, and that is because the "us" in question is in parts to begin with. On the other hand, centering ourselves in that little marble means that we maintain *Control* over our entire being despite the fact that someone holds our wrist. In effect, the wrist they "control" will be but an extension of our more unified power. In short, unless they can gain control of our physical center, they will not control "us."

Better yet, if we are *Centered* and they are not, they will never seize control of that marble. When functioning as a condensed, unified being of body and mind, we certainly need not fear being grabbed *by the arm of* a fragmented being. In fact, in being grabbed we only come to recognize our opponent's instability, and thus intuitively understand how to exploit that instability.

Even more importantly, and I will discuss this further in the *Body-Mind* principle, if grabbed while not *Centered*, our minds literally go to the location of the grab. Thus, when someone grabs our wrist we tend to think about that wrist. In this way, the person not only controls the wrist but controls our mind. Yet such loss of mental control occurs only when the mind wanders around the body. Yet when *Centered* in being, the mind remains at the stable-feeling center of gravity rather than floating to the location of the grab.

There's a simple exercise that demonstrates this point. Stand with good posture, breathe from your center, and think about your center. Locate your mind in your center of gravity. When you feel centered, ask your partner to *slowly* start pinching your hand. See if you can keep your attention at your center. What you'll find is that while you might acknowledge a certain amount of pain, it won't really "hurt" until your attention—your "mind"— moves from your center of gravity to the location of that pain.

Before concluding, I want to note that the marble metaphor ultimately proves somewhat inaccurate. Instead of a marble, we should condense our weight and attention to a single point, and points literally contain no mass. However small we think of a point, it could be smaller still, and as it shrinks so do we become more unified.

Furthermore, I must note that when I say to "think about the center of gravity" or to "focus attention" there, that I do not mean that we literally should think about it. Rather, I mean that our attention simply should be located there—that we should *be* there. It should be the location of our being. But that takes practice, and typically a lifetime of it.

There is yet another level to *Centeredness*; it is the wellspring of internal energy. To my understanding, getting *Centered* denotes a first step towards learning to harness the power of internal energy, something that proves to be a long practice for which there are many methods. Thus, those interested in the topic should pursue meditation, chi gung, Reiki, or some other art form that directly addresses energy movement in the body.

33
Triangulation Point

ALSO KNOWN AS *THE MISSING LEG*, I BRIEFLY touched on *The Triangulation Point* in the chapter on *Reciprocity*. To recap, our two legs cannot support us in all directions at all times. If we stand with one foot on each of TP1's white dots, we would find ourselves stable against the black arrows but unstable if pushed by the white arrows. Conversely, were we to

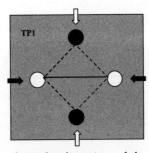

stand on either of the black dots, we would be weak in the direction of the white dots. Therefore, someone in a "horse" or wide-legged stance, could

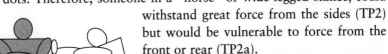

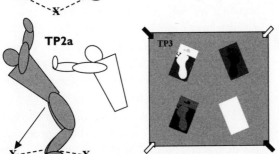

withstand great force from the sides (TP2) but would be vulnerable to force from the front or rear (TP2a).

However, while most easily identified from the "horse" stance, two *Triangulation Points* always exist. For example, if we took a "front" stance, represented by the white footprints in TP3, we would be strong against the black arrows

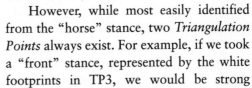

but weak against the white arrows. Were our stance on the black footprints then we would be strong against the white arrows but weak against the black arrows.

In fact, were we standing on the black footprints then each white footprint would represent the precise location of a *Triangle Point*—the point where we actually need another leg for support. The "missing leg" always exists in a triangulated point between the other two legs—see TP1 and TP2.

Yet when we discuss the *Triangulation Point*, the direction of the point carries just as much importance as the point itself. Thus, were we standing in the black footprints in TP2, any force along the line of the black arrows would create instability.

The *Triangulation Point* takes on importance when executing takedowns and throws. While it seems obvious to suggest that we should direct all takedowns to the "missing legs" rather than to the existing legs, many martial artists often overlook this tactic. Say, for example, that Jane wants to apply a simple wristlock (TP4) to Gargantua and that both take a neutral stance—neither foot ahead of the other. As in TP5, we see that the technique can be applied in such a way that the wrist lock occurs directly over Gargantua's *TP*.

TP4 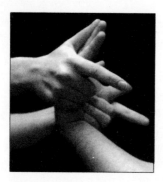 **TP5**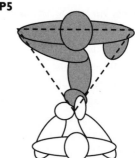

If Jane executes the wrist throw from her present position, *she cannot throw Gargantua into his TP because she is standing in it.* Consequently, throwing *from* the TP itself instead of *into* the TP forces Jane to direct Garagantua into points of relative stability. If in TP6 her force aligns with the arrow then she will end up pressing against Gargantua's massive right leg. Consequently, she would either (1) have to force his leg to collapse, which is unlikely given the

TP6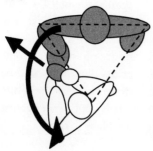

size of Gargantua's legs, or (2) move his body over that leg, which is equally unlikely. Yet even *if* Jane were powerful enough to collapse Gargantua's leg or force him to acquiesce through pain compliance, she still would be throwing in a direction of resistance rather than non-resistance. In short, it would not be optimum.

The curved arrow in TP6 represents another path Jane's technique could take, but it proves no less desireable. Note that the arrow curves outside Gargantua's body before it curves back towards the center of the illustration. As such, Jane still would be exercising pressure against Gargantua's right leg. Worse, as I will discuss later on, both of the arrowed paths are *Centrifugal* rather than *Centripetal*, which forces Jane to move Gargantua around her own body.

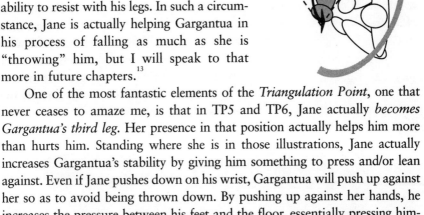

TP7

Instead, Jane could move somewhere along the path of the gray arrow in TP7, thereby getting out of his way and throwing him directly into his *TP*, which affords him no ability to resist with his legs. In such a circumstance, Jane is actually helping Gargantua in his process of falling as much as she is "throwing" him, but I will speak to that more in future chapters.[13]

One of the most fantastic elements of the *Triangulation Point*, one that never ceases to amaze me, is that in TP5 and TP6, Jane actually *becomes Gargantua's third leg*. Her presence in that position actually helps him more than hurts him. Standing where she is in those illustrations, Jane actually increases Gargantua's stability by giving him something to press and/or lean against. Even if Jane pushes down on his wrist, Gargantua will push up against her so as to avoid being thrown down. By pushing up against her hands, he increases the pressure between his feet and the floor, essentially pressing himself into the floor more firmly. This only makes her efforts to throw against his legs *less* effective because he stabilizes himself by countering her force. Generally speaking, therefore, any time we stand in an opponents *TP*, we help the opponent because (1) we cannot throw them into that *TP* and (2) we allow the opponent to use us as a "leg" for additional support.

Of further note, in TP5 & TP6, Jane cannot fully exercise *Heaviness* because to a certain degree she must lift Gargantua in order to put him in motion, meaning that she must move his mass laterally or upwards but not directly downwards.

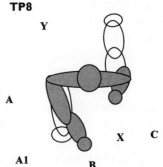

TP8

While TP5 and TP6 depict a neutral stance, the *Triangulation Point* plays no less a role in any stance. As TP8 depicts, a forward stance changes the placement of the weak points—X and Y— but it does not alter the principle of their use. Were Jane to start in position B, she easily could move to position C so as to throw Gargantua to weak point X. Conversely, she could move

---

13. The number of confluent principles this aligns is astronomical. It equally changes the *Ratio* of motion, makes the technique *Centripetal*, applies *Relativity*, and allows us to throw *Down* with *Heaviness,* to name just a few. It also increases the pressure on the wrist itself!

from position B to position A and throw Gargantua to weak point Y. These two options should be relatively clear and straight forward.

Yet what would happen if Jane found herself in position A1 (TP8)? From that position, a likely one after executing an outside parry or block, it would be difficult to reach weak point Y and impossible, given the nature of this particular wrist lock, to throw to weak point X. The involves exercise of a *future Triangulation Point*. From A1, Jane effectively and easily could continue the path of Gargantua's arm through B and along the weak line moving from Y to X. Doing so would prompt Gargantua to step forward with his left foot, and the instant he committed to that step, a new set of *Triangulation Points* would form.

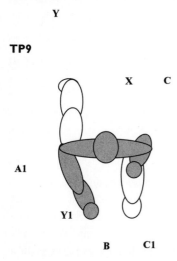

Hence, in TP9, Y gets left behind as Gargantua steps forward with his left foot. Weak point X, which was the front weak point, turns into the rear weak point, and a new weak point forms in Y1. Jane, having moved into B or C1, then could throw to Y1 with ease. Remember, Gargantua need not take the full step for Y1 to materialize. It actuates as soon as he commits his weight.

Yet while the wrist lock does a good job of exemplifiying how we exploit our opponent's weak points so as to better functionalize our takedown and locking techniques, it does not demonstrate how to exercise *Triangulation Points* to increase our own martial power. Looking to *Reciprocity*, we must remember that if the "weak" points make the opponent weak, they must simultaneously make us strong.

They do so in that we actually utilize weak points in generating power when striking, or in any release of energy. When we step into a punch, we actually exercise a controlled "fall" into one of our own *Triangulation Points*, thus exercising *Heaviness*. Of course, we *must* do so with correct *Structure* or we will lose stability and power. Nevertheless, it demonstrates that martial arts functions because of a balance of forces, something I will discuss further in *Yin-Yang*. For now, suffice it to say that while most martial artists recognize the power in driving a strike forward with the rear leg, not as many recognize the *yin* aspect of that motion—the falling action into the *Void/Triangulation Point*. Therefore, *it is because we are weak in area X that we are powerful in releasing/delivering force*.

Interestingly, while we fall into the *Triangulation Point*, we also construct stability from it. As TP10 depicts, the arm with which we strike functions as our "third leg," which takes the weight we drop into the

Triangulation Point and communicates it to the target. While we must not depend on that "third leg" for stability, if we think about striking with all the weight a leg would bare then we can strike with tremendous power.

TP10

Obviously, the same would apply to any and all releases of energy, as in a wrist throw, hip throw, or kick. Yet it must be noted that dropping the weight must be small, a few inches at first, a few milimeters upon higher proficiency. Any more than that unduly can make use fall literally instead of figuratively, thus decreasing our power and slowing our movement.

Ultimately, the applications of the *Triangulation Point* are multitudinous. It plays a role any time we are standing and moving, but its enumerations are far too plentiful to discuss at length here.

34

The (Dynamic) Sphere

THE DEFINITIVE WORK ON THE *DYNAMIC SPHERE* IS A BOOK BY A. WESTBROOK and O. Ratt: *Aikido and the Dynamic Sphere,* and I recommend it highly to anyone wanting to learn about the *Sphere* principle.

Sp6   **Sp7**

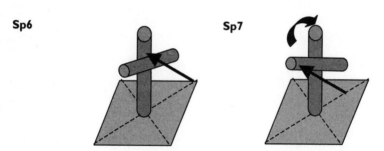

To first understand *Spherocity*, we return to *Spinal Alignment.* In discussing that principle, I noted the body's inclination to turn in one direction or another in response to oncoming force. Sp6 and Sp7 demonstrate that again here. Were force to engage the "T" directly at its post, the "T" would not pivot. However, if the "T" receives force in any fashion but directly dead center then it will be turn along the path of that force, and such rotation represents the outline of a *Sphere.* In this sense, and as I will demonstrate, *Spinal Alignment* and the *Sphere* principle could be said to be *Reciprocal* principles, but remember that *Reciprocal* principles do not cancel one another out, nor do they contradict one another. Instead, they *compliment* one another.

That said, the inclination of the body to turn establishes potential circuits around the body, and the *Sphere* principle identifies those circular paths, which S1[14] demonstrates. Note that the depicted circles do not constitute all the lines of movement, of which there are an infinite number. However, they demonstrate the basic types of paths the body can follow when using the *Center* as the locus of movement and keeping sound *Structure*. Therefore, the infinite number of circuits ultimately form a sphere around the body.

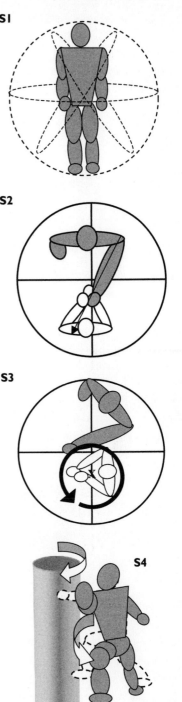

We see, therefore, that were the body to receive force directed anywhere other than at the spine itself, its structure would want to turn away from the oncoming force. Therefore, if we look to S2, we see that while the general attack might be coming straight at Joe from Gargantua, the more specific line of attack, as represented by the arrow, actuallly misses Joe's spine. Consequently, Joe's body wants to turn in order to receive that force. (I should note the presence of additional lines of force, such as the one created by the Gargantua's grip, but we need not contend with them at present.)

S3 represents a most basic concept of the *Sphere* principle, illustrating what would happen if Joe spun perfectly in place around a center axis—"X." Note two essential elements of Gargantua's path: First, it changes. Second, it moves *away* from Joe. It is as if Joe acts as a spinning cylinder of which Gargantua attempts to take hold. The cylinder immediately deflects Gargantua's efforts, sending him twisting off away from the stationary center of the cylinder itself (S4).

14. Westbrook and Ratti. *Aikido and the Dynamic Sphere*. Tuttle: Vermont, 1970. p. 100.

The emerging problem with the pathways in S3 and S4 is that Gargantua moves away from Joe's power. Furthermore, Gargantua neither moves along the path of his *Triangle Guard,* nor does he move to his *Triangulation Point,* thereby making the pathway of his movement less than optimum.

S5

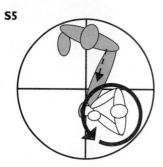

Consequently, Joe would be better moving to the side, rougly into Gargantua's negative triangle, where he could continue Gargantua's arm's line of attack. We see this in S5, where we should note that Gargantua's attack not only continues along its unaltered path (*Leading Conrol*), but Joe can actually encourage Gargantua to overextend along that path. Joe thereby exploits the weakness of Gargantua's *Triangle Guard,* as well as his *Triangulation Point.*

While essential for understanding the basic mechanics of the *Sphere* principle, the above explanation addresses only its basic physical mechanics rather than its full power. Whereas the primary level of the *Sphere* principle involves directing the opponent's force along circular lines while rotating as a whole being, a secondary level concerns the greater strategic notion that only one person should function as a sphere in any given moment. Obviously, we should always be that person. In doing so, we recognize our *Center* not only as the center of our *Sphere* but equally as the *opponent's* center of gravity, taking control of them as part of our sphere, much as a boat dragged into a whirlpool.

S6

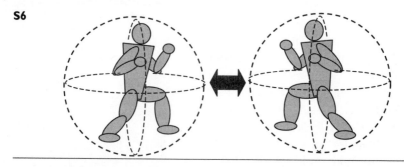

Therefore, as I have previously noted, we can view martial combat as a clash of geometric shapes, and this is an important concept to keep in mind when considering the geometric shape of the *Sphere*. Combat involves the "clash" of two spheres of action. As long as both spheres remain intact then each combatant maintains his or her own *Centeredness* and control of his or her full being. However, once one person becomes absorbed into the other person's whirling sphere, the latter gains control of the former.

Looking now to S3a—a replication of S3—we see that Joe will not defeat Gargantua's sphere if turning as depicted. While Joe *might* be able to exercise greater control of Gargantua because Gargantua has (1) committed to an attack and (2) grabbed Joe, what we see in S3a amounts to two spheres spinning against one another rather than one sphere defeating the other and taking control of its center—the attacker.

S3a

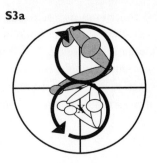

Looking to S5a by contrast, we see that Gargantua's path becomes more eliptical than circular/spherical. He, in essence, ceases acting as the center of a sphere and instead becomes part of the circumference of Joe's sphere. This enables Joe to turn at will, and because of the relationship between the center and the circumference of a circle, the smallest turn Joe makes will result in a large motion for Gargantua. (See also *Spatial Relativity* and *Ratio*.)

S5a

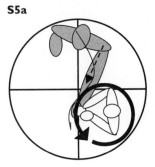

Yet *Spherical* motions need not be so large and pronounced. To the contrary, we ultimately must seek the *smallest Sphere* possible. A capable martial artist will destroy the opponent's sphere and take control with exceptionally slight, nearly imperceptible movements, far to subtle to depict here.

S7

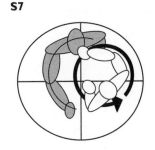

Two essential points still remain, however. First, once Gargantua succumbs to Joe's *Sphere*, Joe can use Gargantua's own intial force to place him in locks and dispel him with throws. Second, while most easily demonstrated in a grappling context, the *Sphere* principle applies equally to striking.

S5b

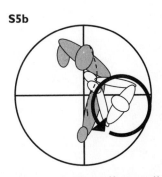

Looking to S7, we see that Joe maintains the integrity of his *Sphere* while penetrating and defeating Gargantua's sphere. Joe counters Gargantua's haymaker, thrown along the circumference of Gargantua's own sphere, by throwing a hook punch. In reality, we do not like the pentagonal shape of Joe's present body structure, but it suffices well to demonstrate the *Sphere* principle in this case. The same hook punch can be thrown elbow down, or the punch could be straight. Hence, S5b, in which we see Gargantua following the same eliptical path as in S5a, Joe steps or "rolls" his sphere aside, and uses the turning action of his sphere to contribute power to his punch. Note, as well, that Joe moves in such a way that the circumference of his *Sphere* coordinates with the line of Gargantua's punch. Any less movement would require deflection, and more movement would be excessive. More importantly, that precise amount of rotation allows Joe to move in direct proportion to Gargantua, which initiates a kind of *Leading Control* to be discussed later on.

35

The Body-Mind

As is the hand, so is the mind, so is the hand.

THIS PRINCIPLE POSES SOME OF THE MOST PRONOUNCED DIFFICULTIES WITH respect to its categorization. In one sense, it easily could be classified as a philosophical principle, given its implications reach into issues of consciousness as much as they do into actual physicality, but the other philosophical prinicples cover those areas well enough. Therefore, I discuss the *Body-Mind* principle here because its physical power impacts our techniques dramatically.

The *Body-Mind* idea seems simple enough at the outset: the state of the mind effects the state of the body; the state of the body effects the state of the mind. Initially, we can view this on a primal level: for example, when the mind perceives a threat, this in turn causes the body to initiate the "fight or flight" response through a sudden release of adrenaline, an increased heart rate, and a rapid breathing. The *body* reacts to what the *mind* observes, *whether or not an actual threat exists*. As the mind perceives, so the body follows.

On a far less primal level, we see the same principle at work when the mind encounters stress, during a bad day at the office, or when confronting a long-term fear, for example. At such times, many people suffer from "tension headaches," neck pain, ulcers, or in more extreme cases, heart attacks or strokes.

Conversely, the state of the body also effects the state of the mind. Physical pain, as in suddenly stubbing a toe or smashing a finger with a hammer, can seize the mind completely, rendering it utterly incapable of rational thought. It also can make the mind make the mouth use some words we typically do not want children to hear! On a more long term basis, pain can darken our mood. Someone suffering from a potent headache might well become cranky. Someone suffering from chronic pain might become downright ornery.

Of course, this manifestation of the *Body-Mind* works in reverse. Anyone who has had a good massage knows the happiness that results. Anyone who has felt pain suddenly dissipate will remember the happiness that comes merely from a return to normalcy.

Yet while such general understandings of the inter-relationship between mind and body might suffice for most people, as martial artists we require a deeper, more specific understanding of how each effects the other. To discuss that exhaustively would require a book in itself, but I can elaborate on the principle enough to point at its relevancy to martial applications.

Consider what happens when Gargantua grabs Jane's wrist. In order to execute and maintain such an attack, Gargantua has to "think" it. Barring absolute Zen enlightment, we must attribute some thought process to Gargantua, however subconscious it might be, which means that while Gargantua probably intended to attack Jane and grab her wrist, he did not *consciously* think to constrict the muscles in his hand. Despite the lack of *conscious* thought, however, his mind still causes the hand to clench because a hand cannot clench on its own. Its muscles need to be told to clench via electrical impulses from the brain. Therefore, the clenching of Gargantua's hand is, in itself, a thought. It might not be the same kind of thought as $E=MC^2$ but it is a thought nonetheless.

In fact, the harder his grab on her wrist, and the more *Intent* he is on seizing her, the stronger the thought behind the grab itself. In effect, the harder he grabs the more he has to "think" about grabbing, and as he devotes more of his mind to that "thought," less and less of his mind remains to think about, or react to, anything else. *This is arguably the greatest principle we can exploit: the capacity for a mind to react decreases in proportion to its intent to attack.*

Stepping away from Jane and Gargantua for a moment, try a simple exercise. Get a partner and ask them to apply a painful joint lock to you. If they do not know how to apply a joint lock, a pinch will suffice just as well. We're seeking any kind of pain that can be applied in slow increments rather than all at once (such as a punch to the face). Allow them to position the joint lock but before they apply it, relax and think about your *Center*. Once you feel well focused on your *Center*, ask your partner to slowly apply the lock. See how long you can keep your mind focused on your *Center* rather than on the pain. You will notice that as long as you locate your mind in your *Center*, the joint lock does not *really* hurt; you might experience some pain, but it remains negligible. Yet at the moment the lock *really* hurts, you will feel your attention—your mind—move from your *Center* to the place of the joint lock. (If this is not a good argument for keeping *Centered*, I do not know what is.)

Or try another simple *Body-Mind* exercise. Stand up and throw a few punches, starting softly and getting harder and harder as you go. As you do so, think about something relatively simple, such as naming the members of your extended family. Notice how increasingly hard punches make it increasingly difficult to think. Finally, throw those punches are hard as you can and make note of the effect. You will find it far more difficult, if not impossible, to maintain a train of thought when exerting maximum effort. (If that is not a great argument for *Relaxation* and *Effortless* technique, I do not know what is.)

These exercises teach us two simple rules: First, we are all stupid. The mind really can attend only to one thought at a time. Sure, we can grab our partner's wrist and still hold a conversation, but only if we grab halfheartedly. If we grab as hard as we can and with full intent, as in the punching exercise, the mind becomes consumed in that one act.

Richard Behrens develops this idea in his book, *Teachings of a Grand Master*, when he discusses the "lower mind" vs. the "higher mind." The former concerns those actions we don't really "think" about, while the latter concerns those "thoughts" requiring our conscious attention. Using that distinction, it is possible for our "lower mind" to grab someone's wrist while our "higher mind" attends to other matters but, barring certain levels of enlightenment, both minds will be consumed in one action were that action to surpass a certain threshold of *Intent*.

Second, the exercises above teach us that *the mind locates itself in the body when acting on/through the body.* Keeping *Centered*, our mind locates itself in our center, at least until a certain amount of nerve impulse—pain— demands its attention someplace else, such as at the location of the wrist lock, at which point the mind moves from our *Center* to our wrist. Note, of course, that I am not talking about the *brain*, which always remains firmly between our ears. I am talking about our *mind*, something far more elusive than the gray matter itself.

Both of these factors now inform the Gargantua-Jane scenario. When Gargantua grabs Jane's wrist, supposing he does so with *Intent*, his mind becomes consumed by the "thought" of grabbing. This makes him less inclined to react well to countertechniques Jane could employ, *provided those countertechniques do not originate from her wrist* (see *Indirect Pressure*). I am certain that many fellow martial artists exploit this principle, knowing that when someone attacks hard in one way, they become vulnerable in other ways. We cannot rightly say that Gargantua will not react to Jane's actions, but we can say that the greater his effort in grabbing, the less likely and less quickly he will do so. In effect, *as his hand becomes clenched, so does his mind.*

Furthermore, Gargantua's mind effectively becomes located in his grabbing hand. It does so not only because the "thought" must be there if the hand is to clench hard, but also because of the power of *Tactile Sensitivity*— the power feeling has over other senses. Therefore, *where his body goes, so does his mind.*

Yet Jane, too, can be victimized by the *Body-Mind*. Just as Gargantua's mind moves to where he grabs, so will Jane's mind be inclined to move there as well, if only because her mind must attend to the sensory stimulation in her wrist. While Gargantua's attack does not produce the pain of a joint lock, the grab still offers enough sensory stimulation to draw Jane's attention.

We therefore see *Reciprocity* at work once again, for just as the *Body-Mind* can be exploited in Gargantua—strong for Jane—so can it diminish her own capacities. In fact, Jane's mind will tend to move to her wrist not only because of the physical sensation, but also, and perhaps more importantly, because of the psychological "feeling" of being seized, controlled, grabbed, etc.

Paradoxically, it is the *perception* of being seized that makes Jane literally seized (*Opponents Are Illusions*). When Jane feels seized at her wrist, her mind moves to that point of concern, to that place of physical stimulation. In moving to her wrist, her mind moves to the same location of Gargantua's mind. Doing so forces Jane to attempt to resist from her wrist, the same place where Gargantua is most powerful—the same location as his *Body-Mind*, *Intent*, and strength. As Gargantua enjoys considerable physical superiority to Jane, Gargantua will win the battle for the wrist.

We see this phenomenon most regularly in choke holds. Martial artists new to the experience of actually being choked, or even just having someone's hands on their throat, often experience difficulty in applying escape techniques. They become so concerned with the choke itself, so disoriented by the sensation of it, that they cease to function normally. Worse, they try to resist the choke from the point of the choke; they fight against the strength of the arm rather than employing proper technique.

Of course, the *Body-Mind* must not only be what we exploit, but also what we *employ*. We must seek techniques that communicate force but do not seize our minds. We must act freely. While generally this has to do with minimizing our overall body tension, most importantly, we must focus on minimizing tension in our hands. Maintaining relatively relaxed hands, clenching them only at moments of impact, if at all, permits the mind to be aware and free.

To that end, *Torsion* becomes an invaluable tool, especially in the application of locks. Any time we can avoid grabbing and otherwise exercise the power of opposing forces between limbs or fingers, we can remain relaxed while still applying effective technique, thereby keeping our mind free to respond to current stimuli.

All said, we must respect the connection between the mind and the body, and in doing so recognize that they are not separate entities but rather interrelated, if not one in the same.

36

The Void

THE *VOID* PRINCIPLE *ALMOST* SEEMS SO OBVIOUS THAT IT SHOULD NOT warrant discussion. Yet it took quite a while for me to discover it and most of the martial artists with whom I work do not seem to recognize it *as such*. Simply, the *Void* principle works on the premise that *the opponent cannot fight/resist us where the opponent is not. Hence, always attack the Void.*

At first that must seem remarkably simplistic. It might appear to be nothing more than a mandate for striking unprotected areas of the body. If the opponent's defenses sits too low, attack high. If they sit too high, attack low. If they sit too far to the right . . . Yet while those would be acceptable interpretations and applications of the *Void* principle, they are only the most rudimentary ones.

More subtlely, the *Void* principle challenges us to manipulate the physical matter of the opponent's body without *directly* engaging it and/or directing our force into it. Despite how it might seem, there's nothing magical about the *Void* principle, but it does require that we re-assess how we apply techniques. Returning to the *Pure Objective* ideal of *effortlessness*, we do not want to "force" opponents to do anything because "forcing" them then signifies that we must be encountering, though perhaps overcoming, resistance. If we must overcome resistance, the techniques cannot be said to be effortless. Thus, we must keep in mind the basic tenet of the *Void* principle: *the opponent cannot resist where the opponent is not.*

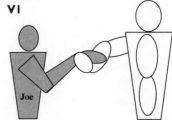

V1

Let's consider a simple wrist lock as seen in V1. Regardless of whether or not you are familiar with this particular lock, we only need understand that Joe wants to apply downward pressure to Gargantua's wrist. Typically, Joe would enter this wrist lock after being grabbed at the wrist, and Joe typically would use his left hand to secure Gargantua's hand, but that is not depicted. Other than that, the particular mechanics of the lock, for the time being, are unimportant.

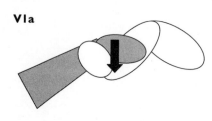

VIa

As in V1a, if Joe attempts to apply pressure directly into Gargantua's wrist (black arrow) then Gargantua can resist that pressure by pushing in the oppositce direction. Worse, because Gargantua will push up against Joe's arm, Gargantua actually will stablize himself by pressing his own feet more firmly against the ground, thus diminishing Joe's ability to de-stabilize him. In other words, Joe not only will encounter difficulty because Gargantua can resist force directed into his own wrist, but also because pushing into Gargantua's wrist helps. Gargantua resists more. As Gargantua can overpower Joe, Joe will have no hope of executing the lock in this fashion.

Alternatively, Joe should not direct force *into* Gargantua's arm, but around it. At this point, however, I must note that a consistent point of contact must be maintained (something typically best accomplished

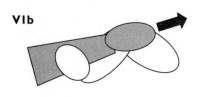

VIb

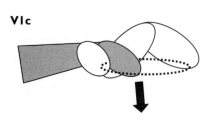

VIc

through *Torsion)*. The point at which Joe's wrist and Gargantua's wrist touch at the start of the technique must be the same place they touch through the entire technique. While it would be easy enough for Joe to simply move around Gargantua's arm by sliding on it (V1b), doing so obviously would not produce the desired wrist lock regardless of whether Joe slid his arm straight forward (as depicted) or more downwards.

What will work, however, is for Joe to direct his force through the *Void* or empty space created in Gargantua's arm structure (V1c & d). In which case, Joe literally directs his force into thin air, and *Gargantua cannot resist force applied into thin air because Gargantua's body mass is not present to do the resisting.* Note once again, however, that Joe *must*

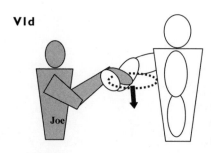

VId

Joe

maintain the point of contact; merely sliding over Gargantua's arm will accomplish nothing.

At first, this proves a difficult problem to reconcile. Maintaining contact at a single point while directing force into empty space poses a number of challenges, though it becomes easier as we become more relaxed and *Heavy*.

Furthermore, the proper exercise of *Void* also typically involves the proper exercise of the *Triangulation Point*. If we properly direct force through the void in Gargantua's arm structure but improperly direct that force to his feet, as represented by the black arrow in fig. V2, we give Gargantua the ability to push against the technique using his legs, as represented by the white arrow. Conversely, if we apply the force to the *Triangulation Point*, as in V2a, Gargantua has no ability to resist because the force never engages his body directly.

Obviously, many other principles affect our ability to properly execute the *Void* principle, with *Indirect Pressure* being a factor of close relation.

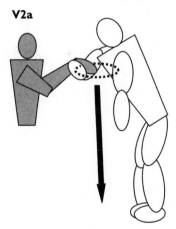

As the *Reciprocal* principle states, however, the ways that we are weak are the very ways in which we are strong. While we do not want to succumb to the *Void*, we actually exercise its power when striking. In fact, without use of the *Void*, we could not punch properly at all.

As in fig. V3, in a forward stepping punch some of our weight actually "falls" into our *Triangulation Point* in order to generate movement and power. While that force becomes stablized by the solid matter of our bodies, it is the *Void* that actually facilitates movement. In other words, our areas of "weakness"— *Void and Triangulation*—prove integral to generating power. Interestingly, when we make contact with a target over a given *Triangulation Point*, that arm actu-

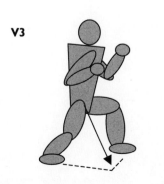

ally serves as our third "leg," taking the weight of the body that was falling into the *Void* and communicating it into the opponent.

Ultimately, the *Void* principle challenges us to look at combat through the perspective of the photographic negative. We need to learn about martial arts not only by paying attention to our physical selves but equally by recognizing the function of the spatial emptiness immediately around us.

37

Centripetal Force

MOST PEOPLE ARE SOMEWHAT FAMILIAR WITH THE CONCEPT OF *CENTRIFUGAL* force, force that moves away from the center point. Tie a ball to one end of a string. Grasping the other end of the string, start swinging the ball around your body. The ball will start in a low, small circle and as you swing the ball faster and faster it will create a larger and larger circle around you until the *centrifugal* force keeps it level to the ground (CT1 & CT2). In reality, the faster the ball whirls around you, the more it wants to move *away* from you.

CT1   **CT2**

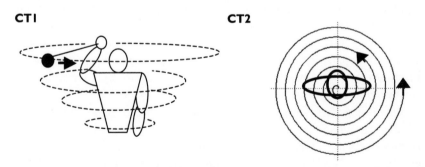

The problem with *centrifugal* force concerns the location of our *Center* of power—two inches below the belly button and midway between our abdomen and spine. As that represents the location of our power, movement away from that source results in a *decrease* of power. Just as a bullet is most powerful when first leaving the gun and an arrow is most powerful when first leaving the bow, so do our techniques hold the most power when close to our *Center*. As discussed many times throughout this text, it is getting our power to reach our limbs and our opponents that poses us the most challenges.

A second problem with *Centrifugal* force concerns the two competing forces at work. As the ball wants to fly off into the distance, the person swinging it must fight that force in order to stop it from doing so. This might not seem all too problematic when swinging a small ball on a string, but it becomes highly problematic when swinging a larger object, such as Gargantua. Obviously, this radically inferferes with *The Percentage Principle*: if we need to use some portion of our power to generate *Centrifugal* force and some percentage of our power to fight that force, the latter power detracts from the efficacy of our technique.

Centripetal force, on the other hand, represents the exact opposite. Water spiraling down into a drain offers an excellent example of *Centripetal* force—force that spirals inward rather than outward. Thus, we would reverse the direction of the arrows in CT2 in order to represent *Centripetal* force. Interestingly, and this will become important later on, *Centripetal* force manifests only in the presence of a *Void*, much as a the *Void* created by an unplugged drain "pulls" the water to it.

Before I go any further, however, I must note that *Centripetal* and *Centrifugal* forces are akin to *yin* and *yang*. While this chapter will speak to the importance of *Centripetal* force, we always use both, and the following chapter will speak at length to *Centrifugal* force.

With that said, we tend to place far too much value in *Centrifugal* force and not nearly enough value in *Centripetal* force, which often seems entirely overlooked despite its remarkable worth. *Centripetal* force (1) facilitates effortlessness, (2) brings opponents and techniques closer to our *Center*, and (3) usually requires less movement on our part than does *Centrifugal* force.

Moving into an example of *Centripetal* force in action, I first want to note two important overlapping principles. First, we must manifest a *Void* (if voids can be made manifest) for *Centripetal* force to emerge. Second, we also must note that the opponent already poses a natural *Void*, that being the *Triangulation Point*.

Examining the CT3 series, we see Gargantua executing a right arm grab to Joe's right wrist (CT3a). In response, Joe turns to his left and steps under Gargantua's arm (CT3b) before turning 180 degrees to face Gargantua and apply a *sankyo* style wrist lock that lifts Gargantua onto his toes (CT3c).

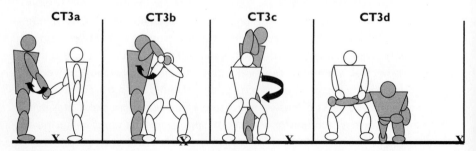

Joe then completes the 360 degree turn and pulls Gargantua into an arm bar. (Of course, this explantion is not meant to teach technique, but only to demonstrate the point.) In fact, we must take particular notice of the locaction of the X, which does not move. In CT3a we see find the "X" directly below Gargantua's arm and over his *Triangulation Point*. Note that Joe moves away from that point in the process of applying the technique. Consequently, the CT3 series demonstrates the technique as it would be done *Centrifugally*.

The CT4 series illustrates the same technique we see in CT3 but from above rather than from the side. Note that the "X" remains in a static position while Joe changes his position relative to it. "Y," which does not exist until CT4c, also remains static and becomes the center point of the circle created by the *Centrifugal* force Joe uses to move Gargantua.

As I mentioned before, in order for Joe to move Gargantua along the circular, *Centrifugal* path illustrated above, he must use some portion of his own power to keep Gargantua from moving too far away. Otherwise, Gargantua might move a small distance in CT4c and then take a step away from Joe and out of Joe's range. Thus, by using *Centrifugal* force in this way, Joe fights himself, at once spinning Gargantua away while simultaneously holding him close.

I should point out that while it appears as though Joe implements circular force against Gargantua, *Centrifugal* force actually moves away in a straight line. Returning to the ball on a string example, releasing the string will cause the ball to fly away in the direction the string points at any given moment. It will follow the exact path of the string itself because the *Centrifugal force moves directly away from the center*. This means that at any given moment, Gargantua's mass wants to move directly away from Joe in a straight line. To stop Gargantua from doing just that and move him from CT4c to CT4d, Joe must devote a certain percentage of his power to keeping Gargantua close to him.

In yet another sense, Joe, in position "Y," actually stands in Gargantua's way. Gargantua must move around Joe in order to reach the arm bar. This obviously lengthens the time it takes to execute the technique, something Joe cannot afford.

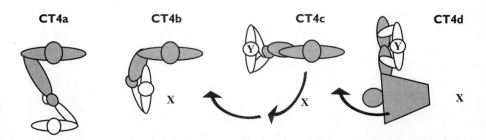

Yet let us examine what happens when Joe executes the same technique *Centripetally*, which means that Joe must create a *Void* into which Gargantua can fall. Fortunately, Gargantua's body dictates the exact place for that *Void*. Looking back to CT3a, we find that the "X" rests in Gargantua's *Triangulation Point*, the very spot to which he happens to be pointing. Let me refer back to *Triangulation Point* and note that Joe's position makes him function as Gargantua's third leg, meaning that he bears some percentage of Gargantua's force, weight, and/or *Intent*.

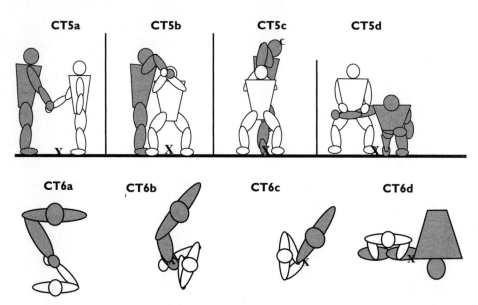

CT5a   CT5b   CT5c   CT5d

CT6a   CT6b   CT6c   CT6d

Looking to the CT5 and CT6 series, we see it possible to execute the same technique while drawing Gargantua into and dropping him down onto the *Triangulation Point*, thereby being *Centripetal*. As a result, Joe can move far less. In CT5&6b, Joe steps off the "X" thereby creating a *Void* into which Gargantua can fall. In CT5&6c, as Gargantua continues to move into that *Void*, Joe steps beneath his arm until finally driving Gargantua down into the "X" in CT5&6d. All said, Gargantua's path would look something *akin* to CT7.

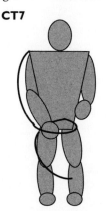

CT7

Not only does this require considerably less effort on Joe's part, in CT5&6c we find that as Gargantua falls to the "X," he actually falls into Joe's wrist lock. Joe, therefore, uses Gargantua's weight to lock Gargantua.

Of course, Joe also never puts himself in the position of having to fight himself by pushing and pulling Gargantua at the same time. Furthermore,

Joe manages to draw Gargantua into his own power *Center* rather than pushing him away from it, which means he simultaneously draws Gargantua away from Gargantua's power center.

Meanwhile, one of the most remarkably valuable elements of *Centripetal* force entails the way speed *increases* as a given object moving at an otherwise constant rate traverses smaller and smaller circles. If we take an object moving at a given speed and increase the amount of *Centrifugal* force on it by forcing it into tighter and tighter circles, that force converts into more speed.

On a more advanced level, that Gargantua grabs Joe's wrist means that Gargantua is sending *Intent* and energy toward that point and beyond, which in this case means down the length of his arm and towards his own *Triangulation Point*. Consequently, Joe need not "throw" Gargantua because Gargantua already intiated the process of falling. Joe need only facilitate Gargantua's fall by (1) ceasing to be Gargantua's third leg, thereby (2) creating a *Void* where he—Joe—used to stand. With proper mechanics and a high level of *Tactile Sensitivity*, Joe will permit Gargantua to throw himself.

Yet we need be advanced practitioners to exercise *Centripetal Force*. We only need recognize that any and all locks, throws, and takedowns may be functionalized by drawing the opponent into ourselves and then removing ourselves from the space we occupied, thereby spiraling the opponent downward like water into a drain. Those who understand this principle well will see how to apply this concept in any such technique.

Yet what about striking? Where does *Centripetal* motion come into play there? Interestingly, it does play a role, albeit a more subtle one. I will leave that discussion for the next chapter, however.

38

Centrifugal Force

MOST MARTIAL ARTISTS SEEM TO POSSESS A SOMEWHAT INNATE OR INTUITIVE understanding of the value of *Centrifugal* force, particularly as it comes into play when striking, such as in the use of bodily torque to cultivate power. However, *Centrifugal* power, if unchecked, can compromise technique. The previous chapter illustrated one way it does just that by establishing competing forces, e.g. having to devote energy to keeping Gargantua close enough to apply the given technique while the *Centrifugal* force pulls him away at a 90 degree angle.

CFI

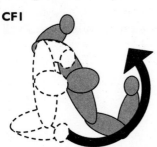

Believe it or not, the exact same problem occurs within our own bodies. We see this occuring to the figure in CF1. Throwing a hook punch, the *Centrifugal* force acting on the figure's right arm and wrist, though generating considering speed and torgue, nevertheless means that the figure must generate two competing forces, one to propel its own arm in a circular fashion and one to simultaneously stop its own fist from flying away from the body in a straight line.

CF2 illustrates another potential problem with the *Centrifugal* force cultivated in the body, this time a result of *Wave Energy*. As the *Wave Energy* chapter illustrated, it moves up the body in a *Centifugal* manner, creating a flicker of rotation in each limb. If the body is tense, improperly *Structured*, and/or the strike lacks *Spinal Alignment*, that *Wave Energy* will not pass *through* the body, it will

CF2

turn it. In essence, the *Centrifugal* force of *Wave Energy* can make us throw ourselves out of our own technique. Thus, we must regocnize that if we generate enough force to move someone else's body, then we also must be generating enough force to move our own bodies, and so that force must be cultivated and channeled properly.

Returning to CF1, some strikers who 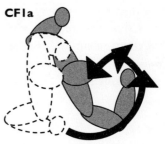 throw hook punches intuitively recogize the power of *Centripetal* force in that they constrict the path of their otherwise circular, *Centrifugal* strike to a decreasing radius spiral (CF1a). Exercising the same amount of force and speed but doing so over an increasingly shorter circle will increase the speed and power of the strike. That, by the way, seems to be the most effective way to integrate *Centripetal* and *Centrifugal* forces when striking with any circular motion, hook punch or other.

To do so most effectively, two actions must occur: First, the body must be *Relaxed* and *Heavy*, manifesting proper *Structure* so that we need not use muscle tension to establish the *Centripetal* counter-force that holds the *Centrifugal* force from flying off into the distance. In other words, as long as we permit the *Wave Energy* to travel through our body freely, we need not fight the *Circular* motion with muscular strength, which would diminish the quality of our strike.

Second, we must contruct the decreasing radius spiral as seen in CF1a but should *avoid* doing so by use of muscular strength. Rather, if we use the *retraction* of the hip motion that generated the *Wave Energy* to snap the circular strike inwards, we will create three positive effects: (1) a decreasing radius circle that increases the speed and power of the strike, (2) a sharp whipping effect, and (3) the capacity to strike our opponents from reverse angles, i.e. because we hit while the radius decreases, we can strike opponent from from the back to front, as in striking the back ribs towards the solar plexus.

Therefore, *Centrifugal* force represents no less important a principle than *Centripetal* force, but we must be careful with its use. It can quite easily gain the better of us and diminish our techniques, and it must be viewed and exercised in balance with *Centripetal* force.

Case in point: I previously mentioned that  *Wave Energy* ultimately constitutes *Centrifugal* force in that it directs force outward. Yet the *Centrifugal* force present actually begins via a *Centripetal* motion. As we see in CF3, which takes places at the inception of the *Wave* motion, the right knee twists *inward* into the *Void* between the legs and *Down*. That inward motion creates a proportionate *inward* spiral of energy that then gets channeled upwards. Imagine, for example, a car getting sucked into the whirling vortex of a tornado and then rising upwards until accumlating enough velocity to break free of the vortex and fly off into the distance. Something similar occurs as we use *Centripetal* motion to generate a vortex in our physiology that then releases energy *Centrifugally*.

I should note that advanced levels of striking largely negate notable body movement and torgue. If we relax and orient the spine properly, the *Wave Energy* can travel up it without any physical rotation in the body. The force simply passes through like water through a hose.

39

Sequential Locking & Sequential Relaxation

(Communial Locking, Chain Locking, Body Seizing)

*S*EQUENTIAL *LOCKING* SPEAKS TO THE IDEA THAT BECAUSE THE HUMAN body works as a compilation of joints, it can be controlled via those joints. Or more precisely, that we can access otherwise distant, inaccessible joints of the body if we manipulate close, accessible ones properly.

Looking to SL1, we see a wrist lock being applied. How does it function? It functions by first taking up all the leeway in the wrist joint. When the wrist can offer no more slack, the elbow moves as much as it can to absorb the force being applied to the wrist. Once the elbow does all it can, the shoulder moves to absorb the pressure. The only force being applied is to the wrist, yet as the receiver's body wants to save the wrist from dislocation, it first yields at the wrist, then at the elbow, then at the shoulder. It yields *sequentially*. Or we could say with equal accuracy that the person applying the technique *Sequentially Locks* the receiver's arm.

SL I

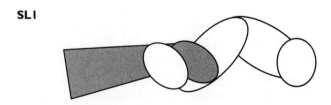

Yet sequential locking affects a great deal more than the arm. In an effort to keep the wrist from dislocating, the body will yield at the spine. Without proper *Spinal Alignment*, the body will do so successfully by twisting out of the lock. With proper *Spinal Alignment*, each joint in the spine—each vertebra—will lock sequentially, seizing the entire body from the hips up. Interestingly, with proper *Spinal Alignment*, we can seize the entire spine virtually instantaneously. The spine can pivot and bend only when it does not directly receive force. Once it becomes the direct recipient of force, it becomes as a solid bar.

Once we seize the spine, we control the entire upper body. Yet as the body still wants to save the wrist from dislocation, it tries to absorb the force against the wrist by yielding at the knees, the next major joint in the body's sequence. This explains why people drop to their knees when receiving a wrist lock (or other joint manipulation). It does not and should not occur because their opponent forced them downward, nor should it be a matter of pain compliance exclusively. It should occur because the body seeks downward mobility in an effort to save a given joint. This affirms *Spatial Relativity*. To drop an opponent, we need not disperse our force over a large surface area of motion. Instead, we need only concentrate our force into the smallest part of a particular joint and the opponent's body will relent.

If the opponent's knees cannot compensate for the force, the opponent will seek out a prostrate position, at which point the opponent loses any further ability to yield to the technique. Hence, complete submission.

Understanding *Sequential Locking* and its relationship with *Spatial Relativity* teaches us how to damage joints if we so choose. As we just saw, the opponent's body needs time to receive the force directed into its wrist (or any other joint). While that required time amounts to less than a second, if we apply force to any joint faster than the opponent's body can yield, we damage the joint rather than *Sequentially Locking* the body. The more localized the pressure—*Spatial Relativity*—the easier that becomes. The faster the application—*Temporal Relativity*—the easier that becomes.

Of course, we do not want to dislocate joints and rip tendons except under the most extreme circumstances. Fortunately, the same lessons apply to submitting opponents. A proper joint lock will exercise only a fraction of an inch of motion and yet drop the opponent's entire body to the floor. What a *Ratio*.

If we think of *Sequential Locking* as a matter of taking up the available slack in the opponent's body, then we see that it applies to virtually all techniques, not just joint locks. Throws are one technique that takes up slack by extending the body, for example, by pulling the arm to take up the slack in the shoulder and spine, as in the case of a standard shoulder throw. Even strikes take up slack, especially by those who do so while particularly tense. They effectively consume the slack in their own bodies, which makes it a perfect opportunity to hit them.

Yet *Sequential Locking* is not without its *Reciprocal*. Just as we can exploit *Sequential Locking* in our opponent, so do we exercise it for our own techniques. Yet unlike the example above, we do so without undo tension and far short of the point of straining ourselves. A properly aligned punch, for instance, will take our own joints to a *constructively* "locked" position, removing enough slack to create the stability required to deliver force. As always, what is our deficiency from one perspective becomes our strength from another perspective.

By contrast, we also must exercise *Sequential Relaxation,* which means relaxing from the *Center* outward, reversing the sequence that would lock the *Center.* We should relax from the *Center* to spine to shoulder to elbow to wrist to fingers. Furthermore, just as *Sequential Locking* connects us to our opponent's *Center,* so does *Sequential Relaxation* keep techniques connected with our *Center.*

Those who would question how we can relax sequentially when previous chapters have argued for consistent relaxation raise a good point. Yet any lifting of the arms (or other motion), unless accomplished purely through *chi,* involves some muscle tension, though perhaps not excess tension, thus permitting *Sequential Relaxation* once again.

40

Peripheral Vision

A SIMPLE PRINCIPLE BASED ON AN ANATOMICAL TRUTH, *Peripheral Vision*, rather than direct vision, should be employed at all times: we should never direct our eyes at a target. Instead, we should look off in a slightly different direction or focus our eyes just short of the target so as to see everything all at once but nothing in particular. In *Principles of Advanced Budo*, Shihan Tony Annesi offers a wonderful phrase of exercising peripheral vision: "Look far to see near, look near to see far." That encapsulates it well.

Peripheral Vision becomes important because the eyes enjoy too intimate a relationship with the mind. When they focus on something, the mind fixates on it. As a result, the mind's attention must shift away from the fixation before responding to any other stimulus, and that takes time. Furthermore, because the mind becomes fixated on a particular thing, *all* mental reactions become slowed, even reactions to motions by that on which the mind is fixated. Put another way that will be explained in more depth later on, any fixation carries with it *Intention,* whereas not focusing the eyes helps keep us in *Non-Intention.*

Essentially, any stimulus coming through focused eyes will be proceed by the cognitive elements of the brain, meaning that we will think about whatever we directly see. By contrast, stimulus coming through peripheral vision still goes through the brain but it does not get thought "about." Consequently, we react more quickly when using *Peripheral Vision* than when using direct vision.

At first, many martial artists find this uncomfortable. Yet we should keep in mind that we need not look at something to see it. Driving along in our cars, we might be *looking* at the car in front of us but we still will *see* the car to the right as it swerves into our lane. Our *Peripheral Vision* picks it up.

Interestingly, *Peripheral Vision* also helps keep us *Relaxed* and *Centered* because the lack of visual fixation encourages a lack of mental fixation, which in turn encourages a lack of physical fixation and stimulates the *Body-Mind*.

Not only that, focused vision also can betray us by revealing our *Intention* to the opponent. If we suddenly look at the opponent's arm, he or she will recognize our desire to block it. If we suddenly look at the opponent's face, he or she will recognize our desire to strike it. In this way, focused vision *Telegraphs* our movements, something the blank stare of *Peripheral Vision* does not.

41

Tactile Sensitivity

WITH *VISUAL SENSITIVITY* REFERRING TO PERCEIVING STIMULI THROUGH the eyes and *Peripheral Vision* referring to using unfocused vision, *Tactile Sensitivity* refers to touch, i.e. receiving stimuli through what we feel. Generally speaking, we want to favor *Tactile Sensitivity* for three reasons: First, it responds faster than *Visual Sensitivity*. Second, it typically offers more information. Third, it is less easily deceived.

Its relative quickness comes from the fact that reflexive actions can occur without involving the brain. If we place our hand on a hot stove, the neuromuscular system recognizes the damage being caused and pulls our hand from the stove *before* the nerve impulses reach and get processed by the brain. For this reason, we can experience a delay between injuring ourselves and feeling the resulting pain.

Of course, *Tactile Sensitivity* will enhance our responses and our techniques only once they become *Reflexive*. They must be drilled into the neuromuscular reflex or else the system will not respond automatically. Once accomplished, however, it becomes better suited to the frantic pace of combat.

More importantly, *Tactile Sensitivity* typically offers more information than *Visual Sensitivity*. If we block the opponent's strike, *Tactile Sensitivity* includes more than the square inch of contact between our arm and the opponent's. It also offers full-body information, including the relative power of the opponent, our state of balance, the opponent's state of balance, the direction of the moving force, etc. While *Visual Senstivity* offers some of that information as well, it offers less, though this fact does not suggest that we need to limit ourselves exclusively to the tactile.

Furthermore, *Visual Sensitivity*, especially in the case of direct vision, gets fooled all too easily. This cannot be fully explained, but anyone who has engaged drills such a *chi sao, hubud, sambrada,* push hands, and other "sensitivity" or "energy" drills will understand it completely.

Working from that premise, *Reciprocity* insures us that we can exploit the power of *Tactile Sensitivity* by tactics such as *Indirect Pressure.* Grabbing our wrist, *Tactile Sensitivity* tells the opponent that he or she has control over us. Provided we do not move or resist *from* the wrist itself, *Tactile Sensitivity* will tell the opponent's mind that it maintains control. The opponent might see our arm move but by the time *Visual Senstivity* overcomes the more powerful *Tactile Sensitivity,* we will have applied a counter-technique. Therefore, while we want to exercise our own *Tactile Senstivity* in constructive ways, we also want to take advantage of the fact that the opponent will pay more attention to feel than to sight. Such "mind tricks" move us a long way towards taking down the likes of Gargantua.

42

Rooting

(Grounding, Nullifying, Channeling)

WHILE THE PRESENCE OF THIS CHAPTER MIGHT SUGGEST OTHERWISE, I AM not going to make a significant effort to explain *Rooting*. To do so would be notably like having to explain a joke. We might appreciate the joke after the explanation but it will never be funny. For it to be funny, we probably "had to be there."

Rooting involves directing force into and from the the ground through proper *Physiokinetic* alignment of the body and proper attention to *Relaxation, Centeredness*, and all of the other principles discussed in this section. Suffice it to say that if we manifest the body properly, we can channel all force directed at it directly into the ground. To that end, *Relaxation* proves critical because energy forced into the body will locate itself in muscle tension. In fact, not only will force find tension, it will find *Intention*, meaning that if we bring our mind to the force, the force will register in our mind. We must not give the force power by acknowledging it.

Remember the pinching exercise in *Centeredness*? As long as we keep our mind in our *Center*, a pinch to the hand will not "hurt." As soon as we move the mind to the location of the pinch, it hurts because there will be no pain without the presence of the mind. Our attention to force directed at us only allows it to clash with our mind, something *Non-Intention* prevents.

Therefore, we never want to receive force. We want to be mere conduits of force, allowing it to pass through us into the ground, which will absorb all the force we can give it and far more.

Conversely, we want to secure our own techniques by *Rooting* them in the earth. I do not mean that we want our own force to channel from the earth, though that might become true eventually, but that we want to drop our weight into the ground so as to become more stable. Having discussed

Newton's Third Law, it stands to reason that any force we generate must be stablized by some counterforce.

In addition to stabilizing ourselves through *Heaviness,* we can use the force we generate to produce the weight we need for stability. If properly *Rooted,* we will push ourselves into the ground as we push against an external object. To use Peter Ralston's example from *Cheng Hsin,* whatever we lift up simultaneously pushes us down, thus stabilizing us.

It might seem as though this contradicts previously mentioned ideas such as *Heaviness* and the *Percentage Principle* in that we want absolutely none of the force we generate to come back at us. True enough. I will resolve the paradox as follows, keeping in mind that explaining a joke will not make it funny: If (1) our stability grants us the ability to project force and (2) projecting force outward produces counterforce against us and (3) we use that counterforce to increase our stablity then (4) we use that stability to generate greater amounts of force meaning (5) the counterforce actually becomes force and (6) we fulfill the percentage principle by generating all force at the opponent.

Ultimately, the opponent's force becomes our force and our counterforce becomes our force.

Now wasn't that funny? As I said, "you had to be there." Do some push hands with a skilled *tai chi* practitioner and you'll "get it," no pun intended.

PRINCIPLES OF TECHNIQUE

A S WITH *PHYSIOKINETICS* AND *PRINCIPLES OF THEORY*, THE ENTIRE BOOK could fall under this section heading. After all, martial arts practice obviously involves techniques, techniques that perhaps better the person in the process, techniques that do or do not follow rigid sequences, techniques that exercise *Physiokinetics*, etc., but techniques nonetheless.

Whereas the discussion of *Physiokinetics* does not necessarily hinge on the presence of an opponent, *Principles of Technique* refer to purely interactive endeavors, endeavors that in some way relate to the presence of an opposing partner. In short, this section specifically concerns itself with physically influencing, and not being influenced by, an opponent in a martial context. In a sense, it could be said to cover the more pragmatic applications of *Principles of Theory* and *Physiokinetics*, yet I do not like the suggestion that the aforementioned principles in any way lack pragmatism. They are no less practical than anything to follow, though what follows does speak more to their application in context.

Simply, *Principles of Technique* will speak to those elements we typically associate with martial arts—movement, timing, footwork, etc. While the particular nature of strikes, locks, and throws differs from style to style, the *principles* of techniques do not. As this section will demonstrate, whether we strike with a vertical fist, horizontal fist, three-quarter fist, knife hand, ridge hand, palm heel, slap, finger poke, etc. bears no influence on the underlying elements of striking itself.

Actually, that previous statement requires some qualification. To the extent that different techniques fulfill different objectives and work from differing ideologies, they also might differ down to their core. In other words, a finger poke might be more suited to a particular task—poking the eyes—than a palm strike, but this section is not concerned with the partic- ular variations. Such task-specific and style-specific discussions would be far too cumbersome to engage here.

In light of that, it would seem appropriate to again note that some styles favor certain principles, and that some styles might express certain principles more effectively than others, or at least differently. Regardless, all principles remain present and each and every one should be cultivated to maximum *Efficiency*.

43

Technique*s* vs.
Technique_

BEFORE I CAN DISCUSS THE *PRINCIPLES OF TECHNIQUE_*, I MUST NOTE THE importance of the absent "s," meaning that this section does not discuss "Principles of Technique*s*." If not for the absent "s," this book would not exist, and I would not be half the martial artist I am today.

For years, I focused on the accumulation of martial arts technique*s*. As I noted in the introduction, I searched for the most effective technique*s* I could find, technique*s* from martial arts of all different nationalities, technique*s* in all ranges of combat, technique*s* to deal with every possible attack situation, and so on and so forth. I was playing the encyclopedia game—cataloguing as many technique*s* as I could. In fact, I foolishly, and often *erroneously* prided myself on knowing more technique*s* than many other martial artists, and enjoyed showing my students how one entry could lead to countless different striking combinations, joint locks, throws, finishing holds, etc., or how one throw could be achieved by a variety of entries, with a variety of strikes interlaced, or how one finishing hold could be achieved from a variety of throws, locks, and takedowns.

While I *in no way denigrate* the value of multiple technique options, I personally operated under the misconception that the quantity of technique*s* mattered more than their quality. Put another way, I valued *quantity* of technique*s* rather than the *quality* of technique_. I focused on the accumulation of different options instead of on understanding what truly made any one given application work. In short, I "knew" countless technique*s* in the general sense—understood the macro motions, how they generally looked, what they generally accomplished and how they generally accomplished it—but did not understand the more subtle and precise micro motions that truly made techniques functional and powerful, especially against the likes of Gargantua. Put simply, my techniques lacked sound technique_.

Furthermore, as I noted earlier, the vast number of techniques I "knew" (or what at least *seemed* like a vast number to me at the time), ultimately became more confusing to me than useful. I could not marry certain techniques from one style with techniques from other styles. Hence, I sought out some reconciliation, and hence this book.

Eventually, I came to understand that whether I "knew" one, ten, or one-thousand techniques at a mediocre level of understanding, I was still just a mediocre martial artist. Consequently, I began to seek "mastery" in terms of the quality of my motions rather than in the quantity of their variations.

Whereas during my early years in the arts I was impressed by martial artists performing techniques I had not seen before, I later became desensitized to new variations. Instead, I found myself impressed by martial artists who performed techniques, even simple ones, at higher levels of mastery.

Yet I must emphasize that I am *not* condemning the accumulation of techniques. To the contrary, such learning pushes our coordination and understanding of the arts, and we obviously never know when and where we will encounter techniques better than our own.

Yet I am taking issue with valuing quantity over quality. At least in my case, such concern with quantity was premature—quite premature. I was performing techniques while lacking an understanding of what made them function. To use an example from the preceding section, I was performing countless techniques that were dependent on a good *Axis* without any knowledge of the importance of *Axis* as a principle. It did not matter, therefore, how many techniques I could perform. Because all techniques function from the same principles, any ignorance of principle manifests itself in every technique. Only now, given that I possess a modicum of understanding of principles, am I starting once again to feel qualified to concern myself with the absent "s."

I could like it to understanding grammar. If I do not know how to use a period, it does not matter how many sentences I write. Each will be problematic, and the lack of proper period placement only will confuse everything I attempt to say.

That said, here are the *Principles of Technique_*.

44

Equal Rights

OPPONENTS HAVE RIGHTS TOO. I AM NOT SPEAKING OF LEGAL RIGHTS AND moral rights, rights which must be respected, but rather of rights to action, reaction, defense, movement, and intelligence. Any effort to diminish the quality of our opponent only diminishes the quality of the art designed to defeat that opponent.

Unfortunately, we all too often diminish the quality of the attacker by failing to grant the opponent the same basic "fighter's rights" that we possess. Perhaps a classic example of this concerns the right to retract techniques, as in instructing our in-class "opponents" to throw a single technique and leave it dangling in the air while we perform a series of strikes and counterattacks.

Real attackers will do everything in their power to avoid personal harm. Thus, we must afford them that equal right to self-preservation. Therefore, we effectively find Newton's Third Law returning to us in a way he probably never considered. "For every action there is an equal and opposite reaction" also means that for every action we take, we must grant our *attackers* an "equal and opposite" ability to react against us, just as we reacted to them. Unless we do something to prevent it, every time we get to act, they get to act/react. To diminish them to anything less only *diminishes our own ability as martial artists.*

After all, learning to defend attackers who throw a single punch and leave it in the air does not pose us many challenges. In fact, we need not learn martial arts at all if our opponents will be that incompetent. They would throw a single punch and we, while it dangled in the air, could walk to the nearest mini-mart, buy a newspaper, roll it up, and return to smack them across the nose with it. Better yet, we could just walk away. Thus, we must give our opponents equal credit as autonomous and self-interested beings. The saying, "tomorrow belongs to no one," must equally apply to every next moment. It does not belong to us; it does not belong to Gargantua. It must be seized, not assumed.

A caveat to this, as to most principles, regards training method and curriculum. *Equal Rights* does not *necessarily* exclude an instructor's option to train students by starting with unrealistically deficient opponents. Such pedagogy could prove valuable with respect to focusing on technique, coordination, *Posture*, etc.

Yet such a caveat would be a temporary allowance only. It also would not allow for "no-opponent-will-ever" statements, something that once again shortens our lines by pre-casting our attackers into unrealistic molds. We cannot afford to assume what opponents will and will not do. While some attacks bear greater statistical probability than others—statistically speaking I will run into haymakers more often than axe kicks—we simply cannot afford to make hastily generalized statements about our would-be opponents. Instead, we would be wiser to give them credit for unpredictability, randomness, craftiness, and a host of other qualities we do not want to face.

Fortunately, no matter how unpredictable the attacker, we need not feel any loss of *Control*, at least not if we focus on principles. We cannot predict what an attacker will do, but we know what principles will be involved. *Principles make no distinctions between types of attack. Principles make no distinctions between types of opponent. Principles make no distinction between circumstances. Principles never vary.* Be the attack some form of punch (straight, round, hook, uppercut, or otherwise) or a grab (wrist, lapel, throat, hair, or otherwise) or hold (bear hug, choke, headlock, or otherwise), we nevertheless can understand the forces at work and exploit them accordingly. Therefore, we need not restrict opponents to certain attacks and/or responses. Let them do *whatever they want*. Let them be unpredictable, random, and crafty in their *techniques* because they'll never be random or unpredictable in their principles.

All else said, our opponent probably will possess at least one trait that we might not, that being the *Intent* to do harm. I will speak to this further later on, but that intent to hurt, as opposed to our more simple desire to not be hurt, creates an imbalance in the dynamic of the fight that will work for us far more than it does against us.

45

Compliment

BRUCE LEE COINED THE NOW FAMOUS ADAGE, "YOUR TECHNIQUE IS MY technique." It is a wonderful phrase. Before discussing it, I'll note that while I think I have a good sense as to Lee's meaning, I do not know his mind and so I only can offer my own interpretation of the phrase. Even so, this discussion will be incomplete because it actually continues in the philosophy section when I discuss *Non-Intention*.

On a surface level, "Your technique is my technique" means that we allow the opponent's action to dictate our response to that action, or better yet, that *we have no action until the opponent takes action*. For example, we cannot block until the opponent punches. We can perform the motion of a block but as nothing actually will be defended, we cannot be said to have "blocked." Therefore, your punch, which is "your technique," prescribes my block, which is "my technique," and that starts to explain Lee's phrase.

The same concept applies when attacking instead of defending. The nature of our attack, such as the type of attack we choose to execute and its target, will depend on the nature of the opponent, the situational context, and the presence of openings. Thus, our attack is the opponent's defense. "Your technique is my technique."

Looking at the concept just a little bit deeper, however, we find that the very nature of our defense must compliment the nature of the attack. I discussed this in *Defense Defines The Art*, an article I wrote for the July, 2002 issue of *Black Belt* magazine. To sum up the point, we cannot use Western boxing against a *samurai*; it just will not hold up against an armored opponent with a long and lethal piece of steel. Instead, *jujitsu* offered unarmed *samurai* a chance of surviving when disarmed because it focused evading the long strokes of swordsmanship, seizing control of hands and arms, executing joint locks and throws against which armor offered little protection, and disarming. Yet put a *jujitsu* practitioner in a boxing ring with 14 ounce gloves on and they will be in as foreign a territory as a Western boxer on a 14th century Japanese battlefield.

While this synopsis leaves something to be desired, *jujitsu* nevertheless did not develop in a vacuum. It developed in a context that required it and gave it life. It would not be accurate to say that *jujitsu* emerged *because of* the *samurai*, as if some Japanese men grouped together in a dark room and decided to develop an art to use when disarmed. It would be more accurate to say, "Because *samurai* was, *jujitsu* was." In other words, *jujitsu* did not emerge in response to swordsmanship. It emerged with it. There was swordsmanship. And so there was *jujitsu*. (See *Yin-Yang*)

Similarly, we must examine how our own technique emerges with the context. That means that we cannot adhere to a motion simply because it is our style, because it has been practiced that way for a long time, or because it is the newest trend in martial arts, or for any other reason. A combative form out of step with combative function cannot be called a "combative" form. As *jujitsu* served as a *Compliment* to swordsmanship in that it served as its necessary antithesis, so must every one of our techniques be the *Compliment* to our opponent's technique.

This means our technique must intuitively address several factors: (1) The context of the fight. (2) The nature of the opponent's technique. And (3) the opponent's anatomy.

It must do so intuitively, though not necessarily improvisationally. While we must at every moment *Compliment* our opponent's technique, we can and should do so by exercising thoughtful, pre-conceived techniques. Our training should develop a repertoire of techniques large enough to permit us to *Compliment* the opponent in the appropriate way and at the appropriate time. Many arts have done just that, be they traditional or otherwise.

This discussion continues in the *Non-Intent* chapter, which delves into the more philosophical elements of this idea. For now, however, we must recognize that any adherence to preconceived techniques that do not meet and *Compliment* the reality set forth by our opponent only undermine the fundamental premise of the fighting arts.

46

Kobo-Ichi

BEFORE DELVING INTO A DISCUSSION ON THIS ISSUE, I MUST DISTINGUISH between two different definitions for "offense" and "defense." In one sense, we can define "offensive" and "defensive" with regards to "aggressor" and "defender," respectively. I want to make it clear that I presume that responsible martial artists will *never* be aggressors, meaning they will never initiate conflict. Therefore, all usage of "offense" and "defense" in this text will refer to "attack" and "defense" rather than who initiated the conflict. In other words, "offense" will not refer to who started the fight but to *techniques designed to affect the opponent*—strikes, locks, throws, etc.— while "defense" will refer to *techniques that protect*—blocks, parries, dodges, etc.

Moving on, I would like to introduce two new and reciprocal terms. The "Offensive Advantage," refers to the benefits of attacking. The "Defensive Advantage," refers to the benefits of defending. Yet as offense and defense are co-dependent, it follows that when speaking of the *Offensive Advantage,* I equally and simultaneously will be speaking of the *Defensive Disadvantage.* When speaking of the *Defensive Advantage,* I equally could be speaking of the *Offensive Disadvantage.*

The *Offensive Advantage (OA)* states that offensive techniques *eventually* will defeat defensive techniques. No matter how small a hole we leave in our defense, offense eventually finds it. No matter how proficiently we defend, offense eventually will overcome us. For example, were we 99% effective in blocking, an unrealistically high percentage and one that obviously would vary depending on the skill of our opponent, we could be said to block 99 out of every 100 strikes. Thus, 1 out of every 100 strikes will get through. Yet that speaks only to the percentage chance; it fails to tell us which one of the 100 strikes will penetrate. It could be the 62nd strike, or the 23rd, or the 4th. In effect, every time someone strikes at us we gamble on our ability to defend it. The unfortunate truth, therefore, is that unless we defend with 100% effectiveness, which no one does and few even vaguely approach, we eventually will succumb to the aggressor. The longer the fight, the greater number of attacks. The greater number of attacks, the more likely they will land. And in combat time, anything longer than a few seconds is a very long time.

Therefore, to counter the *Offensive Advantage*, we must minimize the number of attacks we permit the attacker to launch. In order to accomplish that, we need to act against the attacker in such a way that he or she cannot launch attacks, and "acting on the attacker" sounds an awful lot like "offense." Put another way, purely defensive techniques—those that *only* stop an oncoming attack and nothing more—do nothing to dissuade the attacker from attacking again, and so we presume it only a matter of time until the attacker, by skill or chance, finds the flaw in our defensive skill. Therefore, we cannot be purely defensive if we hope to achieve victory.

Interestingly, all martial arts *inherently* recognize the need to stop the attacker from attacking. Even *Aikido*, known for its relatively peaceful and non-aggressive defense, does not limit itself to defense in the purest sense. Rather, it acts on the attacker to dissuade future aggression, and does so through the use of throws, locks, and takedowns. Thus, all martial arts include techniques designed to defeat the attacker in some fashion—a concession of the need to stop the assault rather than exclusively protect against it.

Yet while offense does come with its advantages, it equally comes with its disadvantages. As we will defend ourselves most effectively when devoting all our arms and legs to protection then any attack inherently compromises some defensive capability because it uses a limb that could be defending. That represents the disadvantage of offense and the *Defensive Advantage*.

Just as the martial arts inherently recognize the need to counter the *Offensive Advantage* by squelching future attacks, so do they inherently recognize the *dis*advantage of offense, which is why martial arts typically defend first and counter second. Against a punch, most martial arts exploit the areas of the opponent's body left unprotected and/or exploit the energy committed to the punch itself. Either way, they recognize that attacking can create defensive deficiencies.

In addition to its physical problems, attacking can create mental flaws, which returns us to the discussion of *Intention*. We must remember that our objective differs from our attacker's *Intention*. Whereas the assailant seeks to hurt, we seek not-to-be-hurt (while recognizing that not-being-hurt ourselves sometimes requires that we hurt the assailant). Yet attackers can and often do become so preoccupied with their desire to hurt us that they compromise their defensive abilities.

All said, offense and defense each possess inherent strengths and flaws. This would seem natural and unavoidable, perhaps, but as martial artists we must find flaws utterly intolerable. While we want to adopt and execute the advantages of both modes, we may permit ourselves no tolerance for their seemingly inherent disadvantages. We cannot afford to play the purely defensive game because we know that (1) pure defense does nothing to dissuade an attacker's aggressive behavior and (2) that the attacker eventually will hurt us. At the same time, we cannot play the purely offensive game because we know that attacking can compromise our defensive integrity.

While resolving this discrepancy between offense and defense seems difficult, we must remember that martial arts study seeks to accomplish what untrained brawling cannot. If the martial arts cannot accomplish more than brawling then we should give up practicing them immediately. Yet the martial arts do not differ from other professional endeavors in this regard. The professional football team plays in ways the amateur or even college teams cannot. The professional plumber lays pipe better and faster than the amateur. The trained psychologist diagnoses mental illnesses that the rest of us do not understand. Therefore, any argument that we cannot eliminate the inherent problems of offense and defense runs contrary to the very cornerstone of martial arts—we can do what the untrained cannot.

Furthermore, if we have to sacrifice defense to execute offense, and vice versa, then we cannot possibly be operating at maximum *Efficiency*. How can we be exercising true *Efficiency* when creating openings for our opponent to exploit? How can we be said to be exercising true *Efficiency* when permitting our attacker to strike at us over and over again? In the same sense, how can we be said to be in *Control* if we are partially unprotected? Or how can we be said to be exercising *Control* if the opponent acts upon us?

Fortunately, we do not have to choose between sound defense and effective offense. In order to remain in accord with the *Pure Objective* and the general objective of the arts, we need only to think of offense and defense as a single entity. In short, every technique must be equally offensive and defensive.

"Equally" becomes the operative and challenging word. Consider, for example, a single block. In the purest sense of a block, it is 100% defensive and 0% offensive in that it defends the attack but does nothing to take control of the attacker and dissuade future aggression. However, if that block knocked the opponent's punch away and exposed part of the opponent's body to counter attack, it would become 100% defensive *and* some small percentage offensive—let's say 20% offensive for the sake of argument. (Two notes: (1) These percentages do not, or at least *should* not, work on a sliding scale. We do not want to sacrifice defense to attain offense. (2) We cannot actually assign quantifiable percentages to techniques.) If we could block hard enough to unbalance the opponent for a moment, thus preventing the next few attacks, we could deem the technique 100% defensive and perhaps 50% offensive. And if we could block hard enough to break the opponent's arm and end the fight then the purely "defensive" block will fulfill both offensive and defensive necessities.

Unfortunately, most blocks fall short of being 100% offensive, if it were not so, they alone would end all conflicts. Instead, they tend to work in conjunction with other techniques, and I certainly would not want to dismiss the value of such combinations. For example, a powerful block that unbalances the opponent and enables us to land a strike certainly permits both offensive and defensive objectives to be fulfilled. While not optimum, as would be one technique accomplishing both ends, the block-strike combination certainly accomplishes more than either part alone.

In a similar respect, we also can compensate for the deficiencies in one technique by simultaneously executing another. If we examine the intercepting fist in Tech 1, we see that the darker figure simultaneously defends the attack and also strikes. The defender's right arm defends by making contact with the attack and redirecting it—100% defensive. It redirects it into the left arm, which also parries—100% defensive. At the same time, the defender's right arm "offensively" punches to the assailants face. So should we categorize this combination as a defensive technique because it protects or an offensive technique because it strikes back? Obviously, both. Proficiency aside, the technique is both offensive and defensive. It would not even work without doing both. It is *Kobo Ichi.*

I use that one technique only as an example. As martial artists, we enjoy a plethora of techniques to serve offense and defense in harmony. On the other hand, the extent to which any given technique does not fully protect us while simultaneously defeating the opponent effortlessly and instantaneously is the extent to which that technique is inefficient and contrary to our aims.

Tech I

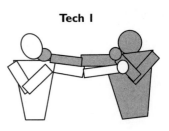

Ultimately, as the chart Tech 2 shows, we can identify five levels of technique. Least effective is merely blocking (or defending in any regard). Above that we find the ability to defend and then to counter, as in to block first and punch second. Above that comes the ability to defend and counter simultaneously, as in blocking with the left arm and punching with the right arm. Above that, we find pre-emptive striking—defeating the attack before it comes to fruition. In such a case, "defending" might become unnecessary. Finally, at the pinnacle, we find the ability to make our "defensive" techniques fulfill "offensive" objectives and "offensive" techniques fulfill "defensive" objectives. I call this *Kobo Ichi.*

(Most effective)

↑

Diffusing confrontation before its inception.

↑

Offense and Defense as one in the same.

↑

Strike then Block.

↑

Simultaneous defense and offense.

↑

Block then strike.

↑

Block only.

(Least Effective)

What we seek as martial artists resembles that of the Zen archers of which Herrigel speaks in his classic text, *Zen in the Art of Archery*. The Kyudo masters with whom he trained had a saying, "one shot, one life." And so it must equally be with us. "One life, one fight, *one* technique."

Thus, we must not permit ourselves any complacency with respect to less than maximum percentages. We cannot rationalize an acceptance of a great offensive technique if it compromises our defensive integrity, nor can we tolerate defensive techniques that do not end conflicts. While we all might be inclined, if not wise, to accept such techniques were there no alternative, we cannot consider such techniques *optimum*. We must seek to achieve techniques that are 100% offensive *and* 100% defensive. We must seek *Kobo Ichi*.

47

Economical Motion

DIFFERENT FROM *EFFICIENCY*, *ECONOMICAL MOTION* CONCERNS OPERATING our bodies so as to waste as little movement as possible without sacrificing speed, power, and efficacy. Obviously, this directly integrates with *Physiokinetics*. In fact, I nearly placed this discussion in that section because the two so rightly intertwine. For example, the discussion of *Axis* relates directly to *Economical Motion* because moving with a tight, vertical *Axis* simply proves more economical than moving with a large, titled one. Similarly, *Spinal Alignment* helps to *Root* power, which means we need less movement and momentum to generate force, which also facilitates *Economical Motion*. I could go on. Every *PK* principle instructs us on how to "apply the body" economically. Therefore, I will not spend time discussing the *Physiokinetic* connections to *Economical Motion;* they should prove accessible upon re-investigation.

To define *Economical Motion* rudimentarily, consider a punch. As martial artists, we typically consider the bar room "haymaker" to be the classic example of the *un*economical punch. First, as Gargantua winds up to hit with all his might, his fist moves away from us rather than towards us. This *Telegraphs*—signals what is to come—the punch to follow. Therefore, it is not only uneconomical in the physical sense, it also is uneconomical in a tactical sense. Second, once it does begin moving forward, it follows one of the longer possible paths to us by looping in a gigantic arc rather than following a straight(er) line.

If we suppose that Gargantua's fist started 1½ feet from its target—that being our jaw—then we find that his haymaker travels perhaps three, four, or even five feet to reach us—one or two feet backwards in retraction and then three or four feet in arc. Viewed this way, moving the fist five feet to cover a distance of a foot-and-a-half does not make much sense.

When viewed on such a dramatic scale, the nature and importance of *Economical Motion* should be apparent. However, we must examine our own movements as martial artists with equal or perhaps even greater scrutiny. For example, if we seek to execute a straight forward punch then every inch we retract equals two inches of additional travel—one for the inch retracted plus one forward again. Thus, every single inch of retraction results in a two inch problem.

In the same respect, once Joe executed a right cross block against Gargantua's right punch (Tech2), it would be uneconomical for Joe to retract his block before launching a right strike to Gargantua's face. In fact, it would pass up a golden opportunity. Being halfway between himself and Gargantua, Joe's fist sits in an excellent position to counterstrike. Supposing they move at the same *Movement Speed*, Joe's counterstrike will land when Gargantua's left attack has traveled only half the distance between them.

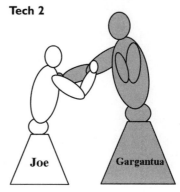

Tech 2

Joe

Gargantua

At the same time, however, having covered half the distance to the target means we may exercise only half the distance to generate power, and it is that *seeming* obstacle to power that makes many people retract before striking, thus diminishing or defeating *Economical Motion*. Yet we should not need to retract to achieve power if we align principles properly, including but not limited to *Spinal Alignment, Centerline, Secondary Pressure, Posture,* and *Heaviness.* Thus, any time we find ourselves executing less-than-optimally-economical motions on the grounds that they lack sufficient power, we first should re-examine our understanding of the principles involved.

Yet *Economical Motion* also must be considered in other ways. For example, if we return to the cross block example then we should question whether or not the block can further diminish the distance Joe's backfist will need to cover. If, for example, Joe's block struck with sufficient force to tilt Gargantua forward then not only would Joe's counterstrike need cover less distance, its relative power would *increase* because Gargantua's face would fall into it.

Thus, we see once again how offense and defense can unite. If, in addition to defending, the block jerks the attackers face into the defending fist, the defensive motion becomes equally offensive. It becomes both *Economical* and *Efficient.* Therefore, *Economical Motion must include not only those motions we make but also those motions we force our opponent to make.* If forcing opponents to increase their motions and to compromise their *PK* can permit us to shorten our motions then we must exercise such options, always.

In summary, (1) our motions must be as economical as possible. (2) *Economical Motion* should not conflict with speed and power provided that all principles align. (3) The most effective way to exercise *Economical Motion* not only concerns our own bodies but also *how we can force the opponent to move more so that we can move less.*

48

Active Movement

BEFORE EMBARKING ON THIS DISCUSSION, I WOULD LIKE TO MAKE A DISTINC-tion between two different types of movement: *passive* and *active*. For my purposes here, *passive movement* will refer to motion that does not change our position *relative to our opponent's*. For example, if Jane were sparring with a bad left arm then she might position herself in a right side forward stance. If the Joe began to circle her, the general movement she would make to keep her right side facing him would be *passive movement*. In such a case, she does not change her relative position; she maintains it.

Some styles take *passive movement* a step further. *Capoeira*, some forms of *pentjak silat*, *kung fu*, and *bando*, and some ring fighters, never take static, stationary stances. Instead, their fighting "stance" changes constantly, ever shifting and thus never offering the opponent a fixed target. While such constant, general motion can serve valuable tactical aims, we still classify it as *passive movement*.

By contrast, *active movement* defines movements that *change our position relative to our opponent*, such as stepping forward to punch, sidestepping to parry, exercising a retreating kick, entering to throw, etc. The discussion to follow will concern itself with *active* rather than *passive* movement, movement that *changes our position relative to our opponent*.

With respect to *active movement*, I see only one time to use it: when the opponent cannot compensate for it. If we lunge forward with a punch when the opponent can equally retreat or sidestep, or in some other fashion compensate for our movement, then our active movement not only proves wasteful but also, as we will see, compromising. In effect, if we use *active movement* to gain a positional advantage, we will fail to meet that goal if our opponent can respond proportionally.

Worse, moving when the opponent can compensate permits the opponent to exploit our movement. In fact, our ability to move in relation to our opponent, and typically in response *active movement*, serves as the foundation for most martial arts technique. It facilitates our ability to exploit the *Offensive Disadvantage* in that we wait for the opponent to attack and then move ourselves into a position that permits us to strike against the targets left unguarded by the attack.

At first, it might seem far fetched to suggest that we should exercise *active movement* only when the opponent cannot move in response, but it can be done. Three different instances permit us such opportunities: The first occurs when the opponent has committed to an attack. At such times, the opponent, though moving, will not be able to compensate for our motion. For example, if the opponent were to lunge forward with a committed punch then the opponent would not be able to alter his or her inertia to compensate for our sidestepping. I must emphasize "committed" as the critical word. At such times, the opponent, though in motion, becomes unable to move *relative to our motion* because of his or her commitment to a particular course of action. We call this "Frozen in Motion."

Put another way, as it takes energy to move when the opponent commits all of his or her energy to a given attack, that opponent enjoys no reserve energy to compensate for our own actions. Though in motion, such an opponent becomes locked into a particular course of action. That the opponent is in motion, while true in one sense, is merely an illusion in another sense. Being locked into a course, they become "static" or unchangeable until that course of action completes itself. Thus, whether we move against someone locked in place or move against someone committed to a particular action, we still can move *relative* to that person easily enough.

The second appropriate circumstance for movement happens whenever the opponent lacks *Balance*. At such times, the opponent must first regain balance before moving. Unfortunately, worthy opponents seldom just throw themselves off balance. It is more likely that we will unbalance them by blocking, feinting, evading, etc.

The third circumstance occurs whenever the opponent cannot perceive our motion, as would be the case if our speed exceeded the opponent's reaction time, or if we were moving imperceptibly in any variety of fashions.

Regardless of how a given scenario plays out, *active movement* achieves *nothing* if the opponent can move in response. If we move actively—committing our own energy to the motion—then our opponent can exploit our motion through his or her own *Active Movement*, thus subjecting us to the *Offensive Disadvantage*.

Unfortunately, we often see martial artists engaging in *active movement* and accomplishing little with respect to the relative position of the attacker. Instead, movement should be decisive and definitive, and occur only when safe. (See *Zanshin*)

49

Positioning

*A*CTIVE *MO*VEMENT STATED THAT WE SHOULD MOVE ONLY WHEN THE OPPONENT cannot compensate for our movement. Similarly, *Positioning* dictates a singular place to locate ourselves during combat: where we can affect the opponent *and* where the opponent cannot affect us. While I do not assert that our positioning alone should make us wholly untouchable, to seek out anything other than a position of safety seems ludicrous.

While attaining proper *Positioning* might not be easy, it also might not be as difficult as it sounds. A martial artist who kicks well enough to keep a non-kicking opponent at a distance can be said to have fulfilled the *Positioning* principle, so can the same be said about the martial artist who can control the *Primary Gate* while in close range along the *Centerline*.

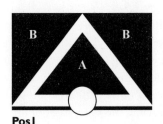

Pos I

In that sense, prior discussions of the *Triangle Guard* afforded us some understanding of where to position ourselves so as to achieve proper *Positioning*. Consider fig. Pos1, which depicts the positive *Triangle Guard* in white and the negative or implied triangles in black. While we cannot exist in the positive triangle because our opponent occupies that space, we can locate ourselves in the negative or black triangles, namely positions A or B.

Essentially, Jane achieves just that, penetrating Gargantua's *Triangle Guard* and *Positioning* herself at what would be point A. While Gargantua still may be able to launch attacks, Jane's direct and close access to unprotected *Centerline* targets should thwart those attacks before Gargantua can articulate them. (Pos2)

Pos2

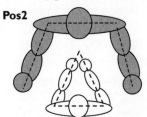

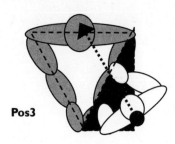

Pos3

Alternately, Jane could move into one of the two B positions, as in Pos3. Notice that while Gargantua's force and triangle are directed forward, Jane's force and triangle are directed straight at Gargantua's spine. This brings up a critical element of proper *Positioning*, namely that we must keep ourselves oriented towards the opponent. There are, however, exceptions to that rule. If the torso is not the primary target, as might be the case in entering into certain wrist locks, then different angling becomes permissible, though not preferred. More on that in the chapter to follow.

Yet the *Triangle Guard* is not the only *Physiokinetic* principle that informs positioning. The *Sphere* principle does as well. Looking to figure Pos4, we see just how the *Sphere* instructs us as to how to enter. Typically, the opponent's *Sphere* is smaller than that depicted, which I enlarged to more clearly illustrate how we use the curvature of the *Sphere* to guide our movement. The

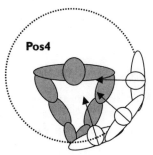

Pos4

Sphere also instructs us as to how to move behind the opponent, should such opportunities become possible.

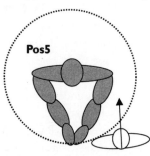

Pos5

Contrast this against Pos5, in which Jane moves outside the *Sphere*, unnecessarily distancing herself from Gargantua and, worse, facing her away from the opponent.

I suspect many readers already recognize the intimate relationship between *Positioning* and *Active Movement*. We cannot achieve the former without moving distinctly. In fact, movement should happen so quickly that it should be as a quick cut between two frames of a movie, the first showing the martial artist in one position, the second showing the same martial artist in an entirely different position. The actual movement between the two positions should be imperceptibly fast. Obviously, the slower we move the more the opponent can compensate for our movement, i.e. reposition against us.

Like so many other areas, proper *Positioning* can itself determine the fight. The combatant holding the superior position typically wins. However, this discussion of *Positioning* is incomplete without the discussion to follow: *Angling*.

50

Angling

*A*NGLING—OUR ORIENTATION TOWARDS OUR OPPONENT DURING PROPER *Positioning*—seems to be a principle about which we martial artists often become too lackadaisical. Given the speed at which combat occurs and our desire to apply our techniques, we often all too willingly sacrifice proper *Angling* in favor of overcompensating when avoiding oncoming attacks, meaning that we move too far away from the opponent and turn inappropriately. To a certain extent, this proves understandable. Proper *Angling* must be subtle. While we might feel more comfortable establishing relatively large distances between ourselves and oncoming attacks, we ultimately should play a game of inches.

I will limit my discussion of *Angling* to three particular angles, namely 22½ degrees, 45 degrees, and 90 degrees. While I want to permit for many contextual exceptions, we generally should value those angles in the order presented. The 22½ degree angle, therefore, stands as the eminent position for entering into techniques. Note, however, that I said eminent when "entering," which means that some techniques might appropriately move into other angles over the course of their execution. For example, virtually any application of a hammer lock will result in an eventual 90 degree angle between us and our opponent.

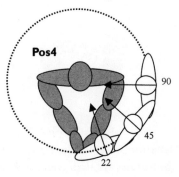

Why do I otherwise favor the 22½ angle? Because it changes our *Positioning* just enough to avoid an oncoming attack but without sacrificing our access to our opponent. Looking back to Pos4, we see that when

Jane positions herself just 22½ degrees off of Gargantua's *Centerline,* she will have evaded the force of his assault and moved into the *Void* of the negative part of his *Triangle Guard,* but still remains oriented towards his *Centerline* so as to access all of his targets, both those on *Centerline* and those across his body, such as his right shoulder. This access diminishes at the 45 degree angle and becomes largely non-existent at the 90 degree angle. Of course, other targets present themselves as we move to larger angles but as we must move through 22½ to get to 45, we should consider what we can do in the former (*Efficiency*).

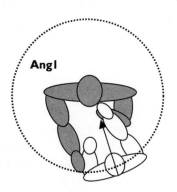

(Interestingly, despite the illogical nature of arguments by analogy, I once heard a culinary expert discussing how 22½ degrees is the perfect angle at which to sharpen a blade. It forges a perfect balance between sharpness and durability. In fact, in my art we find the 22½ degree angle to surface nearly everywhere, including the proper alignment of bones when striking, the path for entering into wrist grab defenses, and more.)

Looking at the same concept a bit more closely, as in Ang1, where Jane can (1) maintain her *Triangle Guard* while (2) successfully defending Gargantua's right punch, (3) squelch his left arm, and (4) maintain access to his *Centerline.*

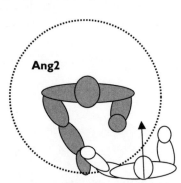

Both of Gargantua's arms also remain available for Jane's techniques.

Contrast this against Ang2 (and Pos5), which might be the position we would seek if "sidestepping" and attack by moving directly to the side and then delivering an outward left block. This position cultivates an illusory feeling of safety. Far away from Gargantua's right hand attack, we feel secure, yet we lack the ability to effectively counter and the distance between Gargantua's left hand and our face seems notably short, shorter in fact than the distance between either of our hands and his face.

Yet Ang2 does not present nearly as many problems as Ang3, which not only leaves Jane improperly *Positioned* outside of Gargantua's *Sphere* but also leaves her particularly vulnerable to his next attack. For that matter, in order to successfully counter-attack, she first would need to turn 45 or more degrees towards him.

I should note that these same problems manifest irrespective of whether Gargantua attacks with his right hand (as depicted) or his left. That said,

Angling akin to Ang3 can be permissible under certain advanced conditions of *Leading Control*, but that is too subtle a discussion for this text.

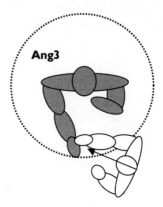

Meanwhile, two additional rationales for the 22½ degree angle still require discussion. First, most combative situations leave larger angles *initially* inaccessible. How many times have we seen kickboxers able to move to 45 degree angles? Rarely if ever. Strikes at closer ranges simply come at us too fast for such dramatic sidestepping.

More importantly, *in order to reach the 45 degree angle, we first must transgress the 22½ degree angle*. As we *must* pass through the 22½ degree angle on the way to the 45, and as we have demonstrated that the 22½ degree angle offers effective *Positioning* for defending and countering, and as we must uphold *Efficiency*, moving to the 45 without seizing the opportunity to act at the 22½ seems wasteful.

None of this is meant to depreciate the value of working at 45- and 90-degree angles, each of which serve important functions in martial arts. The question becomes one of how we achieve those angles when they are necessary, and in that regard we need to consider (1) the general tactical value of the 22½ degree angle and (2) the fact that we transgress it on the way to other angles.

At the same time, in order to execute certain techniques, we do at times need to orient ourselves away from the opponent's *Centerline* and towards other body parts, such as the limb we might be manipulating. In one sense, this holds to the *Triangle Guard* principle in that we always want to keep it oriented towards our technique. More often, however, we need not orient ourselves away from the opponent to achieve proper technique, nor need we change our *Positioning* in order to be in proper position.

Case in point: If applying an arm bar, one option could be to change our own orientation to direct our force at the arm itself. The Ang4 series depicts just that. As shown, Jane acquires Gargantua's arm with improper

Ang4

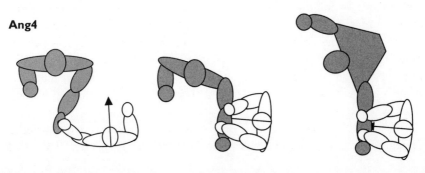

orientation and then steps around it to a 90 degree angle, at which point she applies an arm bar technique that bends Gargantua over.

Ang5

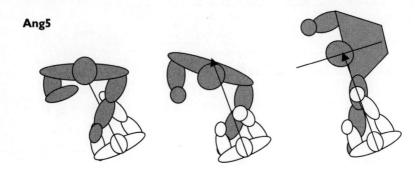

By contrast, the Ang5 series shows that Jane need not misalign herself in order to apply the arm bar. Rather, she need only (1) establish the 22½ degree angle and direct her force into Gargantua's arm and *he* will turn away from her, thereby establishing a 90 orientation between the two of them *while leaving her aligned with his primary targets*. Obviously, other principles, such as *Reciprocal Spinal Alignment* and *Indirect Pressure* help make this functional, but the premise with respect to *Angling* remains unchanged. We need not compromise our *Positioning* and *Angling* in order to achieve desired orientations. We can make our opponent move around us instead. *Angling*, therefore, not only concerns how we orient ourselves towards our opponent but also how we orient the opponent towards us.

51

Leading Control

*L*EADING *C*ONTROL MEANS DEFEATING THE ATTACKER BY EITHER NON-opposition or *encouraging* the *Intention* behind the attack, often by redirecting that *Intention* without the attacker's awareness. Put differently, it involves controlling the opponent by encouraging and then exploiting their actions through redirection or misdirection.

As *Aikido* is best know for *Leading Control,* let's first examine it as *Aikido* might contend with a same-side wrist grab, and we will use the same initial example we saw in the chapter on the *Sphere* principle. In LC1, Gargantua has seized Jane's wrist, his *Intent* and general anatomical commitment moving forward, as represented by the arrow. Even though his wrist grab might pull down or backwards, it must follow the arrow's path to reach her before doing so, and it is that *Intention* that Jane exploits.

LCl

In LC2, Jane, offering no resistance to the wrist grab itself, rotates her body and "joins" with Gargantua in his forward motion. More to the point, she actually *subtly* encourages him to move in the same direction he intended to move, which "forces" him to move *more* than he intended, which begins to mentally and physically unbalance him. That ultimately enables

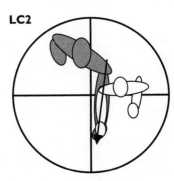

LC2

LC3

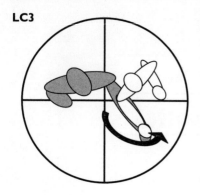

LC3, in which Jane uses Gargantua's original forward intent to "lead" him into a technique by changing "their" combined course of action. In short, she established control by joining him, "encouraging" him, and then redirecting him. She controlled him by leading him, which quite amazingly means that he, in effect, "followed" her, something we seldom see Gargantuas doing with respect to the Janes they attack.

Yet while the above illustration depicts a somewhat classical *Aikido* application of this principle, the principle obviously need not be applied using *Aikido*, nor need it involve any grappling.

Consider, for example, a way I've seen *Kosho-Ryu Kempo* exploit this same principle, at least so far as I can depict *Kosho-Ryu* accurately here. Among other things, *Kosho-Ryu*, as well as certain styles of *pentjak silat* and *kung fu*, has made an art of seizing on the opponent's intent to attack by feinting movement in one direction and then moving the other way. As we see in LC4a, Gargantua has cocked his right arm and has committed his *Intention* and anatomy to punching Jane square in the face. Jane, recognizing his intent, does nothing to change Gargantua's intent to hit her, mean-

LC4a   **LC4b**   **LC4b**

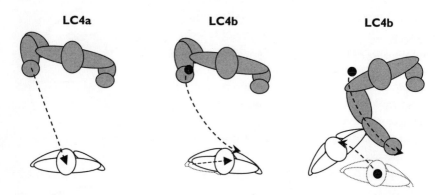

ing she does not, at this point, raise her hands to block or parry, which would *Telegraph* her own *Intention*. What she does in LC4b, however, is just slightly feint motion to her right. Picking up on Jane's (supposed) movement and direction, Gargantua's mind intuitively changes the course of the punch so that it will make contact with Jane where she theoretically will be when given her supposed movement. Unfortunately for Gargantua, in LC4c Jane reverses her direction and evades Gargantua's punch entirely, safely stepping to the outside of his body.

Just as we saw in LC1-3, Jane seized control of Gargantua's actions by exploiting his original *Intention*. She effectually controlled him by leading him (to do what he intended to do originally, which in this case, was to strike at her).

Some styles of *Pentjak Silat* approach the same principle with a similar tactic. They might parry a first attack in a manner that leaves a distinct and deliberate opening in their defenses, much as LC5a leaves an obvious path for Gargantua to throw a second punch at Jane's face. Because aggressors *instinctively* seize available lines of attack whether they really want to or not, the *silat* practitioner tricks the opponent into attacking a certain place and then exploits that motion, as in LC5b.

LC5a   **LC5a**

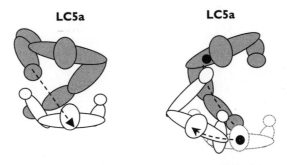

Target Replacement also exercises this same principle. You'll find it discussed in *Teachings of a Grand Master: A Dialogue on Martial Arts and Spirituality*, by Richard Behrens. It exercises *Leading Control* by inserting a false target between the attacker and his intended strike point, as in between the punch and the face it is trying to hit. In LC6a, we see the initial trajectory of Gargantua's strike. In LC6b—once Gargantua has committed—we see Jane place her palm in that trajectory. In LC6c, as Gargantua strikes, Jane recedes her hand *along the trajectory of the initial strike*. As she does so, she moves the rest of her body off that trajectory and delivers a counterstrike to exposed targets. Though seemingly magical, once an opponent's mind locks on a trajectory, it will attack the nearest target in that trajectory regardless of the attacker's original intent. Thus, Gargantua becomes fixated on Jane's hand rather than her nose. Behrens states that

LC6a   **LC6b**   **LC6c**

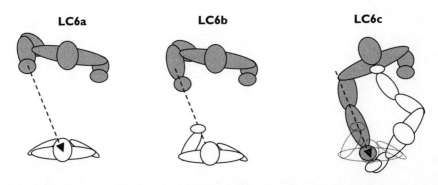

eventual mastery of this technique could actually result in changing the course of the punch by moving the target hand, or in extreme cases dropping the attacker to the floor by lowering the hand proportionately.

Of course, there are countless other ways that various styles exploit this principle. These are but a few *rudimentary* examples, but they serve to demonstrate the importance of *Leading Control*. Remember, that as combat primarily concerns *Control*, the ability to control the opponent via his own attack, if not "before" his attack, must be valued over merely stopping an attack already in progress. Furthermore, what could be more *Efficient* than defeating the attacker via his or her own *Intention*?

52

Complex Force

WHILE SUFFICIENT MEASURES OF ANY KIND OF FORCE CAN CAUSE DAMAGE, the human body actually receives *simple* types of impact relatively well. By *Simple Force,* I refer to straight, non-rotating energies that hit the body flatly. A basic vertical-fist punch demonstrates *Simple Force* quite well. It strikes exclusively with forward energy, involving no rotation or other motion.

I do not mean to suggest that *Simple Force* cannot be effective. Yet as the body receives that kind of force most effectively, it becomes the least effective force regardless of how much of it we employ. In fact, when using *Simple Force,* "how much" must become the primary concern and it forces martial artists into the "more force is better" trap. Of course, more force *is* better. But as martial artists, delivering force to the opponent cannot simply be a matter of *how much*; it also has to be a matter of *what type.*

We want to deliver the right kinds of force to the body, namely those which exploit vulnerabilities in human anatomy. To that end, we seek to exercise *Complex Force*—force that not only moves forward into the opponent but also involves *at least* one additional form of motion, namely *Spiraling, Scissoring, Carving, Vibrating,* and/or *Sheering.* Each of those five forces is a principle of its own.

Though uncertain as to why the body receives *Simple Force* best, I suspect it comes from the fact we do not encounter *Complex Force* in nature. As *simple* forms of impact exist in nature, the body developed natural defenses to it—hard skeleton, flexible joints, muscular "padding." Yet such did not occur with respect to *Complex* force.

Of all the *Complex Forces,* most martial artists will find *Spiraling* the most recognizable if only because it exists in the most popular martial arts strike: the corkscrew punch.[15] Yet other techniques apply that same force equally well, and we should seek to implement it during any and all strikes, locks, and throws. (Note that *Centripetal Motion* is a kind of *Spiraling Force*. That fascinating correlation demonstrates that the body is not only prone to *Spiraling* impact but equally vulnerable in terms of its stability.)

Note that "during" becomes the operative word. If we, for argument's sake, throw a corkscrew punch but finish the corkscrew motion before impact or at the moment of impact, the functional element of the corkscrew becomes lost. The corkscrew must rotate *during* impact, and for it to be a true spiraling motion (rather than a circle motion), it must penetrate as it turns. (Does that mean the corkscrew punch must first impact palm up and turn only after making first contact? No. It can rotate while closing in on the target but at least some rotation must occur post-impact. I must note, however, that some anatomists find the corkscrew punch to place an unhealthy amount of strain on the wrist, something that can be resolved with a slight change to the punch's delivery, all the while maintaining the spiraling motion.)

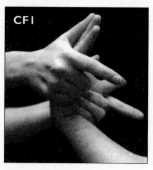

CF1

Joint locks benefit from *Spiraling Force* no less than strikes. Look closely at any joint lock and you will find *Spiraling Force* involved, however subtly. As in CF1, the force applied against the wrist advances in a decreasing radius circle—the classic definition of a spiral.

Professor Wally Jay refined and popularized this very idea with *Small Circle Jujitsu*, which for our purposes here might be a small misnomer. It should be titled, "Small Spiral Jujitsu" because all of Professor Jay's techniques exploit *Spiraling Force* dramatically well.

Scissoring represents the second force the body does not like and it involves receiving two opposing forces simultaneously. We need not look far to discover an example of *Scissoring* as CF1 demonstrates it quite well. The right hand applying the lock moves forward while the left hand applying the lock pulls backward. The opponent's hand gets rolled between the applier's two hands, getting pushed and pulled at the same time. It is, in effect, being *Scissored* between two opposing energies.

We see other obvious examples of *Scissoring* force when viewing throws, such as a hip throw, in which our upper body leans forward and pulls the opponent while our hips push backward. Hence, the opponent's body becomes *Scissored* between two opposing forces, as in CF2. Were only the top *or* bottom

---

15. I should note that many of the martial artists with whom I work do not maximize the power of their corkscrew punch because they do not turn it *exclusively* on the radial axis (*Radial Principle*). Instead, they allow the *path* of the punch to follow a spiraling arc, which actually decreases the amount of spiral on impact.

top *or* bottom force applied against the opponent, the throw would not work. Interestingly, this actually combines two simple forces, but the combination of two *simple impacts* creates the *Complex Force* we seek.

CF3

Though more difficult to apply, *scissoring* proves no less useful when striking. We might see it when trapping the face between a hand and an elbow, or when trapping a punch between two arms while blocking. Some advanced applications exercise two different hand motions in a single strike in order to "pinch" nerve points.

Moving on, the body equally dislikes *Carving* energy—force that grinds into the body through rotation and *Torsion*. We see this energy exemplified in traditional blocking, in which the blocking arm rotates on its *Minor Axis* and *Carves* into the striking arm, essentially turning the bone of the blocking arm into the bone of the striking arm. The blocking bone not only rotates against bone of the striking arm but also "penetrates" that arm. Given that the body does not like that *Carving* energy, the better we delay the block's rotation *until the moment of impact,* the more *Carving* energy we will deliver.

That same carving energy can be applied in joint locks and other soft/hard tissue manipulation techniques. Often, such grinding motions can enhance the entry into locking techniques, if not also their ultimate application, but such techniques are too subtle to illustrate here.

Sheering force probably receives the least attention of the *Complex Forces.* I want to credit Mr. Bob Orlando, a *Pentjak-Silat* instructor, with an excellent explanation for *Sheering* in which he likened it to a plow. Unlike a windshield wiper, the angle of which changes with respect to the windshield as the wiper moves, the angle of a plow remains constant—fixed. As a truck moves a plow down a snowy street, the plow does not push or wipe the snow off to the side of the road. Instead, it *sheers* the snow away by use of its forward motion.

Mr. Orlando offered a wonderful example of how martial artists might apply *Sheering* power. When delivering a forearm strike to Gargantua's ribs, Joe would not exercise *Sheering* by swinging his arm from left to right (CF3). Instead, *Sheering* would occur only when Joe moved his arm forward while maintaining its angle relative to his body (CF4 & CF4a). Whereas in CF3 his

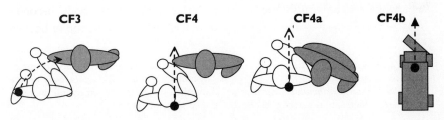

| **CF3** | **CF4** | **CF4a** | **CF4b** |

arm moves like a windshield wiper, in CF4 & CF4a, his arm moves like a plow (CF4b).

Note, as well, the other structural differences between the two motions. While I will not detail them here, CF3 exercises other structural principles, such as proper use of the *Triangle Guard*, *Triangulation Points*, and *Spinal Alignment*, to name just a few. Even without those other principles at work, however, Joe's strike in CF3 only represents *Simple Force* because it makes contact with the body while moving in one direction only. Yet his strike in CF3 & CF3a manifests *Complex Force* because it not only strikes *into* the ribs, it also slides along them.

That impact could be even more *Complex* by also *Carving* against the ribs during impact, which Joe could implement by beginning his forearm strike in the palm up position (CF3) and rotating it to palm down during impact (CF3a), thereby grinding his forearm against Gargantua's ribs.

Sheering can be applied no less effectively in many striking, locking, and throwing contexts, not the least of which being the execution of blocks. I have seen martial artists immediately double, even triple the power of their blocking through the use of *Sheering*.

The fifth and final *Complex Force* is *Vibrating*. I list this last because it typically involves a subtle, nearly imperceptible mixture of the forces above, and I want to credit Kyoshi Joe Mansfield with pointing this out to me as I conceptualize it here, though it is actually something I also saw Sensei Jim Tirey apply a few years earlier but did not recognize it as such. In applying a choke hold to take his opponent to the ground, Sensei Tirey essentially shook the opponent in the process. "Shook" is actually a problematic term because it implies large motions, but *Vibrating Force* is much subtler than that. We need only create enough movement in the opponent to confuse the neuromuscular response and equilibrium. It might even be imperceptible to the human eye. We *vibrate* a technique—a choke hold, a wrist throw, even a strike—so that it (1) prevents the opponent's body from identifying a single energy to respond to, while (2) forcing the opponent's mind to concentrate on stopping the *Vibration*, such as by holding still, rather than on countering the technique!

Ultimately, all *Simple* motions can and should be empowered through the proper exercise of *at least* one of the *Complex Forces*. Better yet, we should invoke all five at all times, because *it is not how hard we hit, but how we hit hard that matters.*

53

Indirect Pressure

A LSO KNOWN AS "SECONDARY PRESSURE" AND "NON-LOCAL MOVEMENT," *Indirect Pressure* involves moving our body from a location other than where we connect with the opponent. This means not moving from the fist when striking with the fist, or not moving from the neck when grabbed at the neck, or not moving from the wrist when grabbed from the wrist, etc.

Examining a wrist grab, we must first return to the *Body-Mind* principle if we are to understand how and why *Indirect Pressure* works, to say nothing of why it is so important. Looking at IP1, we see Gargantua with a firm hold on Joe's wrist. As *Body-Mind* teaches us, however, Gargantua's mind actually becomes "located" in two concordant places: (1) where his body is tense, and (2) where his intent is focused. In this case, both 1 and 2 happen to be the same place: Joe's wrist. Joe would be ill-fated to attempt to move from his wrist, the focal point of Gargantua's mind and strength. Considering the power of *Tactile Sensitivity*, and recognizing Gargantua will immediately sense any resistance Joe offers, Joe should not attempt to exercise wrist muscles at all. Therefore, IP2 represents Joe's inability to move against Gargantua's wrist grab.

Yet that Joe would be unwise to attempt movement *from* the wrist, as in through

IP1

IP2

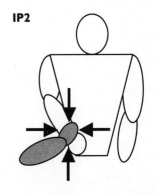

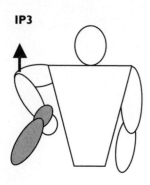

IP3

muscles in the forearm and hand, does not mean that Joe's wrist cannot be moved. It can be moved, provided *it* is not doing the moving. The source of the movement must come from a place other than the wrist itself—other than Gargantua's focal point. Instead, it could come from movement in the elbow (IP3). In other words, because Joe cannot move his elbow upwards without also moving his wrist upwards, he therefore can move his wrist upwards *by* moving his elbow upwards. Moving from the elbow by using the triceps, Joe will not tip off Gargantua. Gargantua will not sense Joe's elbow movement because Gargantua's *Body-Mind* fixates on Joe's wrist. In order for this to function, Joe must use *only* those muscles that control his elbow and none of the muscles that control the wrist, forearm, or hand. If he uses any of the latter muscles, Gargantua will feel Joe's effort to move. Provided Joe does this properly, he will move freely until Gargantua's visual acuity catches up with his *Tactile Sensitivity*, which takes at least a fraction of a second or more.

Moving the elbow against a wrist grab is a basic example of *Indirect Pressure*, one I learned from someone in Washington D.C., only to later discover that it, along with two other techniques he showed me, probably actually originated in *Yanagi-Ryu Aikijujutsu*, under *Soke* Don Angier.

Yet while I trace this particular entry to *Yanagi-Ryu*, the principle remains universal. We see it in many different contexts throughout the martial arts world. The premise always remains the same: never move from point of the opponent's focus.

Similarly, never strike with the weapon of impact. When punching, for example, impact with the fist but do not strike *with* the fist. Instead, make the elbow the source of the motion. At first, some martial artists have difficulty distinguishing between the two, and understandably so. After all, any strike will involve motion in both the hand and the elbow. The distinction, therefore, comes from the source of that movement. If when striking we bring our *Body-Mind* to our hand and think about moving the hand fast then we will use direct pressure. If we instead focus on moving the elbow so as to move the hand and do not bring attention to the hand (and do not exercise muscles from the elbow down) then we will exercise *Indirect Pressure*, which ultimately proves far more effective.

Why? Several reasons: First, when the opponent receives the blow, his or her body *instinctively* will sense and react against the strike if the weapon of impact is tense. Think of it this way, if you saw that you were about to be hit by a Nerf baseball bat, your defensive reaction would not be nearly as pronounced as it would be if you saw that you were about to be hit by an aluminum bat. In the latter situation, most people would attempt to evade more determinedly, and most people would tense up more to ready themselves for impact. In either case, our visual acuity would make a threat assessment and our brains would instruct our bodies to react accordingly.

The same process of reaction happens through *Tactile Sensitivity*. Our bodies react instinctively to physical sensation, as in touching a hot burner vs. a pool of cool water. Consequently, if our *Body-Mind* resides in our fist as represented by tension, the opponent's body immediately will react to the moment of impact, typically by tensing up. However, if our *Body-Mind* remains in our elbow, the opponent's *Body-Mind* will not *feel* a dramatic impact no matter how dramatic the impact might be. Consequently, it will become more vulnerable to it.

By the same reasoning, we actually lose power when striking with direct pressure. If we move our *Body-Mind* to our fist by focusing on it as the agent of the strike then we also not only tense the fist to ready it for impact, but tense our bodies to support that impact of the fist. Yet it is moving from the fist itself that causes the sensation of a hard impact for which we must anatomically prepare and compensate. If we do not move our *Body-Mind* to the fist then we will not feel the repercussions of our strike and we therefore do not need to anatomically prepare ourselves to receive it. (*Power Paradox*)

Note three points about this scenario: First, the problem compounds. If we strike with direct pressure—from the fist and with the fist—we prepare anatomically and the opponent prepares anatomically. As the opponent braces for the impact, we try to hit harder—more direct pressure—which only prompts both parties to brace more. Hence, a vicious cycle.

Second, using direct pressure proves antithetical to so many other principles. In fact, it makes them impossible. For example, we tend to act from the fist in order to provoke a greater sensation of impacting against the opponent, but as we know from the *Power Paradox*, the more we feel the impact the *less* powerful we must be. Furthermore, the tension produced by direct pressure only consumes power within our own bodies that we otherwise could transfer to the opponent, hence a violation of the *Percentage Principle*. Not only that, striking with direct pressure affects our own anatomy in such a way that it typically causes us to *Telegraph* our *Intention*. The list continues: various manifestations of direct pressure contradict every conceivable martial principle.

Third, I should note that some fist tension can still prove useful. Properly timed, which typically means just after the actual moment of impact, a fleeting moment of primary/direct pressure can have devastating results.

Striking with *Indirect Pressure* must be learned over time. To realize this principle properly, and without serious risk to the hand, other principles must be aligned properly, especially those concerning the anatomical structure of the strike itself. Therefore, students learning to exercise this principle typically transition from direct pressure to *Indirect Pressure* as they improve.

As a final point about *Indirect Pressure*, it absolutely need *not* concern moving from the elbow rather than the hand. Looking at it more specifically, moving the hand from the elbow—one joint up—would be *secondary* pressure. Moving the hand from the shoulder—two joints up—would be *tertiary* pressure, which bests secondary pressure because it is farther removed from the weapon of impact. Moving from the spine would be *quaternary pressure*, and moving from the *Center—truly* moving from *Center*—is *quinary pressure*. (Note that this is different from *Wave Energy*.) I have seen a meager few martial artists who can truly move with *quinary pressure*, a group of which I am not a part. It is remarkably impressive. *Indirect Pressure* also can be achieved by moving from the legs or knees, shifting the entire body forward.

Ultimately, our power grows as we retract the source of power farther back into our bodies, i.e. moving from primary to secondary to tertiary, etc. Unfortunately, most find it exponentially difficult to retreat from step to step. That said, most can learn to exercise *Indirect Pressure* in the secondary form with a little training, and that one movement from primary to secondary pressure affords a considerable leap in power.

54

Live Energy
(Live Force, Snap, Zhing)
& Dead Energy

THE DISTINCTION BETWEEN *LIVE ENERGY* AND *DEAD ENERGY* ROUGHLY equates to the respective difference between getting hit by a bullet and getting hit by a sledgehammer. While a sledgehammer obviously can penetrate, it actually pushes more than it penetrates. Hit in the chest with a good swing from a sledgehammer, we would find ourselves knocked back a few good yards. Bullets, by contrast, penetrate more than push. Struck in the chest with a bullet, it might pass through us entirely and leave us standing in place. I am not suggesting that bullets also do not push. Many produce significant "knock back." Yet bullets favor penetration while sledgehammers favor pushing. Any type of force contains both *Live Energy* and *Dead Energy*.

Typically, as martial artists we want to deliver *Live* rather than *Dead Energy* because it will penetrate more successfully into the opponent and it proves far more difficult to *Root*. Whereas a *Dead Energy* punch to the nose might break the nose and send the recipient back a short distance, a *Live Energy* strike would break the nose and leave the opponent otherwise (relatively) unmoved.

This occurs partly because of *Temporal Relativity*. Whereas *Dead Energy* spreads our power over a relatively long period of time, *Live Energy* condenses our power into a shorter period of time. If we strike someone in the nose faster than their face can move away from the force, the nose will break and the body will move little. Similarly, if we suddenly place more force against the nose than the body can *Root*, the nose will need to "absorb" that force entirely on its own. If we strike with more force than the nose can absorb, the nose breaks.

While some practitioners reserve *Live Energy* for striking, it equally can be applied to grappling and locking techniques. If executing a wrist lock in such a way that we want to drop our opponent to the ground but do not want to damage the wrist, we typically exercise *Dead Energy* more than *Live Energy*. Elongating our force through *Dead Energy*, as in applying consistent force from the start of the standing lock to its finish on the ground, permits the opponent's body enough time to yield so as to save the wrist from injury. To release the pain on the wrist that comes as a result of the downward pressure applied against it, the body drops lower and lower, thereby decreasing the unnatural angle at which the wrist is bent. As a result, the wrist, though in pain, avoids damage.

By contrast, if we want to damage the wrist, we might "snap" the lock on using *Wave Energy*, focusing a sharp moment of *Live Energy* against the joint. If we "snap" the wrist faster than the body can move in order to compensate for the force against it, the wrist bears the full brunt of the force against it, which consequently results in a sprain or ripped tendons, or both. A fully *Live* lock would snap so quickly that the wrist would rip, sprain, or break while the opponent otherwise remained nearly motionless, and would recognize the damage only after it had been done.

Of course, we need not necessarily work at either extreme. We can apply just enough *Live Energy* into the wrist to seize it and cause pain, while applying enough *Dead Energy* to maintain the lock and submit the opponent. Other variations exist, as well.

In essence, *Dead Energy* vs. *Live Energy* represents the difference between a push and a punch. If we push someone, we move from 100% power at the start of the push to 0% power at the end of the push. The exact opposite holds true when striking, which starts with 0% power and works towards 100% power. To understand this, try a simple exercise: starting right next to a partner, place your hands against his or her shoulders and give a firm, complete push. Notice how most of the "push" occurs at the beginning of the motion. Then step away from the partner and do a palm strike to the shoulder, and notice how the power increases as the hand moves closer to the target.

At advanced levels, even pushes become *Live Energy*. I've been "pushed" by *Tai Chi Chuan* practitioners that made it feel as though an explosion went off in my chest, something I realized while hurdling backwards through the air.

Ultimately, we want to apply *Live Energy* in all techniques, yet we must remember that *Live Energy* and *Heaviness* do not conflict. It is relatively easy to produce "snap" devoid of *Heaviness, Extension & Penetration*, but it's also pointless. Instead, we must "snap" the full weight of our bodies in all techniques and yet remain in enough control of that energy to apply it appropriately given the technique and its context.

55

Torsion & Pinning

MOST MARTIAL ARTS INVOLVE SOME KIND OF GRABBING, AND SOME MARTIAL arts rely on it quite heavily. In fact, some martial artists possess such strong grips that they can rip the bark off trees, and we can only sit in awe of that kind of prowess and power. Yet grabbing poses certain difficulties with respect to martial principles, and so I confess to holding some strong reservations as to its worth. That said, I know of martial artists who can execute magnificent grabbing techniques that penetrate to the bone and rip tendons, and so while I wonder if we should not allow for such specialized grabbing, I nevertheless must speak to *Torsion* as a grabbing alternative.

Grabbing in martial arts raises three dominant issues. First, grabbing typically requires us to produce tension, which runs contrary to principles such as *Relaxation*. In fact, given how difficult it can be to tense the hand alone, grabbing encourages us to tense other parts of our bodies, especially the upper torso, shoulders, and neck. Second, as a result of that physical tension, we also end up tensing the *Body-Mind*, especially given the intimate relationship between the mind and the hand. This inhibits *Non-Intention* and mitigates desired mental states such as *Mushin* because as our hand seizes the opponent, so does our mind become "seized" in the *idea* of seizing the opponent. Third, our opponent's *Body-Mind* instinctively senses grabs and reacts against them. Given the power of *Tactile Sensitivity*, coupled with the fact that grabs interject a considerable amount of direct pressure, the opponent has no choice but to feel them.

If we combine the second and third issues, we discover that our opponent will recognize our grab on more than a mere physical level. As our *Body-Mind* will locate itself in the grab and as the grab will express *Intention*, the opponent will feel *Intention* even if only on a subconscious level. This will *Telegraph* our desire for *Control*, which only helps the opponent to resist.

Despite the issues it raises, we certainly must appreciate some of the outcomes grabbing seeks. Locks, throws, holds, and their ilk can serve remarkably well, and we do not want to discard such tactics. Fortunately, we have an alternative: *Torsion*. While more literally defined as tension produced from twisting, as in twisting one end of a rope while the other remains fixed, *Torsion* more generally refers to the tension established between two opposing forces, such as two reeds bending against one another. The more they bend, the more *Torsion* manifests itself between them.

Tor1

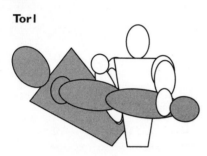

Generally speaking, the same techniques that can be applied through grabbing can be applied through *Torsion*. Examining Tor1, we see Jane grabbing Gargantua's left wrist and attempting to execute an arm bar with her right arm. Given the size of Jane's hands as relative to the size of Gargantua's wrist, Jane might find it difficult to secure a firm grip at all.

Furthermore, supposing that she can pull his wrist back so as to apply forward pressure with her right arm, the tension in her hand will force her to use direct pressure instead of *Indirect Pressure*. For that matter, she also cannot move her left hand through a *Void* as it obviously must remain secured to Gargantua's physical self.

Tor2

In contrast, Tor2 demonstrates how Jane could apply the exact same technique through *Torsion* by securing Gargantua's limb with the countervailing forces between her two forearms. To those who have not experienced this first hand, it might appear as thought there's nothing actually holding Gargantua in place, but when properly applied the arm bar will prevent him from flexing or rotating his arm in any way, thereby preventing him from escaping. Not only that, exercising *Torsion* permits Jane to use *Indirect Pressure* from her left elbow, as well as to weave her left hand into *Void* spaces rather than directing the force into Gargantua's arm.

Additionally, because Jane need not tense her arms to grab, her *Tactile Sensitivity* will remain more aware, thus making her more attune to Gargantua's efforts to counter her technique. Similarly, her hands have not "seized" anything, nor has her mind become "seized" by the idea of grabbing. I am sure I am not the only one to have witnessed martial artists holding onto a technique long after they should have relinquished it for another. They do so because if the hand latches onto something, so does the *Body-Mind*, thus making it reluctant to let go. Yet by exercising *Torsion*, Jane's arms remain sensitive and her mind remains equally fluid.

As if that were not useful enough, because Jane never applies her power directly into *Gargantua's* arm, using *Indirect Pressure* and *Void* applications instead, Gargantua will experience a difficult time sensing Jane's technique. Given a couple of seconds to think it over, he obviously would have no problem deciphering her technique, but she should afford him no such luxury.

In addition to *Torsion*, *Pinning* also can play a role, such as how she might be *Pinning* Gargantua's arm to her body by using her left forearm to press it against her ribs. *Pinning* earns respect as its own principle but its root worth differs little from *Torsion*, so I mention them alongside one another.

Most grappling techniques can be applied through *Torsion* and/or *Pinning* rather than grabbing, yet if grabbing becomes imperative then we should exercise single-handed *Torsion* rather than a traditional grab. We accomplish this by closing the hand so that the fingertips touch the tip of the thumb, roughly what we would do if using the hand to simulate a mouth. If we "grab" in this fashion, we never make contact with the opponent with the tips of the fingers, using the balls of the fingers instead. Rather than creating a closed, circular force that seizes and expresses our *Intent*, this functions by the pressure between the two opposing parts of the hand—*Torsion*—and leaves the hand sensitive and the mind fluid.

56

Speed

FROM A CERTAIN PERSPECTIVE, *SPEED* CAN BE THE DIVIDING LINE BETWEEN success and failure in technique. Note that I said, "in technique," which means that we cannot rely on the attribute of *Speed* alone to bring victory. Yet speed *reciprocates Timing* in that if we move fast enough our opponent will not be able to respond to our actions, and if the opponent cannot respond to our actions, we (should) win.

This chapter includes several principles concerning *Speed* in martial arts, the first of which is *Movement Speed* —the rate at which our body traverses distance, as in how many feet per second a fist travels when punching. When most people think of *Speed*, they think of this, and with good cause. Moving faster does equate to moving faster, after all.

I hope readers already recognize the many ways in which previously discussed *Physiokinetics* inform our ability to increase *Movement Speed*, such as proper *Structure*, a tighter *Axis*, *Relaxation*, the use of *Indirect Pressure*, and so on. Of course, *Wave Energy* also impacts *Movement Speed* significantly, though we must be careful to avoid *Telegraphing* our motions.

Yet *Speed* involves a great deal more than the rate at which our bodies and limbs traverse distance. In fact, *Movement Speed* represents just one factor of *Effectual Speed*—the holistic time it takes to complete a given technique. Obviously, faster *Movement Speed* can improve our *Effectual Speed* but *Movement Speed* alone will not suffice.

Consider what happens when we introduce *Timing Speed*. I will not discuss this at length as *Timing* earns its own chapter, but the faster we *Respond* to our opponent, the faster we can put our technique into effect. Let's say Joe can execute a given technique in .5 seconds compared to Jane's one second. However, let's say that Jane reacts to Gargantua's attack .5 seconds faster than Joe. Joe will move his limbs .5 seconds faster, but Jane will move her limbs .5 seconds sooner. Consequently, both will complete the technique at the same time.

None of which speaks to *Spatial Speed*. If Joe possesses twice the *Movement Speed* as Jane, meaning that he moves twice as fast, but Jane can accomplish the same technique while traversing only half the distance through better *Economy of Motion*, then both will end at the same time supposing equal *Timing Speed*. Put another way, if we can execute the same technique while covering only half the distance, we become twice as fast as before. Personally, I see this as one of the biggest advantages martial artists possess over the untrained, most of who fight with remarkably large motions. All other factors being equal, if we keep our motions just half the size of their motions, we *Effectually* become twice as fast. If you have ever fought someone twice as fast as yourself, you know how crippling that becomes.

While I do not want to delve into particular techniques and how we might be able to shrink them, I will refer back to principles such as *Positioning, Angling, Primary Gate, Axis, Centripetal Motion,* and *Centerline* as places to begin thinking about how to make the same technique smaller without sacrificing effectiveness. Philosophically, it would not hurt to examine concepts such as *Non-Action* and *Non-Intention* for more insight into decreasing the *Effectual Speed* of our techniques.

All of this boils down to the notion that we must not devote our energies merely to *Movement Speed*. As *Effectual Speed* involves *Movement Speed, Timing Speed,* and *Spatial Speed*, we must be ever attentive for ways to apply each one to our techniques, keeping in mind the truism that our opponent cannot react to techniques that happen faster than his or her sense of *Timing* perceives.

Of course, if we follow *Speed* to its logical end and keep the *Pure Objective* in mind, our goal must be to execute all techniques *Instantaneously*, meaning zero *Effectual Speed*. While impossible, it should serve as a useful razor with which to cut out, modify, condense, accelerate, etc. all motion in our technique.

57

Timing

*T*IMING REFERS TO THE SPEED OR POINT AT WHICH WE RESPOND TO THE opponents actions. If, for example, we realize the opponent has thrown a punch only *after* it hits us in the head then we have poor *Timing*, to say the least. If we recognize and counter techniques at their immediate inception then we have good *Timing,* to say the least.

Timing holds such eminent importance in martial arts that it nearly deserves a book of its own. Arguably, without proper timing, we have nothing. We might be able to compensate for speed, strength, range, proficiency, and other factors, but if we lack the ability to react to our opponent then all of our techniques, no matter how magnificent otherwise, become useless. The most beautiful, powerful, effortless block in the world accomplishes nothing if executed too late.

Kosho-Ryu Kempo offers an excellent phrase that refers to timing. They say, "It's not how you move, it's *when* you move." While I cannot entirely discount the "how" of moving, they make a good point. Given the choice between moving well and moving at the right time, I would choose the latter. As martial artists, obviously we want to do both (something with which I have no doubt that the *Kosho-Ryu* practitioners would agree).

The golden rule for *Timing* concerns *Active Movement.* We must move "when" the opponent commits his or her *Intention* to attack. Without the opponent's commitment to a particular course of action, we cannot exploit the opponent's force, lack of balance, or the fact that he or she has become *Frozen In Motion*—locked into a certain course of action. *Frozen in Motion* is something I discussed in the *Active Movement* chapter, and it means that once committed to throwing a punch, the opponent will largely follow through with that motion. Though in motion, he or she otherwise will be unresponsive, i.e. frozen.

Therefore, we should *not* react to arms and legs, per se. We need not and should not wait until opponents physically deliver the punch in order to execute our response. Instead, we can and should execute our response at the moment they *Intend* to take a course of action, such as when they commit to throwing that punch but before the punch itself takes form.

Other authors have touched on important ways to recognize such "tells," such as a sudden fixation in the eyes or a widening of the eyes, a sinking in one or both knees, a retraction of a shoulder, a dropping of the chin, as well as more obvious "tells" such as a cocking of the fist or any other sort of winding up. Such methods prove largely reliable and should be learned and respected.

Hierarchy of Timing

Recognizing the long term intent to attack. ("That guy wants to get in a fight.")

↑

Recognizing the immediate *Intent* to attack—the point of commitment.

↑

Recognizing the physical inception of the attack.

↑

Recognizing the attack happening.

↑

Too late.

The first critical point about effective *Timing*, however, is that we must react to the *Intent* to attack rather than to the attack, or at least to the earliest possible sign of the attack.

Second, we must wait until the opponent becomes *Frozen In Motion*, i.e. locked into a particular course of action. Physically committed. As soon as the opponent cannot change his or her action, we can exploit the frailties of that action. We do this by persuading the opponent that the attack will succeed, that it *will* hit (grab, throw, etc.) us.

Of course, sensing an opponent's *Intention* can prove difficult at best. Some less apt fighters do a wonderful job of telegraphing their plans but more skilled combatants learn to hide their true intentions much the way good card players keep a "poker face." In fact, many skilled fighters will throw feints or non-committed techniques designed to provoke reaction and to freeze us in motion. When at the mercy of such techniques, our own good *Timing* might betray us. On the other hand, if we become skilled in exercising such techniques, we can use *Timing* against the opponent. Offensively, we can do so through feints, just as the opponent might do to us.

Defensively, the same concept becomes a bit trickier in application, but possible nonetheless and profitable beyond measure. To evoke commitment, we must wait until the *last possible moment* before executing a defensive technique. At first, this might seem in contrast to the previously mentioned idea of sensing the opponent's *Intention* rather than waiting for actual physical motion. While that's still preferred, good fighters will not commit their own *Intention* until they become certain of success, which often means *after* the aggressor begins the physical technique, but before it lands. They might begin to throw a punch but do so half-heartedly at first, waiting to see whether or not they think it will land. Only once persuaded that it will land will they truly commit to it. Therefore, we still want to sense their *Intention* as soon as possible, even if it manifests after the start of physical motion.

Fortunately, we can force the attackers' *Intention* to manifest itself. We can manipulate their *Timing* rather than merely relying on our own. *Aikido* offers an excellent example of how to accomplish this through its famous "J-step" technique, which involves swinging the rear leg behind the body so as to pivot the body off the line of attack, even by up to 180 degrees. Yet the initial motion of the "J-step" actually often moves *forward*. When confronted with an oncoming punch, the *Aikidoka* might step forward fleetingly before rotating. the sudden close in distance tricks the opponent's mind into believing the strike will land, which prompts total commitment. Yet that initial forward motion actually serves the *Aikidoka's* evasion, which then facilitates some counter-technique used to defeat the opponent.

Aikido aside, we need not wait for the opponent to commit and we need not be at the mercy of the opponent's *Timing*. Rather, we can seize *Control* of the situation, including our own *Timing* and the opponent's.

58

Rhythm

WHILE *TIMING* CONCERNS HOW QUICKLY WE CAN REACT, *RHYTHM* DEFINES the pacing at which we execute those reactions. Ultimately, the two overlap a great deal. I will offer some very rudimentary examples of how changes in *Rhythm* change the nature of a given technique, but I do so only to exemplify the principle in the hopes that readers will experiment with the premise on their own.

When we speak of *Rhythm*, we typically do so in terms of "beats," as if actions occur in time with the ticks of a metronome. A "beat" could occur every second, half-second, one-sixteenth of a second, etc. The time interval between beats matters little. What matters is that beats occur at a consistent pacing—the same time interval between each one. We *start* with the premise that we and our opponent each get to take one action per each beat. As we will see, it also becomes possible to act on the half-beat, the quarter beat, the one-eight beat, etc., so as to interject more motions per full beat than the opponent. Thus, if we act on every half-beat, which would mean half-beat, beat, one-and-one-half beat, second beat, second-and-a-half-beat, etc., we would be moving at twice the pace of our opponent.

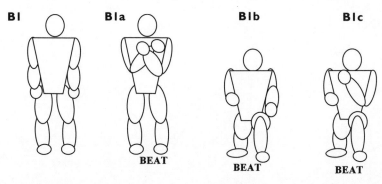

B I   B Ia   B Ib   B Ic

BEAT   BEAT   BEAT

Most martial arts truly become functional when deriving more actions per beat than the opponent. Consider, for example, a simple downward blocking motion, probably something we see in *karate* but not foreign to other arts. (As always, it is the *Principle* that matters, not the particular application, so please do not fuss over it.) The B1 series depicts Joe starting in a standing position (B1), doing an "x" block in front of his chest (B1a), stepping forward with his left foot and doing a left downward block (B1b), before finally executing a left inward chest block (B1c). For our purposes right now, B1a, B1b, and B1c each would occur on different beats.

In application against two punches from Gargantua, the same sequence might look like B2, this time depicted from the side. Joe does the "x" block in B2a, a downward block against Gargantua's right punch in B2b, and a cross/inside chest block against Gargantua's left punch in B2c. In the B2 series, Joe and Gargantua move at the same pace and on the same beats, with each frame receiving its own full beat.

Yet let's examine what happens if Joe changes his *Rhythm* and begins acting on some half beats instead of acting on full beats. B3 would depict Joe and Gargantua in the ready position (not shown). Nothing changes in terms of *Rhythm* between B2a and B3a, and nothing changes between B2b and B3b. However, in B3c, Joe acts on the *half-beat*, not waiting for the next full beat that we see in B3d, where Gargantua *would* throw the left punch as in B2c. Changing his *Rhythm*, Joe also changed the nature of the technique itself. What was a down block into an cross/inside block became a down block into a hammer lock. That became possible only when Joe changed his *Rhythm* and made two motions on one of Gargantua's beats instead of matching Gargantua beat for beat.

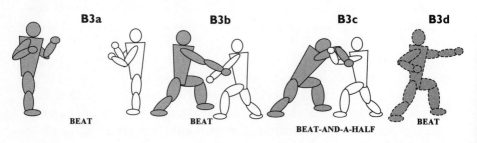

In effect, their respective *Rhythms* went from B4 to B5:

B4	Beat	Beat	Beat
Gargantua	Wind Up	Right Punch	Left Punch
Joe	"X" Block	Left Down Block	Left Cross /Inside Block

B5	Beat	Beat	Beat
Gargantua	Wind Up	Right Punch	(Left Punch would execute here if Joe did not prevent it)
Joe	"X" Block	Left Down Block	Left Cross/Inside BlockThat Creates Hammerlock

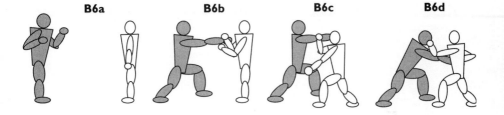

B6a **B6b** **B6c** **B6d**

Yet let's examine what happens if we change the *Rhythm* yet again. As before, both start at ready position in B6 (not shown). In B6a, as Gargantua acts on the first beat by retracting to punch, Joe chooses not to act at all. On the next beat, Joe executes his "X" block against Gargantua's low left punch (B6b). In moving his hands into the "X" position, Joe uses his left hand's rising motion to form the "X" in a defensive manner. Joe strikes the underside of Gargantua's punch with his left hand and lifts it until it is outside his right hand, thus parrying Gargantua's punch. Using the second half of the second beat (B6c), Joe executes his left down block, which now becomes a strike to Gargantua's lower targets, such as the pelvis, groin, or thigh. As he does so, he grabs Gargantua's right arm, thereby preventing Joe from acting on the third beat. On that third beat (B6d), Joe's cross/inside block now becomes a hammer fist to Gargantua's face.

Keeping in mind that this serves to teach *Rhythm*, *not* technique, it demonstrates how a change of *Rhythm* can entirely change the application of otherwise identical motions. In many ways, *Rhythm* might be one of the more overlooked elements of traditional martial arts in that changing the pacing of the techniques reveals otherwise "hidden" applications in forms.

Yet *Rhythm* holds other essential lessons for us, most importantly, that we *never allow the opponent to set the Rhythm*. Looking to the above examples, as long as Joe moved on Gargantua's beats, he possessed little chance of victory. Only when Joe began to determine the *Rhythm* of his actions did he penetrate Gargantua's defenses.

Just as we must not work at the opponent's pace, so must we *derive more actions per beat than the opponent*. If we execute more action in the same period of time we should emerge victorious. Obviously, doing so relies on effective *Economical Motion, Speed, Positioning*, etc. While the examples above only demonstrated how to access a half-beat, we equally can access quarter, eighth, sixteenth, etc. beats. We need not operate on the dominant beat itself at all if we so choose.

Operating outside the normal beat structure will do wonders to disrupt our opponent's Timing, Positioning, and Angling. Thus, we not only will extract more motion per beat but will find ourselves in dominant positions in which to execute those actions.

All said, *Rhythm* could not play a more important role in what we do. As with so many other principles, if we control *Rhythm* alone, we can *Control* the conflict.

59

Balance

I N SO MANY WAYS, THIS TEXT ALREADY ADDRESSES ISSUES RELATED TO BALANCE. To recap just a few such elements, proper *Breathing* helps balance us by dropping our center of gravity and making us more stable. Obviously, *Centeredness* contributes in the same fashion. *Proper Posture* serves us well in that it keeps our weight centered between our legs rather than dispersing it onto *Triangulation Points*. Conversely, the *Triangulation Point* teaches us where to direct the opponent's energy so as to produce a state of unbalance, just as *Centripetal Motion* teaches us where to best direct the opponent's unbalanced force so as to incur the least risk of unbalancing ourselves. I could go on.

Yet two critical principles remain with respect to *Balance*. First, *Balance permits free, powerful movement.* There's a monument in Florida called, "Coral Castle," at the entrance to which stands a rather unique revolving door, one built out of a 15 ton block of coral so perfectly balanced on a pivot that it can be turned with the touch of a finger. Like that coral block, no matter our size and weight, we can turn effortlessly and quickly if balanced properly. This not only relates back to *Physiokinetics*, it also relates to the *Percentage Principle* in that any portion of being devoted to keeping ourselves upright when otherwise unbalanced is a portion that cannot be devoted to other actions.

More importantly, *the opponent must never be balanced.* Fortunately, most opponents are not to begin with, and that should be exploited. Mentally, the opponent probably needs better balance or else he or she would not be attacking—a mentally unbalanced thing to do. Physically, maintaining perfect balance while launching attacks, to say nothing of *aggression*, proves difficult.

Yet regardless of our opponent's initial state of *Balance* or imbalance, *Balance* must be discouraged. Not only does creating an unbalanced opponent facilitate locking and throwing maneuvers, but *the more attention the opponent's Body-Mind must spend on not-falling, the less attention it can pay to attacking and defending.* Every parry, block, evasion, etc. should unbalance the attacker in some fashion, as should every strike, lock, and throw.

Aside from acting powerful and exploiting *Physiokinetic* weaknesses, most unbalancing relies on effective *Timing* and *Rhythm*. For example, most opponents probably will expect that their attack might be defended near its completion but will be surprised if we disrupt it just as it launches. Interrupting an opponent's *Rhythm* seizes the opponent when he or she is in flux, at which point we will find them unstable. What better moment to disrupt balance? Thus, "unbalancing is surprise."

"Unbalancing is surprise" means that we shake the opponent's expectations by interrupting *Timing* and *Rhythm*. While the opponent might expect to be hit, countered, or blocked, he or she probably will expect combat to occur at a certain pace nevertheless. Changing that pace by surprising the opponent with movement and counters at otherwise "odd" times will leave the opponent mentally unbalanced.

To be sure, we want the opponent *both* mentally and physically unbalanced. At such times, we must be sure to exercise proper *Angling* and *Positioning* or the opponent might well topple into us, but supposing we remain correct in our action, we should seize control of the opponent without difficulty, moving a 15 ton block of coral with the tip of a finger.

60

Reactive Control

A S *CONTROL* CONSTITUTES ONE OF THE DOMINANT PRINCIPLES OF THEORY, it raises questions about *how* we should approach establishing it. While *every* principle in this book speaks to *Control* in some regard, *Reactive Control* speaks to it more directly.

One of the easiest and most common ways opponents control us involves keeping us reacting to their attacks. This accentuates their *Offensive Advantage* for as long as they keep us reacting to and defending against what they want to do to us, they need not worry about what we might do to them. Furthermore, they know that as the *Offensive Advantage* states, they will win eventually because some of their attacks eventually will succeed. In forcing us to play purely defensive keep-away tactics, opponents' exercise *Reactive Control*, which means that they control us by our defensive reactions, keeping our minds and body in a process of dealing with what *they* do. In this way, *they* get to dictate to what *we* react.

In no way can we justify this. In no way can we tolerate it. As long as we react to what our opponent does, we cannot establish *Control*. Therefore, we must be the ones to exercise *Reactive Control*, which means keeping the opponent on the defensive. I do not mean that we should prolong combat, nor do I mean that we should start it. Yet I do mean that once combat begins, we must put the opponent in the reactive state instead of the active state. This can mean anything from forcing them to react to our counterstrike, to having them contend with the wrist lock we are applying, to having them grow concerned with our distancing, etc. As a conglomeration of other chapters, the opponent does not get to set the *Rhythm, Distancing, Movement, Timing, Positioning,* or anything else. We set it. We do not compensate for them; they compensate for us. Such is the only path to true *Control*.

61

Natural & Unnatural Motion

NOT TO BE CONFUSED WITH *NATURAL ACTION*, THIS PRINCIPLE CONCERNS the importance of permitting the opponent to move in accordance with his or her natural anatomical inclinations. At first this might sound awfully passive but it has nothing to do with practicing so-called "soft" arts such as *Aikido* and *Tai Chi*. Instead, it concerns the critical principle of *Imperceptibility*. As we do not want to tip off the opponent as to the nature of our technique, the less we disrupt their own anatomical intention, the less they will know! Obviously, at some point, opponents will become aware of what we did, but hopefully not until they have been defeated.

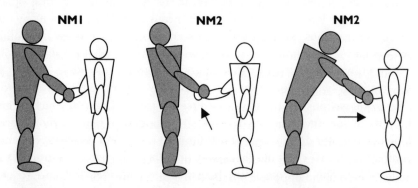

Consider a simple wrist grab (NM1). If Joe moves his wrist by pressing it in forward in any way, it will cause resistance against Gargantua's shoulder, upper back, and upper chest (NM2), which will tip Gargantua off to the fact that Joe wants to move at the wrist. Conversely, if Joe pulls forward in any way, it will pull against those same areas in Gargantua's body, equally tipping him off (NM3). In both options, Joe moves against Gargantua's natural physiology, and doing so only tells Gargantua that Joe wants out.

Yet the same natural arc discussed in the *Primary Gate* chapter exists in this context. Gargantua's shoulder normally moves as a pivot joint, and as long as Joe exploits it as such, he can move relatively undetected, not to mention with greater ease. Gargantua's body will be less inclined to instinctively resist motions it naturally makes vs. those that contort it.

Of course, *Natural Motion* applies equally to striking. If we permit the opponent's actions to run their course undisturbed, we can better exploit natural holes in their defenses and techniques that take advantage of their retracting motions. For example, a soft parry that redirects a punch within the *Natural Motion* of the opponent's physiology will leave the opponent's *Body-Mind* largely undisturbed, thereby not signaling our intention to defend and counterstrike, which makes it easy to follow that punch back to the opponent's body on the path it normally would take. Not to say that "soft" techniques are always preferred over "hard" ones; it is just an example.

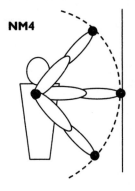

Therefore, while we use *Natural Motion* to lull an opponent out of perceiving our action, we use its reciprocal, *Unnatural Motion,* to shake the opponent's consciousness. If instead of parrying we exercise a block that not only shocks the arm itself but sends a jolt back to opponent's body, the opponent can become momentarily frazzled. Either the opponent's mind will be sur-

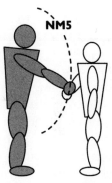

prised by the sudden disruption in its body's motion—note that I am not necessarily talking about pain—or we will force the opponent's *Body-Mind* to locate itself at the place in the body where the most disruption to *Natural Motion* occurred. Or both. No matter the circumstance, we will disrupt the opponents technique, physiology, and *Intention*.

Of course, all martial arts techniques ultimately cause some kind of unnatural effect on the opponent's body through the disruption of the *Body-Mind*. In fact, we must examine the percentage of our motions that actually permit the opponent's *Body-Mind* to remain intact. Any such percentage is too high.

The point behind the principle of *Natural* and *Unnatural Motion*, however, concerns always doing one of two things: (1) executing technique by lulling the opponent's *Body-Mind* through a continuation of his or her *Natural Motion*, or (2) executing technique by disrupting the *Body-Mind's* expectation of *Natural Motion*.

62

Weak Link

(Fourth Joint)

BUILDING ON *NATURAL MOTION*, THE *WEAK LINK* PRINCIPLE STATES THAT some joint in the body always remains weak despite strength in other joints, and that we should seek to exploit that weakness. As most techniques involve some use of the arms (kicks aside, obviously), I sometimes refer to this as the "Fourth Joint" principle because the shoulder often constitutes the weak joint. Counting the hand as one joint, then the wrist and then the elbow, we find the shoulder to be the fourth joint in the sequence.

Referring back to *Natural Motion* and the natural arc of the arm as it rotates in the shoulder joint, were Jane grabbed at the wrist, and were Gargantua's shoulder the *Weak Link,* she would find it relatively easy to move his hand along the path depicted in WL1. Any other movement would force pressure into Gargantua's other joints, such as the wrist or elbow.

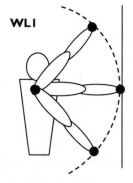

While most people typically do not clench more than three joints, it can happen. If Gargantua also clenches his shoulder joint, he might be weak in any one of the vertebra or, more likely, at the hips. Supposing he tenses his entire body head to toe, something that requires a great deal of concentration and energy, the link in question would become the "joint" between his feet and the ground, where we could tilt or move him with relative ease.

For better or worse, we will find the *Weak Link* only if we do not force techniques into contrived directions. We must allow the motion of our techniques enough liberty to exploit the opponent at points of weakness rather than seeking out artificial paths that might serve the opponent's strengths.

If we listen to the opponent's body, such paths become clear. If we exercise preconceived paths and pay attention only to ourselves, such paths remain elusive. While this might seem to contradict the idea of *Opponents Are Illusions*, it does not. As long as we move in principled ways that exploit our opponent's weaknesses, our opponent possesses no power over us. Yet if we move in contrived fashions, our opponent gains real power.

As with all principles, this one equally applies to striking and blocking. If we block with *Heaviness* and with proper *Angling*, we can exploit the joint in which the opponent is weakest, forcing the opponent to bend or twist from that joint. Partly, the place of reaction depends on where we strike the arm itself, but there is always a *Weak Link* and we can always access it.

63

Non-Telegraphing

"TELEGRAPHING" HAS COME TO BE AN ACCEPTED TERM FOR TIPPING OFF the opponent with respect to what we are about to do. For example, cocking the hand back prior to a punch telegraphs the punch to follow, as does dropping the chin, shifting the weight to one leg, dropping the shoulder, and other factors.

For what I take to be obvious reasons, we do not want to offer our opponents the slightest inkling of the technique to come because doing so only helps them defeat us. Yet this extends to more than just techniques themselves. If a situation begins to escalate and we threaten to beat the person up or suddenly adopt a fighting stance, we telegraph our intention to fight. In fact, a savvy fighter will tell a great deal about how we intend to fight based on the stance we take. Therefore, and aside from our responsibility to verbally de-escalate all potential conflicts, we must hide our intentions.

Sometimes, that even means disguising them. We can exploit an opponent's propensity to react to us by intentionally starting to *Telegraph* one movement while actually executing another. If we retract the right hand as if to throw a hook and then release a quick left jab, we might just catch the opponent by surprise.

Yet most of the time we simply want our techniques to occur without prior suggestion. To such an end, proper *Physiokinetics* could not play a more important role. Any *Physiokinetic* misalignment will force our body to do more than is otherwise necessary in executing any technique.

Furthermore, *Non-Intention* plays an equally critical role. If we think about doing the technique, even think *while* doing the technique, our actions will become contrived. While not *Non-Intention* exactly, a good way to trick the brain around thinking about a technique is to envision the technique as complete. When punching, for example, we will decrease the amount of motion involved if we do not worry about punching fast, hard, or correctly but move as quickly as possible to the finished position of the the punch, "skipping" everything that occurred in between. By doing so, the brain rushes the body to the terminal position rather than taking the body through the steps required to reach it. If the steps involved in the technique are the same as those naturally required to reach its end, which they should be if the technique is sound, then the body will do them automatically, with exceptional *Efficiency*, and without *Telegraphing*.

Of course, the absolute best way to hide our intentions from our opponent is to have no intentions at all, something I'll discuss in *Non-Intention* later on.

64

Extension & Penetration

A SIMPLE PRINCIPLE, *E&P* SPEAKS TO THE IMPORTANCE OF DELIVERING FORCE beneath the surface, whatever that "surface" might be at the time. For instance, striking someone holding a foam chest shield, most new martial artists tend to aim for and stop at the front surface of the shield, making contact with it but not penetrating deep into it. More experienced martial artists might strike more deeply into the target, while highly experienced martial artists do not strike the pad at all but rather the person holding it. For them, the pad does not serve to benefit the one doing the striking. It merely serves to benefit the one being hit.

When facing a real life situation, we must not focus our technique on the outer layer of the opponent's body but rather on extending through the body. If striking to the front of the body, we do not try to hit the stomach or chest, we want strike to the spine. Or as I tell my students, we want to penetrate deep enough to strike the opponent's soul. (Of course, all strikes must be appropriate to the context.)

Yet *E&P* does not refer only to the physical elements of striking. In truth, to strike the opponent's spine we need not (and probably can not) physically move our hand that deep into the body in order to penetrate as desired. Elements of power discussed throughout this text suggest how to *Extend and Penetrate* deeply, such as *Indirect Pressure* and *Spinal Alignment*, and more importantly, *Relaxation*. If we hold our force within ourselves by tensing the body, to say nothing of the striking limb itself, we can consume more force than we release, and the true power of our technique will not penetrate the surface of the opponent. Meanwhile, highly skilled martial artists can strike less and less deeply physically while nevertheless penetrating more and more in terms of delivering force.

Yet *E&P* refers equally to locking techniques, where we want to communicate our force far beyond the surface of the joint, and even beyond the joint itself. Considering the arm bar in EP1, if we direct our force into the elbow itself, which means that we *Intend* for our force to go into the elbow, then our force will stop *at* the elbow. Imagine a

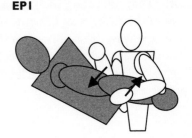

EP I

baseball bat stopping when it hits the ball rather than swinging through it and the problem with failing to penetrate the arm becomes clear. Therefore, we should not focus on applying force to the joint; we should focus on applying through it. In that sense, a true communication of power will send force all the way to the person's *Center*. While we can explain that in terms of *chi*, we also can explain it in terms of *Physiokinetics* because if we can send *Wave Energy* out of the body then we can send it *into* the body. This, in effect, becomes the *Reciprocal* use of *Wave Energy*—sending it in reverse.

The necessity for *E&P* applies no less to throws and takedowns. Whereas beginning martial artists usually try to get their opponent to fall down, and more experienced martial artists attempt to make their opponent hit the ground hard, highly experienced martial artists attempt to throw their opponent through the ground. Some say that we should attempt to throw opponents as deep as they are tall.[16]

At first, it might seem difficult to understand how such technique can even be possible. Yet were someone standing ten feet away from us, we could throw a ball to that person or throw a ball well beyond him or her. The difference not only concerns the amount of force in the throw but also where we *Intend* it to go.

In this way, *E&P* refers us back to *Gravity, Triangulation Point,* and *Centripetal Force*. While some situations and/or techniques might call for dispelling an opponent into the distance, if we throw someone away from us then we cannot use the ground as an ally. We cannot *E&P* into the ground. To accomplish that, we must throw down—straight down—an endeavor facilitated by understanding other principles herein.

Yet true application of *E&P* will not occur until we incorporate *Non-Intention* and ultimately extend our techniques into infinity. When executing a strike, we should not actually think about hitting this deep or that deep. We only should extend the motion of the strike completely. The technique extends to its completion, not slowing down, stopping, or altering its

---

16. Of course, the opponent will not literally penetrate the surface of the ground. This refers to the depth of force rather than the actual physical outcome.

path. That something such as an opponent's arm or body might be in the way of the strike is an irrelevancy to us (and a problem to whatever might be in the way). This only occurs when exercising proper *Non-Intention* in that the technique must "happen." Any objective other than the "happening" of the technique itself will be artificial and consequently undermine the proper execution of the motion.

SECTION IV
PRINCIPLES OF PHILOSOPHY

N OT SURPRISINGLY, *PRINCIPLES OF PHILOSOPHY* GENERALLY REFER TO THOSE
same elements of Eastern philosophy that many practitioners associate
with the arts, primarily Zen Buddhism and Taoism. Rather than recapitu-
lating many of the existing understandings of such philosophies, I hope
instead to demonstrate that martial arts practice is, in its essence, a kind of
physio-philosophy. In fact, what I like about martial arts is that it removes
philosophical principles from the abstract, from discussions exclusively
relating to the mind, and instead grounds them in physical application.

This, however, forces us to ask whether or not martial arts practice
must involve the study of Eastern philosophy. In one sense, the answer is a
resounding "no." Many martial artists of the past were just skilled fighters.
Many did not pursue any kind of spiritual enlightenment or higher intellec-
tual calling, and neither do many present-day martial artists. We see box-
ers, kickboxers, and a slew of other practitioners acquiring considerable
skill without direct attention to tenets of Zen.

From another perspective, however, Eastern philosophy cannot be separated from martial arts in that *whether the martial artist recognizes it or
not,* he or she practices, or at least moves towards, physio-philosophy. For
example, the first chapter in this section concerns *mushin*—the concept of
the empty mind. While I will speak about that principle in greater depth in
the pages to follow, I will now note that repetitive physical training in any
martial art can produce the empty state of *mushin*. In fact, any martial artist
who becomes highly proficient will manifest *mushin* to some measure.
Furthermore, a state of *mushin* will improve the practice of any endeavor,
regardless of what it might be, martial arts included. Thus, the issue of
mushin, much like all other principles, exists regardless of whether or not
we recognize it and give name to it. *Yet we give name to it so as to better*

understand it and our relationship with it, and thus, perhaps, attain it more readily.

With that in mind, I will restrict my discussion of philosophical principles to those that I can relate directly to martial technique. Doing so by no means suggests that other philosophical principles pale in relative importance, but the abstract nature of such principles have been discussed widely and well by a host of authors more qualified than I. Yet I hope to marry principles directly, or as directly as I can, both to technique and to the other principles discussed herein.

Given that this section comes towards the end of the book I do not want to give the impression that principles of philosophy hold greater importance than principles discussed earlier. All principles matter equally. Thus, their placement represents a matter of organization, not one of emphasis.

65

Mind

*The power of the mind is infinite,
while brawn is limited."*

—KOICHI TOHEI

WHAT ARE WE FIGHTING WHEN WE FIGHT? WHAT MUST BE DEFEATED?
What is it within our opponent that keeps us from victory? It is the
mind. The body alone, free of thought, is a useless sum of muscle and bone,
sinew and synapse, blood and flesh. It can do nothing without the power of
the mind behind it, yet as long as the power of the mind imbues the body
with fortitude, the body remains formidable.

The opponents who challenge us do so first and foremost through a
mental action, an act of will or *Intention*. As long as their will remains, we
will need to contend with them. We can strike them, lock them, grapple
them, shed their blood, and break their bones but if they still possess the
will to continue at us, they will do so. In this sense, we apply physical martial arts techniques to their bodies in an effort to reach their minds. We
interact with their *Body-Mind* through pain, injury, or submission until
their body convinces their mind to relent.

No matter how we look upon it, by the way, this seems a brutish venture and it represents some failure of our collective humanity that we could
not engage our opponent's mind without resorting to physical tactics.

Nevertheless, through some means, we must reach the opponent's
mind, and once we persuade it to end its pursuit of conflict, so the conflict
can end. For that reason, philosophy (and also psychology) becomes essential. *We must not permit the opponent to access our minds.* How does an
opponent do that? By "making us" scared or angry or *Intentful*. If we
become mentally imbalanced, so will we become physically imbalanced,
i.e. unprincipled. If we become unprincipled then an opponent will exploit

our deficiencies in precisely the same manner in which we seek to exploit his or hers.

Therefore, embracing *Philosophy* as an element of martial arts practice accomplishes two ends: First, the nature of philosophical inquiry sharpens the mind much in the way that exercise shapes the body. Like every other muscle, our minds become stronger through use. Second, the particular philosophical principles I discuss, as well as so many other ones common to martial arts, help free the mind of traps the opponent can exploit. If we manifest *mushin, kime, non-intention*, and other states of mind then we become impervious to becoming mentally imbalanced, even to misperception.

On another level, possessing a powerful mind can in and of itself begin to dominate the opponent's mind because the opponent will sense our clarity of action, lack of *Intention* and emotion, and our lack of fear. As we really only need defeat the opponent's mind anyway, accessing his or her mind in this purely mental fashion moves us towards our cause, typically before physical combat even begins.

66

Mushin

SO MUCH HAS BEEN WRITTEN ABOUT THE CONCEPT OF *MUSHIN* BY THOSE FAR more adept at its philosophical depth than I that I certainly do not want to reiterate their points. Instead, I would encourage those of my readers most interested in *mushin* as a purely philosophical concept to take up readings on Zen and Taoism that develop the concept at length and in its purest form. Books by other martial artists, such as Musashi's, *Book of Five Rings* and Hyam's, *Zen in the Martial Arts*, also offer valuable insight. What I will focus on here, however, is the intimate and ultimately essential interrelationship between *mushin* as a philosophical concept and the practical application of martial technique.

"*Mushin*" combines two other Japanese words, the first being "mu," which essentially means "no," and the second being "shin," or "mind" in English. Thus, *mu-shin* means "no-mind" and refers to a state of awareness transcendent of conscious thought. We often find this likened to a "oneness" where mind, body, and action become one in the same, where we let go of awareness of the self as something apart from our surroundings. In "mushin," the ego is lost. In letting go of the conception of the self—the awareness of the "I"—the mind becomes free of cluttering thoughts that mitigate action.

We might think of a typical mind as a churning body of water, covered in foam, fraught with violent waves. Were we to drop a stone into such a tempest, it would go unnoticed; its "plunk" would be overwhelmed by the crashing of the waves, and its ripples would be overpowered by their currents. By contrast, were the pool still, the effect of the stone would be quite noticeable. Its "plunk" would be clear and crisp, and the ripples would spread instantly and undisturbed. In turning to ripples, the still water literally would become the effect of the stone.

The general thinking in the martial arts community is that stilling the mind of thoughts, making it uncluttered and free like a still pool, will enable freer and more accurate responses to the attacks "cast into" it. I certainly take no issue with such reasoning. In fact, it makes sense from two different perspectives: A mind that intellectually considers an attack will *not* successfully react to it. It will be far too consumed with thinking *about* it to permit the body to respond *to* it properly: "Gargantua is throwing a punch. It's a haymaker. I need to step to my right and block. Block hard! Now!" Can you imagine engaging thought processes such as these during combat? Such lengthy mental considerations will delay our responses, as would consciously thinking about the need to slam on the brake when the car in front of us suddenly stops short. We do not consider braking or consciously note the need for braking, we just brake.

Conversely, a mind focused on anything other than the pending attack obviously ripens the situation for impending doom. Even a strike by an unskilled brute will take but a fraction of a second, and so any thoughts we might have of dinner, that itch on the bottom of our foot, the attractive man or woman across the room, etc. will distract us from the pressing issue of the moment.

Unfortunately, I think many people confuse true *mushin* with *Reflexive Action*, and while we prefer *Reflexive Action* to non-reflexive action, it is not yet *mushin* in the purer sense. *Reflexive Action*, though it occurs without conscious thought, can equally become a fixation of the mind, much as a thought: the mind perceives a particular stimulus and then "thinks" through programmed response, performing a certain technique by rote habit. In such a case, the "thought" is the "technique" and that "thought-technique" occurs regardless of whether or not it constitutes the proper action in the context. It is a pre-programmed response that happens instinctively at the pulling of a certain trigger, and thus it is a mind bound to a particular course of action.

We can think of such instinctive reaction—pseudo *mushin*—as a kind of post-hypnotic suggestion to say "the rain in Spain falls mainly on the plain" whenever we hear the word, "banana," and to ask "how much wood could a woodchuck chuck if a woodchuck could chuck wood" every time we hear the word, "pineapple." Such responses would be instinctive, reflexive, and devoid of conscious thought—seemingly *mushin* in manifestation. But they would be rote, inappropriate, and unresponsive to everything that happened after the initial trigger of "banana" or "pineapple." The mind would continue to produce the entire saying regardless of what other factors came into being. The mind, in essence, would fixate.

So it is with reflexive martial arts technique. If in response to Gargantua's punch we launch into a reflexive, pre-programmed block-and-counter combination, we have effectively committed ourselves to saying, "the rain in Spain falls mainly on the plain" all the way through, start to finish. Such fixation makes us unresponsive to whether Gargantua actually committed to the punch, faked us out, changed his technique mid-way through, or if our combination works effectively at all.

Instead, a mind in *mushin* remains completely uncluttered, free of programmed movement, reacting instantly and fully to everything happening at every second, and unencumbered by its own training. It is devoid of desire, anticipation, emotion, and expectation. It is devoid of programming. In this way, *Mushin* and *Reflexive Action* reciprocate one another.

Yet *Mushin* does not result in any lack of technique. *Mushin* does not make us lax; it does not permit us to "do whatever." Rather, it exercises technique instantaneously and responsively to the stimuli of every moment. That is what makes *mushin* so difficult. It is *relatively* easy to be free of mind and just flail around, and equally easy to develop reflexive, "rain in Spain" kind of reactions. What is difficult, however, is to be both free of mind and precise in technique.

Yet that is not exactly the discussion with which this book is concerned. Rather, I want to examine *mushin* in the context of the other sections of this book, primarily that of *Physiokinetics*. As with so many other principles discussed, it is from a certain perspective entirely accurate to say that this entire book could be lumped under the heading of *mushin* alone.

Case in point, we could consider the entire section on *Physiokinetics* to be speaking to the issue of *mushin* because any misalignment of *Physiokinetic* principles would impair our ability to enter the no-mind state. Why? Because improper *Physiokinetics* produce unnecessary muscle tension and require otherwise unnecessary mental attention. Improper *Posture*, for example, requires more-than-minimum muscle tension to keep the body upright, as a result the mind must attend to muscles, directing them to maintain the body, directing them to be tense, etc. A mind thinking about having to maintain tension is not an unfettered mind.

By the same reasoning, if we execute a wrist-throw takedown towards a location other than a *Triangulation Point* then our muscles encounter undue resistance from the defender. We cannot then rely on technique itself in the purest sense, having instead to supplement it with additional force, and thus fragmenting our mind.

The same holds true for all *Physiokinetic* principles. If properly applied, each will free the mind of superfluous work that could impede its emptiness. Were all properly aligned, the mind would, in essence, become the body, and vice versa, as there would be no disharmony between the "two."

I should point out, however, that I do not believe, and certainly am not qualified to determine, that poor *Physiokinetics* intrinsically conflict with *mushin*; it might be possible to manifest poor *Physiokinetics* and also be in a state of *mushin*. However, I do believe poor *Physiokinetics*, and its ilk, to impede *mushin*. In fact, I would go so far as to say that those who attain a state of *mushin* without having proper *Physiokinetics* prior to that attainment typically acquire proper *Physiokinetics* upon attaining it. The mind rights the body, forcing it into proper position so that the mind can flow freely.

Obviously, this relates us back to the *Percentage Principle* in that the mind cannot be in a state of no-mind if some part of the mind must be focused on this or that, *or even if the mind is conscious of itself.*

67

Kime

KIME REFERS TO "TOTAL FOCUS" OR "FOCUSING ON A SINGLE POINT." IT IS to channel the full power of the mind into singularity such as a martial arts technique. This reciprocates *mushin*, although at first it appears to be its direct opposite. It would seem, in fact, as though *kime* and *mushin* cancel each other out. After all, how can the mind exist in a state of "singular focus" and "no-mind" all at once?

Before resolving the seeming conflict between the concepts, let us first understand *kime* a bit more specifically. To reach that understanding, you first must know that I have three cats, and have had cats nearly all my life. Every so often, I find myself holding an unwilling cat in my arms. Sometimes this is because the cat in question needed some medicine, or because I needed to put it in a pet carrier, or for some other similar reason. Regardless of the motivation, I always find it hard to believe how much force a cat of roughly ten pounds can generate when it does not want to be held. After all, I weigh 165 pounds, which means that just one of my arms must weight *at least* ten, and yet sometimes the cat gives me a decent run for my money. I suppose I could secure the cat more easily were I not concerned about hurting it, but that little ten pound animal demonstrates a remarkable amount of force.

In fact, I used to have a cat, Yang, who loved to play tag with me, which for us meant that I would twiddle my fingers in front of his face and Yang would try to smack my hand before I could pull it away. Yang never used his claws against me, just his paw, and every once in a while he hit me pretty hard with it. To this day I cannot believe how hard he hit my hand with just one paw. My wife could hear the "thwap" from another room.

Why do cats possess such power? *Kime*. When one of my cats struggles to free itself from my well-intentioned clutches, it puts its full being into freeing itself. When it reaches out to tag my hand, it only reaches to tag my hand and it puts its full being into that singular action. I am not suggesting that the cat always does it as *hard* as it can, only that it puts its full being into whatever it does. Anyone who has spent time with cats knows that when playing, they put their full selves into playing. When relaxing in the sun, they put their full selves into relaxing in the sun. When sleeping, they put their full selves into sleeping. And anyone who has seen a cat stalk a mouse and move with absolute singular purpose has seen *kime*.

And yet that they invoke their full being does not mean that they lack *mushin*. Their minds remain uncluttered, unfettered, and unfocused. They remain responsive. Alert. Aware. They spend *zero* attention to what occurred before and what might occur next. They "are."

I can relate *kime* to *Physiokinetics* in the exact same manner in which I related *mushin* to *Physiokinetics*. Yet *kime* also begs for a discussion of *Technique*, particularly with respect to *"Kobo Ichi."* As I noted before, it seems as though the dominant reason so many of us fail to exercise the singular power of *kime* in our techniques stems from a lack of balance between offense and defense. If when blocking we reserve (understandable) concern for the opponent's next attack, for the portions of our bodies we might expose, for the need to counter-attack, etc. then we cannot be devoting the fullness of our being into blocking. Likewise, if when attacking we reserve (understandable) concern for committing to a course of action (*Frozen in Motion*), for revealing our *Intention*, for leaving targets unprotected, etc. then we cannot commit our full being into action.

Other principles impact similarly, but this should offer the concept. Therefore, the principles of proper technique become critical facets of achieving *kime*. If we are to commit our singular focus to a given technique then that technique must be *singularly powerful and complete*. Otherwise, how can we and *why should we* invest ourselves in it as such?

68

Non-Intention

I BEGAN TO DISCUSS THIS IDEA IN THE *COMPLIMENT* CHAPTER, WHERE I BUILT off of Bruce Lee's adage, "Your technique is my technique." That statement not only carries the previously discussed technique-based meanings, it equally applies to a mind set, to a state of being, one that builds off of *Mushin* and *Kime*.

Lee's statement bridges us into the notion of *Non-Intention*, an absolutely essential state of being for us as martial artists. Yet before delving into *Non-Intention*, let us first explore *Intention*, a principle in its own right, which I coarsely define as some "dedicated direction of the mind." For our purposes, *Intention* must be considered a kind of *fixation* of the mind, a determination to act in a given manner, as in a *dedicated* decision to attack us. An opponent devoid of the true *Intention* to attack will not attack.[17]

Note the critical emphasis on the word, "dedicated." Without real commitment to act, there is no real *Intention*. For example, I sometimes encounter people who, upon learning that I practice martial arts, like to play around by tossing some limbs in my direction in a vague and half-hearted mockery of combat. I never play that game. While there are tactics that make it easy enough to contend with such trifles, they are trifles nonetheless. Without *Intention* to attack, we only experience unrealistic simulations, and the martial arts do not concern unrealistic simulations. Drills and exercises remain possible, of course, but they require what Bruce Lee called, "real emotional content."

---

17. Exception: A spiritually enlightened attacker who is at one with himself or herself and all the universe can attack without *Intention* because there will be absolutely no distinction between the self and the actions of that self. I do not think we stand much chance of encountering such a person. And if we do, I imagine he or she will not want to mug us.

Similarly, rarely does a year go by that a newer student does not approach me with a look of doubt, if not one of outright frustration. When I inquire as to the nature of the problem, the student recounts trying to apply a technique on a friend and having it fail miserably. As a result, the student's faith in my teachings, if not in all martial arts, becomes jeopardized.

Oftentimes, students meet with ill-results simply because they lack skill. Victimized by movie montages that turn Ralph Machio into "The Karate Kid" in a mere ninety minutes, students expect to leave their first class ready to drop Gargantua in a heartbeat. Yet this reason for the student's lack of success does not impact this discussion.

Intention does, however, offer a separate explanation for why the student could not apply the given technique to his or her friend. Quite simply, the friend lacked the *Intention* to do the student harm. The friend did not really *Intend to attack,* only to engage in a playful exercise. Even if grabbing (striking, tackling, etc.) hard, that friend probably did so playfully, knowing what to expect, and without being consumed by a dedicated desire to hurt. While experienced martial arts can compensate for such artificiality, novice martial artists cannot. Truthfully, why would they want to? These are trifles.

We equally see that *Intent* gives life to the body. As discussed earlier, the *Mind* makes the body move, fills it with energy, commits it to action, etc. If Jane attempts to put Joe in a wrist lock but he goes completely limp, relinquishing all *Intention* to engage Jane and turning his body into a noodle, Jane will experience considerable difficulty. In withdrawing his *Intent,* his *Mind,* Joe effactually ceases to be present at all. As "Jane's technique is Joe's technique," if Joe offers no technique then Jane possesses no technique.

Note that I am not pointing to *Relaxation* on Joe's part. I'm really discussing utter disengagement from the combative context. As Jane wants to use Joe's motion, strength, force, etc. in her technique against Joe, the absence of such forces thwarts her. For this reason, I always ask my students to grab me like they want to hold me. Merely clasping your arms around someone, even if done so hard, does not constitute a "hold." There is no hold if there is no *Intention* to hold on.

Thus, it is the opponent's *Intention* that we exploit more than anything else. Every principle in this book teaches us how to exploit the opponent's mental fixation. *Indirect Pressure* does so by moving our body from locations other than where the opponent fixated on contact. *Active Movement* and *Timing* do so by exploiting the moment in which the opponent becomes fixated on a course of motion. *Reactive Control* does so by advancing on the opponent and forcing him or her to commit to a given defense. Etc. In short, as we cannot execute a wrist escape against an opponent who does not grab our wrist at all, it is only half-possible to execute a wrist escape against an opponent who does so half-heartedly. Thus, as martial artists, we *want* the opponent to fixate on a course of action. Once the opponent locks into a fixation, any fixation, he or she becomes static—*Frozen in Motion*. Meanwhile, we can become dynamic, active, and responsive.

Reciprocally speaking, this sends us a mighty warning. Just as we seek to exploit the opponent's *Intention*, so does it become possible for the opponent to exploit our own *Intention*, which is why we must have "non." Note that I did not say that we should have "none" or "no intention." "No intention" is exemplified by what Joe did—becoming utterly limp mentally and physically.

Rather, I speak of "non-intention"—action without act*ing* or action without mental *fixation* on a particular course of action. Lee's statement elucidates this idea. When the opponent acts against us, we should not *decide* a course of action, nor should we *pursue* or *fixate* on one, follow one, exercise one, etc. Nor should we *try* to apply a certain technique, a favorite technique, an appropriate technique, etc. We should act without *acting*, meaning that our actions should manifest themselves because our opponent's technique has manifested itself. As we do not desire the opponent's technique, and as our technique merely emerges in *Compliment* to the opponent's technique, then we should not desire our technique either. It should just happen or not happen.

Think about a dam holding back a reservoir of water. Were we to punch a hole in the dam, the water would gush out that hole. The water would not decide to gush out, and it certainly would not *Intend* to gush out. Nor would it "not intend" to gush out the hole. *Intention*, as a concept, simply cannot be applied to the water. As hole, so gushing water.

Likewise, the water would not have to decide how to do it, or when, or with how much force, or how fast. The water would gush at the rate the water in that circumstance would gush. No faster. No slower. No sooner. No later. The water acts with "non-intention." The gushing "happens."

Even to say that the water gushed out *because* a hole appeared would be inaccurate because that suggests a separation between the emergence of the hole and the gushing of the water. Yet there was no such separation. No time differential.

Therefore, facing the opponent's strike, we must not *Intend* to execute a given technique, or any technique for that matter. "As there is attack, so there is defense." As I said, technique "happens." If we train properly to the point of *Reflexive Action*, and if we fully understand the attack, and if our principles align, the technique will emerge along with the attack as if they are one in the same, as if we and the attacker planned it all ahead of time.

On the other hand, if we *Intend* on executing a high block before we see the attack, the opponent can exploit that fixation by throwing a low attack, even if serendipitously. If when grabbed at the wrist we *decide* to execute Escape A instead of Escape B then our opponent can exploit or fix-ation on A by changing to a variation better countered by Escape B. As long as we choose, we can be wrong, or if not wrong, fixated.

Instead, "technique happens." When "technique happens," it is not possible to entertain questions of "right" technique or "wrong" technique. Such irrelevant labels separate us from action by making us think *about* technique rather than simply becoming technique. Therefore, if "technique happens" then technique is "correct." If technique does not "happen" then technique is obviously not correct.

Let me put it another way. When reading this chapter, were you *Intending* to read this chapter, or was reading "happening"? Were you *Intending* to read or were you just reading? You certainly were not "not intending" to read. Were you thinking *about* reading the words or were you reading them? As chapter, so reading. As living, so breathing. As sleeping, so dreaming. (And if you are wondering if we can say that there is "a chapter" aside from your reading of it then you have understood this chapter quite well.)

Of course, as *Intention* works against us, *Reciprocity* dictates that *Non-Intention* must work for us. As implied above, it does so first by keep-ing us free from fixation, and thereby giving the opponent no *Intention* to exploit. Simultaneously, it keeps our mind free and responsive. Yet it accomplishes something else, as well. For a variety of reasons, actions born of *Non-Intention* invariably are more powerful than actions we *Intend*. Primarily, this holds true because during *Non-Intention*, mind and body act as one—*Body-Mind*. No distinction exists between doing something and thinking about doing it. It just happens.

Many newer martial artists suffer from slow hand speed. When instructed to throw a strike as fast as they can, it still drawls its way to the target. Yet place their hand on a hot stove and it will jerk away almost imperceptibly fast. The difference comes from trying to be fast (*Intention*) vs. being fast (*Non-Intention*). In the former, the student tries to move quickly and, while doing so, also must try to conform to the given tech-nique, all of which requires considerable mental energy. In the latter, there is no "technique" for removing a hand from the stove, nor is there *Intention* to do so. As hot stove, so moving hand. To be fair, none of us will execute fast technique until it becomes part of us rather than something we must *Intend* to do.

Yet that only affirms the point. *Non-Intention* bests *Intention*. Consider another example, this time a wrist grab. During seminars, I often grab one participant with a same-side wrist grab (and with *Intention*) and ask him or her to move, even escape. Whether or not the student escapes, he or she experiences relative difficulty in moving. Then we try it again and I ask the participant to forget about moving his or her wrist and to forget about escape. I instruct the student to forget all of it and just scratch his or her opposite elbow—*just* scratch the elbow. At first, the participant usually does the same thing as before and tries to move, *Intending* to break free of the grab. Eventually, I get the student to *just* scratch the opposite elbow as if not grabbed at all, as if he or she just had an itch. At that point, the student moves rather effortlessly and reaches his or her elbow with little difficulty because the student stopped *Intending* to move and *just moved*. We changed the technique from one that focused *Intention* on the wrist being grabbed to one that focused *Intention* on the scratching the opposite elbow. While this is not exactly *Non-Intention* in the pure sense, it is *Non-Intention* to move the wrist and break free of the wrist grab, and that not only "tricks" the participants *Body-Mind* into moving freely, it also tricks my mind because it prompts the participant to move with *Indirect Pressure*.

Yet the point remains the same. We must act *Non-Intentionally* at all times because doing so (1) naturally exploits the opponent's *Intention*, (2) prevents the opponent from exploiting our *Intention*, and (3) makes us more powerful by intrinsically connecting our mind and our body.

69

Yin and Yang

*Y*IN AND *Y*ANG REPRESENT ALL ETERNAL *COMPLIMENTS* AND *RECIPROCALS*. They define each other and give life to each other. As typically defined, *Yin* represents that which is passive, dark, soft, yielding, empty, etc., and *Yang* represents all that is active, light, hard, assertive, full, etc.

Yet there are two popular misconceptions about *Yin-Yang*. The first is that they can be discussed separately, if not actually separated. While we can discuss the *Yin* aspect of a thing, we cannot do so devoid of reference to and understanding of its *Yang* aspect. For example, we can rightly call "darkness" a *Yin* quality, but any discussion of "darkness" must involve reference to and understanding of light—*Yang*. In fact, as we define "darkness" as the absence of light, the mere use of the term "darkness" implies the concept of light. Hence, we can never discuss *Yin* without *Yang*, nor can we separate one from the other.

The second misconception concerning *Yin-Yang* involves the belief that they oppose one another in some kind of eternal conflict, as if "emptiness" and "matter" clash. While each does represent the opposite of the other, each also gives life to the other, and together they construct wholeness. For example, it would be erroneous to consider the empty space in a drinking cup in opposition to the water that eventually fills it. While true that the emptiness gets overcome and eliminated by the water that fills the cup, an empty drinking glass has not fulfilled its implied purpose. Only when filled does the glass fulfill its destiny. Therefore, that the water fills the void only makes it functional and fulfills its purpose. Similarly, a full glass of water constitutes equal meaninglessness for its implied purpose remains unachieved. Only by drinking the water and returning the cup to a state of void (*yin*) does the meaning of cup-and-water become realized. Hence, an empty cup alone (*yin*) remains unrealized in its potential until filled (*yang*), which means that *yin* will be unfulfilled until overcome by *yang*. At the same time, a full cup (*yang*) will remain unrealized in its potential until drank, thus returning to *yin*.

In this way, we cannot view *yin* and *yang* in opposition to one another. They do not negate one another, nor are they opposites. More accurately, we can think of them in terms of binary. *Yin-Yang* does not represent -1 and 1, which cancel each other out and create zero. Instead, *Yin-Yang* represents zero and one. Instead of representing something and negative something, *Yin-Yang* represents nothing and something, or something and the absence of something. Consider light and darkness. If we view light and darkness as equally opposing forces that cancel each other out (1 and -1) then we could say that adding darkness to light will create grayness (as adding -1 to 1 creates zero). Yet darkness, the absence of light, cannot be *added* to anything. We cannot "turn the dark on" in a room; we can only turn the light on. Absent of light, the room will be dark, just as in the absence of something, we will have nothing.

Therefore, *Yin-Yang* must be considered a singular cycle of force. While it might seem paradoxical to suggest that a "singular" thing can be a "cycle," such is nevertheless the wonderful nature of *Yin-Yang*, which represents opposites as togetherness. It is simultaneously the two and the one.

As T. P. Kasulis explains in *Zen Action, Zen Person*, "cause and effect" are both a two and a one. Were I to drop a ball, we could say that my dropping of the ball represented the cause and the falling of the ball represented effect. While some would argue that the cause—the dropping of the ball—happened before the effect—the falling of the ball—such an assertion would be erroneous. We cannot say that the ball has been dropped (cause) until the ball begins to fall (effect). Only when we see an effect can we also say that we see a cause. This does not mean that effect exists before cause, only that we can call nothing a "cause" until an effect emerges, and vice versa. Therefore, "cause and effect" becomes a misnomer. It would be more accurate to write, "causeandeffect" or, equally, "effectandcause" because the two emerge together, at once, giving life to one another simultaneously.

How does *Yin-Yang* apply to martial arts? One way involves the idea of *Compliment*, that "your technique is my technique," as Lee said. The opponent's technique implies, even creates our technique, establishing a singularity in the same way as "causeandeffect." (Lee should have said, "Yourtechniqueismytechnique.") We must possess a repertoire of techniques and be adaptable enough as martial artists to fully *Compliment* the opponent's technique, much in the same way that the water that fills the cup does so completely, without gap, without *Intention*. Our "technique" must emerge in conjunction with the opponent's technique, not in the sense of responding to it or defeating it, but in the co-existing creation of wholeness.

On another level, *Yin-Yang* defines the very nature of combat and its objective. Anyone attacking us does so in a state of *yang* because *yang* by nature represents aggression, the active, the assertive, etc. Though we can fight through *yin* tactics, one in this context cannot *attack* through *yin* means—passive, peaceful, harmonious. By adopting a state of *yang*, the attacker equally and simultaneously attempts to force us into a state of *yin*, which means that the attacker only will manifest/maintain *yang* as long as we manifest/maintain *yin*. Put another way, the attacker's actions cannot be defined as *"yang"* except in contrast to some existing complimentary state of *"yin."*

Thus, the attacker will not accomplish victory or dominance (*yang*) unless we suffer defeat or submission (*yin*). Hence, we must find some way to change the attacker's state from *yang* to *yin,* which means that we must become *yang*—victorious.

Some arts, for example, turn the attacker from *yang* to *yin* by manifesting more *yang* energy than that opponent. A strike to the opponent's body (*yang*) that makes the opponent's pain exceed the opponent's aggression will turn that *yang* aggression into *yin* submission. Other arts achieve a final state of *yang* through *yin* means, as in receiving the force of a punch and redirecting it, thereby allowing the punch to deplete itself. Such a technique uses the *yang* energy of the attack in *yin* ways to return the attacker to *yin* and establish a *yang* position in the relationship.

Yet in terms of this text, *Yin-Yang* holds particular meaning. The misconception of this text might be that it attempts to introduce many principles into the martial arts, that it treats principles as *Yang*—that which is active. Principles are not *Yang*; principles are *Yin* in the way darkness is *yin* and zero is *yin*. We cannot add principles. We cannot create them. They exist in the absence of unprincipled action, just as darkness exists in the absence of light. When we add extraneous motions, extra thoughts, undue tension, fear, etc. we interfere with principles. Thus, principled martial arts exist in the *absence* of unprincipled martial arts. As I said in the *Michelangelo Principle*, to be principled, we need only stop doing everything that is unprincipled.

70

Oneness

As I teach techniques to newer students and challenge them to manifest good *Posture* and sound *Breathing* and *Indirect Pressure* and *Convergence* and *Active Motion* and every other principle, they often ask, "How can you expect me to do so many different things at once"?[18] To which I respond, "I do not want you to do many things at all. I only want you to do one thing—the technique."

I think anyone who has been involved in the martial arts for some time can sympathize with that student. After all, most techniques involve many different motions. They probably require us to move our hands in certain ways and adopt a certain stance and position ourselves in a certain place and do a variety of other different things. Yet as experienced martial artists understand, techniques do not involve many different motions at all. Techniques involve only one motion: the motion that is the technique. To say that we are doing many different things when doing *a* technique could not be more wrong.

Consider earlier discussions of *Breathing* and *Posture* and how utterly erroneous it would be for someone to say, "So I need to *Breathe* properly *and* manifest proper *Posture* at the same time?" As there cannot be proper *Breathing* without proper *Posture*, and as there cannot be proper *Posture* without proper *Breathing*, how can it be that we can do one without the other? Put another way, as *Breathing* properly will create proper *Posture*, to speak of one occurring without the other is impossible. More accurately, there is "breathingposture" or there is not.

---

18. Newer students actually do not need to apply every principle at the same time. It really just feels like that.

In that same sense, to suggest they are many parts of any technique only creates artificial distinctions within a singularity. So could be said of every "single" principle within this text.[19] *Oneness*, therefore, speaks to achieving singularity, turning the supposed "many" into one,[20] just as every martial artist at some point turns the many different parts of a technique into a single technique. Suddenly, what were *many different* principles and motions becomes "technique" and "technique" alone. This transition from doing many things to doing one thing seems to me the defining distinction between the advanced student and the beginning student, the former having put the "pieces" together and the latter still working in "pieces."

Yet true *Oneness* involves a great deal more than eliminating the artificial distinctions between parts. To achieve it fully, we must eliminate the distinction between our self and the now singular technique. Just as we can make no distinction between *Breathing* and *Posture*, so can we make no distinction between self and the technique the self "performs." This refers back to the cause-and-effect example. Just as no cause manifests itself until an effect manifests itself, so does no martial ac*tion* exist without a martial act-*er*.

Therefore, just as the more advanced martial artists can turn the many into the one with respect to the "parts" of a technique, so must we all strive to turn the two into one with respect to the artificial distinction between the self and the technique the self performs. This means that we cannot "do" the technique because that creates distinction between the "we" and the "doing." And we definitely cannot think *about* doing the technique, which only adds a third artificial part—"we," "doing," and "thinking about doing." We must become the technique and the technique must become us. We must not do it nor think about doing it. Rather, "technique happens" or "wetechniquehappens" or "thereismartialartsnessoccuring."

Following the same logic, *Oneness* must extend to all things, such as the "opponent." If a technique is a singularity rather than a collection of parts, and if we and technique is a singularity, then we and the opponent also must be a singularity. "Your technique is my technique." As such, if "we" cannot be separated from "technique" and "technique" cannot be separated from "opponent"—for how can there be a technique without an opponent—then we-technique-opponent must be a singularity.

Following the same logic, *Oneness* must eliminate distinction between the self and the entire universe, or should we further entertain the illusion that there is self apart from universe, as if there could be *Breathing* without *Posture*, or martial action without martial artist, or technique without opponent, and so on.

---

19. Of course, to refer or understand "Oneness" without understanding the many is impossible. See *Yin-Yang*.

20. More accurately, since *Oneness* constitutes the natural state, it means to cease creating the many out of the reality that is singularity.

Of course, true *Oneness* with all the universe seems like a lofty goal. Perhaps some enlightened earthlings have achieved this. I certainly have not. But higher and higher levels of oneness can be achieved. Martial artists who can unify the "parts" of a technique achieve certain power. Martial artists who unify themselves with their technique achieve even more power. In all honesty, I have seen perhaps two such people, and it is awe inspiring.

Yet *Oneness* must remain a goal. If that prompts you to ask, "How can *Oneness* and 'goal' be separate?" or "How can there be 'levels' of '*Oneness*'" then you are starting to understand.

71

Zanshin & Being

ZANSHIN IS A JAPANESE TERM THAT REFERS TO "TOTAL ATTENTION TO THE moment." It involves bringing the entirety of our conscious into any given instance, which consequently increases our awareness of that moment. Yet true *Zanshin* involves more than "being aware *of* the moment," which maintains a distinction between ourselves and the moment about which we are aware. Instead, it entails "being-the-moment," meaning that all distinction between the self and the moment in which the self exists become erased. This is an extension of *Oneness* in that any distinction between a conceptualization of "self" and "moment" would cease to exist. If thinking *about* the self then we are not *being* self, and if we are thinking *about* the moment then we are not one with the moment.

In drawing all our attention into the moment, we become fully aware of everything that happens in it. *Aikido* founder, Morihei Ueshiba had a standing challenge with his students that none of them would ever be able to sneak up on him. None of them ever did. Usually, they would attempt it and he would just laugh.

Or take the old adage about the martial arts master who accepts a disciple under the condition that should he ever catch the disciple sleeping, he would teach the disciple no more. At first, the disciple slept as little as possible. Later on, he learned to be aware of the slightest sound in the house, even while sleeping. Eventually, whenever the master would just think about checking on the disciple, they both would laugh. The disciple's awareness had expanded to *Zanshin*.

Yet I do not think we can separate awareness of the moment from *Being* in the moment, or more accurately, being-the-moment. There's an old saying in the martial arts, one that comes from *Tai Chi,* I believe, and it says, "Stand like mountain, flow like water, move like the wind." This speaks to *full attention to the moment*. When standing, *stand*. Be standing. *Zanshin* standing. Total standing. When moving, *move*. Cat like. Be movement. *Zanshin* movement. Total movement. When flowing, *flow*. Seamless. Be fluidity. *Zanshin* fluidity. Total fluidity.

How often do we see martial artists who when "standing in place" are really only kind-of-standing, somewhat stable, sort-of having established position. On a physical level, they might be shifting their weight around and/or failing to maintain a particular stance or position. On a more abstract level, they might be thinking about moving or transitioning. This is not *Zanshin*. This is not *Being*.

There can be no sort-of-standing. We are standing or we are not standing. We are moving or we are not moving. We must not conflate the two. Likewise, we are punching or not punching. We must not "kind of punch" or punch halfheartedly. Punch or do not. Stand or do not. Move or do not.

Zanshin and *Being* connect to other martial principles in innumerable ways. Consider *Positioning*. If we find that we do not "stand like mountain" when positioned, might that be because our *Positioning* does not afford the necessary *Angling* and "*Kobo Ichi*" capability? Might it be because we lack proper *Rooting* and *Heaviness*? Might it be because we are exercising *Centrifugal* motion that draws us away from ourselves under circumstances where *Centripetal* motion would be more effective? And so on. How can the totality of our being commit to standing until we stand in the right place at the right time and in the right way?

Zanshin. "Stand like mountain, flow like water, move like the wind." Total focus. Total commitment.

72

Non-Action

(We Wei, Water Principle)

NON-ACTION IS NEARLY THE SAME AS *NON-INTENTION*. AFTER ALL, THE effect of *Non-Intending* to do something must be that we *non-do* it. Perhaps the classic example of *Non-Action* comes in the parable of the wise old man and the waterfall. The emperor, having heard of a wise old man in the country, sent soldiers to find him. Arriving at his village, the peasants inform the soldiers to seek the old man at the waterfall, where they soon find him atop a gigantic falls. No sooner do they see him than he jumps off, plummeting into the water below. Given the height of the falls, the soldiers determine that the old man either died on impact or drowned in the churning waters, and so they begin to cry out of fear of retribution from the emperor. Yet a moment or two later, the old man walks onto shore and shakes himself off like a wet dog.

"Why are you crying," he asks the soldiers.

"We thought you dead," they respond. "How on earth did you survive that?"

"Oh, that's nothing," says the old man. "Instead of fighting the water, I become it. When the water pushes me down, I do down. And when the water pushes me up, I come up. Thus, I move with the water as a leaf in the wind."

Thus, *Non-Action* challenges us to accomplish a given end not just through minimal effort but through non-effort. Once again, it would be accurate to say that "technique happens."

Consider the joint lock technique discussed in the *Void* chapter. We move through the space surrounding the arm because doing so proves easier than moving through the arm itself. After all, we cannot move through solid matter. Yet *Non-Action* involves *less* than merely taking the easiest path. Supposing we find ourselves in the position V1c depicts, we need not actively enter the *Void* and "apply" that lock in the active sense of "doing" something. Instead, because the *Void* exists, and because we should be *Heavy, Relaxed, Centered, Non-Intentful*, and so forth, the arm will go into the *Void* because that is the path the arm will take, almost as if the *Void* sucks our arm into it, which is what *Voids* really do anyway.

It should be as water flowing down a drain, which the water does because of the *Void* beneath it. It does not put effort into flowing down the drain. It just flows. Of course, it flows *Centripetally*. And just as the *Centripetal* path represents the natural one for water, so is the human body most vulnerable to falling *Centripetally*. Therefore, to "throw" someone down, we should not need to construct *Centripetal* motion actively, nor should we have to throw someone actively once *Centripetal* motion is established. Rather, we need only allow *Centripetal* motion to happen.

Of course, *Non-Action* does not apply only to grappling. *Wing Chun's* famous motto, "When there's space, strike" equally serves as a statement of *Non-Action*. *Chi sao*—a drill where two participants try to strike one another from a position of wrist-to-wrist contact—refers us back to the water against the dam. As a hole manifests, so does water stream through. So it is in *Wing Chun*, where striking does not occur because there is a space, nor does the *Wing Chun* practitioner decide to strike. The emergence of the space is the simultaneous emergence of the strike. "Causeandeffect."

In this sense, *all* principles of martial power equally serve as principles of *Non-Action* because all of them help us non-act. After all, anything else would be in-*Efficient*.

73

Character

OUR VENTURE THROUGH THE PRINCIPLES OF MARTIAL POWER COULD NOT BE complete without discussion of *Character* development as part of training. Unfortunately, *Character* involves so many different points that it really deserves a book of its own. While someday I may undertake to write such a work, for now I devote this humble chapter to it. Those who understand how martial arts can and *must* develop *Character* will see this chapter as a doorway to an infinite universe (if they have not passed through the door already, that is).

Of course, there are those who argue that *Character* need not be an issue in martial arts. Such people "just wanna learn how to fight." Yet that seems to violate some of our other principles, such as *Efficiency*. Supposing that we are practicing martial arts one way or another, we might as well build our *Character* in the process. Nothing will be lost by doing so. We have *only* to gain. In fact, just as there is no argument for being inefficient, so does there seem to be no possible argument for *not* developing *Character*.

Yet even those who embrace *Character* as a conceptual objective of the arts seem to throw the word around rather liberally. What does it really mean? What are we talking about when we talk about martial arts building *Character*? As I said, such a discussion requires more than I can devote to it here, but we start by examining pain. While I do not advocate masochism and do *not* advocate adding pain to martial arts as a way to attain great *Character*, all martial arts involve some pain over the course of training. Anyone who has been punched, locked, or thrown knows what I mean, as does anyone who found him or herself moaning about muscle aches after a day of hard training.

Several positive effects come from the pain in training, not the least of which being compassion. While many students enter martial arts thinking about how "cool" it will be to put someone in a joint lock, those same students sometimes surprisingly realize that joint locks actually hurt. In fact, because those students typically work with more experienced martial artists, they typically learn how much joint locks hurt long before they learn to apply them. In this way, we learn the precise nature of what we might do to an opponent. By feeling techniques ourselves we develop empathy and compassion for those to whom we must apply those techniques. Such compassionate recognition does not prevent us from applying techniques should the need arise, but it does teach us to respect the truly grotesque nature of pain and violence.

Before going further, I should note that as with any other principle in this text, *Character* can or cannot be brought to light. Some instructors teach martial combat without deference to *Character*, just as there are those who do not appreciate *Efficiency, Structure, Complex Force*, etc. Such "Cobra Kai"—the villainous academy in *The Karate Kid*—schools train students to be merciless to opponents, yet what pride may we take in learning mercilessness? In what way has stripping ourselves of mercy made us better people? Just as the superior martial artists has the option to harm or not harm, so does the superior martial artist possess the option and inclination to be merciful.

Yet pain instructs more than compassion alone. It also teaches us to detach ourselves from our emotions. If when encountering pain our emotions rage out of control, they will seize our *Mind* and we will forget everything we learned. A purely emotional response is not a martial one. Yet in being hit, locked, and thrown repeatedly through training, we learn to detach our emotions from pain, to gain greater *Control* over ourselves. Otherwise, pain quickly would undermine *Non-Intention, Centeredness, Posture, Breathing, etc.* In fact, most schools I have visited involve positive, strict but friendly atmospheres, even while applying painful techniques to one another. Consequently, the participants habituate themselves to maintaining a positive mindset even when receiving painful techniques.

Not only that, volunteering ourselves to be the subject of techniques employed by other martial artists teaches us trust, especially when such techniques typically hurt and almost invariably can damage. We not only learn to let go of our fears and trust in our fellow men and women, we also learn to be trustworthy, to exercise the power we have over others responsibly, in ways worthy of *their* trust in *us*. By contrast, every martial arts class has seen its share of the new student who arrives with more strength and enthusiasm than personal responsibility, who applies techniques too hard and too fast, who at the very least risks injuring classmates, if not actually inuring them. Such a student has not learned that power is choice. Power is not just what we do, it is what we choose *not* to do *(yin)*.

For this reason, I laugh when some people suggest that the martial arts teach people to be violent. Of course, some schools do teach that, but martial artists are typically highly cooperative, harmonious people. After all, if placing oneself in compromising, painful, dangerous positions so that someone else can learn an art form is not cooperation then I am hard pressed to understand what is.

Yet not only does martial arts practice affect our *Character*, our *Character* effects our application of martial arts. Many techniques will not work properly, if at all, if we lack *Centeredness, Relaxation, Heaviness, Non-Intention*, etc., and only when fear, anger, pain, and their ilk no longer control us will we manifest those principles and apply techniques properly. In this way, martial arts not only *teach* stronger *Character*, they require it.

Ultimately, martial arts can teach us everything in terms of *Character*. The martial arts leave nothing out provided we approach them *reflectively* and take the time to examine ourselves, our relationship with each other, our relationship with power, etc. Under such circumstances, martial arts becomes the bridge to the person we want to be.

74

The Empty Cup

MANY AUTHORS HAVE SPOKEN TO THE PROVERBIAL "EMPTY CUP," THE ZEN "beginners' mind," born of the Zen proverb of the master who pours tea for the novice. As the cup overflows, the novice protests, and so the master says, "Like this cup cannot accept more tea, so will you learn nothing unless you first empty your mind." Like that student, we must empty our minds of the knowledge, answers, and "truths" we "know" if we want any hope of further learning.

Yet we should not equate the "empty cup" to mere open-mindedness. While the latter covers some aspects of the former, it also leaves some of the metaphor unfulfilled. For example, "open-mindedness" in the martial arts community typically connotes openness to other styles. i.e. the recognition that any one style does not constitute the be-all and end-all of the martial arts world. While we absolutely must remain open to other styles, *introspective* open-mindedness holds no less value in that we must be willing, even eager to accept deeper insights into the style(s) we call our own.

In a way, it is easier to remain open when looking at *other* styles. Because they are the "other" and not "ours," we can at once appreciate them and dismiss them. We can take from them techniques that we find useful and we can dismiss everything else by saying, "my system is good too."

Yet we cannot dismiss alternate perspectives on our own art quite so easily. More is at stake. We put a great deal of time and effort into practicing our art form and that makes it difficult to keep an open mind about elements that might require rethinking. If we perform a certain technique a certain way, the way everyone in our style does it, the way the tradition of our style dictates, and then learn that the technique could be improved, mustn't we empty our cups under such circumstances?

Never will truth conform to style. Styles must conform to truth.

Therefore, to deny stronger understandings of any martial technique because it defies tradition (or because it is traditional), or for any other reason, only represents a full cup and a mind unwilling to learn and grow.

Perhaps it helps to remember that the spirit of an art does not change with modifications in technique. The martial arts serve to keep us safe and build our character, and if fulfilling those objectives means changing a punch from X to Y then we fulfill the spirit of the martial arts as well as the spirit of our particular style.

At the same time, the cup metaphor serves a deeper metaphor. As we saw in the *Yin-Yang* chapter, a perpetually empty cup serves no function. To fulfill its purpose, it must be filled. Yet a full cup serves no function. To fulfill its purpose, it must be emptied—drank. We fill the cup. We empty the cup. We fill the cup again. We drink from it, take in its nourishment, discard what we cannot use of it, and repeat the process.

Not only that, an "empty cup" also represents unrealized possibility. We never know exactly what its contents will taste like. It brings us continual surprise. And that might be the strongest argument for emptying the cup as often as we can. The most pressing of truths seems to be that *we do not know what we do not know*. At any moment in our lives we can learn that one new idea that entirely reshapes everything we ever believed.

For instance, tomorrow I could learn yet another principle that I should have included in this text. Or perhaps I will see something that makes me reconsider every principle herein, something that makes me rethink, perhaps even recant, everything I've written. And so it seems fitting to end the discussion portion of this text with the *Empty Cup* principle. After all, what better time to remind my readers and myself that I do not know what I do not know about martial principles.

For now, however, I have emptied my cup, spilling it into this text so that I am once again *yin*. I hope your cup has been empty so as to receive this, and I hope to have filled it with ideas worth drinking.

SECTION V
A SAMPLE OF TECHNIQUE

THIS BOOK WOULD NOT BE COMPLETE WITHOUT AT LEAST ONE EXAMPLE OF A technique expressing the principles of martial power. However, certain provisos must be mentioned before venturing forward. First, I will not be able to discuss *all* principles at work in every part of the technique. Not only would doing so require another book, but some of the philosophical and theoretical principles go without mention; they affect our approach to martial arts but cannot be exemplified in pictures. For example, this format favors what can be visually depicted over what can be felt, and yet the how principles feel actually means a great deal more than what they look like. It is impossible, for example, to visually depict the difference between direct and *Indirect Pressure,* a difference that would be plainly apparent when actually experiencing a martial technique.

In the same regard, many principles exist in too subtle degrees to be visually apparent. Consequently, we exaggerated some elements of the photography to make them more apparent.

In order to capture the most precise positioning possible, these photographs were not taken in real time, but posed. Consequently, some of the pictures take a slightly artificial tone. In a few positions, I literally had to hold up my friend and student, Ed Dewey, because he otherwise would have fallen. This affected my own anatomy, though I do not know to what extent that will be perceptible.

As you view this technique, please use the book as a reference guide. I will not at each point explain the principles discussed; I'll only name them and speak briefly to how they apply. My goal involves offering some relative understanding of principle in action, but does not involve trying to teach this particular technique, nor does it involve trying to get people to do this technique this way. In short, there's more than one principled way to apply the hammer lock depicted, just as there are innumerable variations on the entry, strikes, tactics, etc. Therefore, I hope readers will use this as a conceptual example more than a literal one and then consider how to apply principles to their own arts.

Most importantly, the decision to depict improper variations was difficult. The martial arts community involves too much bickering as it is. At the same time, some point of comparison between principled and unprincipled seemed necessary. If readers exercise this technique in the ways I depict as problematic in terms of the principles in this text, and that works fine for them, then I am in no position to criticize, nor am I so inclined.

In the following section, numbers 1-17 depict the principled execution of technique, while letters A-R depict unprincipled misapplications. To begin with figure 1: As Ed (left) and Steve (right) face each other, note the immediate distinction between their stances. By beginning with his hands close together, Steven immediately begins to manifest the *Triangle Guard* and to capture the *Centerline*. Furthermore, he protects his groin and brings his hands closer to being able to defend higher targets. Other defensive stances can be adopted.

Figure 1

Figure 2

Figure 3

As Ed begins to throw a left punch to Steve's chest, Steve seizes on Ed's retracting motion and takes the opportunity to capture the *Primary Gate* while simultaneously bringing his hands into the *Triangle Guard*. In figure 2, note how much more protected Steve is than Ed. Whereas Ed's hands have separated and retracted, putting a good portion of them behind him, Steve's hands remain in front and directed towards Ed's body. Already, Steve is establishing proper *Angling*. Seen from another angle in figure 3, which also depicts the beginning of footwork, it becomes clear that Steve remains *Centered and Structured*, while Ed's body is already tilting. Of course, Steve exercises *Active Movement*, waiting until Ed committed to the punch before moving.

Figure 4: Here we see Steve having completed the first motion of the technique by *Angling* at 22½ degrees while *Positioning* himself by moving around Ed's sphere. Note that Steve's body faces Ed's with *Spinal Alignment*, while Ed's body does not face Steve's at all. While not easy to see in the pictures, close inspection does show the *Spatial Relativity* difference in their two motions, with Steve's being smaller. Similarly, Steve's actions involve *Non-Telegraphed, Economical Motions*, whereas Ed's movements are considerably more gross. Note as well the *Rooted* position in which Steve stands as he extends his hands into position via *Indirect Pressure* and maintains both a small *Axis* and small *Minor Axes*. Also take note of the fact that Steve is establishing *Tactile Sensitivity* and is exercising *Peripheral Vision*.

Figure 4

Contrast figures 1-4 against figures A-D. In figure A, Steve takes his arm off the *Centerline*, away from *the Primary Gate*, and out of *Spinal Alignment* in order to block Ed's punch. In doing so, he exposes most of his primary targets. In figure B, aside from improper *Structure*, Steve blocks Ed's arm pentagonally from the outside in, which leaves him no *Triangle Guard*, thus no way to root

Figure A

Figure B

Figure C

Figure D

force into his feet. Though subtle, you might notice his hips reacting as a result. Furthermore, he steps back slightly, which defeats the possibility of establishing *Reactive Control* and works at Ed's *Rhythm and Timing* instead of *Controlling* it himself. Already in figure B) we see that Steve lacks *Spinal Alignment*, something further exaggerated in figure C, in which Steve's perpendicular stance exposes his face to Ed's right counterpunch. Furthermore, Steve's left arm and left leg are completely out of play. He must first re-*Angle* himself and re-*Position* himself to use them. Notice as well that Steve has moved at least as much as Ed rather than moving with better *Ratio*. Figure D shows an alternate angle of figure B. It might be difficult to tell from the depiction, but in figure C we see that it is Ed's *Sphere* that is penetrating Steve's *Sphere*, whereas figure 4 depicts just the opposite.

Figure 5 depicts just one of many kicks that could be interjected to disrupt Ed's *Rhythm* and *Unbalance* him. This particular kick would strike to Ed's inner right thigh, but other targets obviously could serve equally well. Note Steve's alignment and the subtlety of the angles.

Figures 6 and 7 depict how a strike to Ed's body can be delivered at this point. The strike equally could go to Ed's face or a similar target. Note Steve's *Spinal Alignment* and his *Control* of the *Primary Gate*. Also note that Steve's strike goes towards Ed's rear *Triangulation Point*, and that Steve's feet align

Figure 5

with that point, creating stability for Steve while simultaneously exploiting Ed's instability. Obviously, Steve would exercise *Heaviness, Wave* Energy, and other principles to execute this motion.

Keep in mind that all motions to this point have occurred on just one beat, during which time Steve effectively defended and counterattacked while achieving a safe and *Angled Position* with *Spinal Alignment.* If we contrast this against the position in which Steve ends in figure C, which also occurs at the end of one beat, we see a dramatic difference in the amount accomplished thus far.

Figure 6

Figure 7

Figures 8-10, offer a close-up view of Steve's hand work and body position. Note that in figure 8, Steve is in prime position to deliver a strike to Ed's jaw. Furthermore, he keeps Ed close to him, setting up for *Centripetal Force* and also keeping him close to his *Center.* Not only that, Steve moves with considerable *Economy of Motion*, insuring that Ed misses him but only by a small margin. If seen from above, Ed's strike would pass nearly directly down the left side of Steve's *Triangle Guard*, thereby lulling Ed's *Natural Motion* until it is entirely disturbed in figure 9.

In figure 9, Steve exercises *Heaviness, Minor Axes,* and *Complex Force* when striking down with his right forearm. He's exercising, *Carving, Sheering, and Scissoring* force, all of which helps compromise Ed's arm.

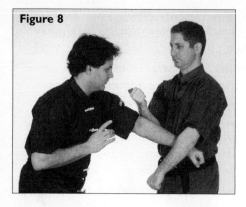

Figure 8

Figure 9

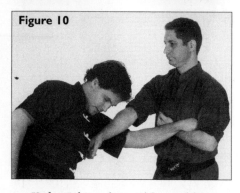

Figure 10

Also note that were Steve in poor *Structure*, his head might be leaning towards Ed's right hand, or he might not maintain *Balance* when contending with Ed's force and weight.

Also note that Steve partially grapples Ed's arm. This creates *Torsion* as he strikes down on it and punches through it. Ultimately, this can rip tendons in the wrist. Though difficult to see in figure 9, Steve maintains his *Triangle Guard* as he strikes to Ed's chest, which would use *Complex, Indirect,* and *Heavy* force in hitting figure 10. Not only that, but in figure 9 the angle of Steve's strike to Ed's forearm aims directly at Ed's *Triangulation Point,* thereby disrupting Ed's remaining *Balance* and beginning *Centripetal Motion.* Also note that the path Steve's left arm follows is through the negative spaces in Ed's *Triangle Guard,* thereby exercising the *Void* principle.

Overall, note how much Steve accomplishes on Ed's one beat, something he could not do were his motions not more *Economical* than Ed's, and were he not exercising principles that did not require large movements to generate power. Obviously, this technique represents *Kobo Ichi* and possibly could accomplish the *Pure Objective.* And finally, in the interest of true *Economical Motion,* Ed actually moves into Steve's punch, which Steve encourages by collapsing Ed's forearm, all of which only increases the impact to Ed's body.

Examining figures E-G, we see what happens if Steve exercises improper *Positioning, Angling, Structure,* etc. Note that improper *Structure* in his body and a manifestation of a pentagonal arm structure instead of the *Triangle Guard* means that Steve cannot sway or bend Ed's stronger arm. Coupled with poor *Positioning* and *Angling,* Steve simply gets hit by Ed's strike figure F. At this point, he also works Ed's *Rhythm.* Most likely, given his body structure, Steve will be forced back by Ed's strike, thereby giving Ed yet one more chance to attack (*Offensive Advantage*).

Regardless of whether or not Steve successfully defends Ed's left strike, his now compromised position puts him in jeopardy of being hit by Ed's right hand figure G.

Figure E

Figure F

Figure G

Figures H-J: In an alternate series of events, these building off of position figure C, Steve could block from the side figure C and grab hold of Ed's wrist with his left hand figure H and then try to strike Ed's arm in a similar fashion to what we see in figure 9. However, Steve's force no longer goes to Ed's weak point—*Triangulation Point*—and Steve's body lacks the alignment and *Structure* to apply most principles of power and *Economical Motion*. Therefore, it probably would take Steve longer than the allotted beat to execute this motion. Supposing however that he had the time to do it, his downward pressure would put force into Ed's right leg, permitting Ed to resist. Furthermore, Steve lacks *Spinal Alignment*, which means that he cannot really communicate his force to Ed's *Center* through *Extension &*

Figure C

Figure H

Figure I

Figure J

Penetration. Of course, Steve also has turned his body away from the point of contact with Ed's arm, thereby weakening the entire application.

As figure J demonstrates, this entire motion also compromises Steve's defensive integrity, permitting Ed a clear and easy shot to Steve's jaw. Not only that, closer inspect of figure J reveals that Ed actually pulls his left arm back to throw his right punch, which pulls Steve into that strike and undermines his *Balance*. Were Steve stable, Ed would not be able to accomplish this.

Figure 11 depicts a another possible strike Steve may insert in place of or along with the other strikes already shown, preferably the latter. Obviously, we want to achieve maximum *Efficiency*. Note that Steve's right arm has retracted but in doing so is now working towards putting Ed into a hammer lock, as seen in . . .

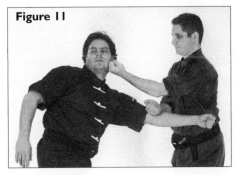

Figure 11

Figures 12-13: Steve has now worked his right arm between Ed's elbow and body. We first note that Ed's left elbow sits almost directly on top of his *Triangulation Point*, which not only disrupts his *Balance* and makes it easier for Steve to manipulate him, it also means that Ed is succumbing to *Centripetal Force*, spiraling down into that *Triangulation Point* that he himself created by launching the attack! To enter this position, Steve moved his right arm through Ed's *Void* and negative triangles, all the while exercising *Secondary Pressure*. As I earlier mentioned the presence of the *Sphere* principle, figure 12 now demonstrates quite clearly that Steve has maintained his *Sphere* and is now at the *Center* of both their positions. Note that Steve is not grabbing Ed's arm as this would trap Steve's *Body-Mind*, construct artificial tension, tip Ed off to the technique, and disrupt *Non-Intention*. Also, Steve maintains the *Triangle Guard* throughout the entire motion, now keeping his right fist

Figure 12

Figure 13

pointed to *Root* Ed's weight and force. Of course, Steve exercises the *Weak Link* principle, using *Torsion* to maintain control of Ed's arm but otherwise moving his fist through the *Void*, thereby placing no force into any part of Ed's body except the weak shoulder joint (and/or hip). Steve also could deliver a left strike in figure 13.

Figures K-Q demonstrates what could occur if Steve attempts to enter the hammerlock by moving around Ed instead of drawing Ed in *Centripetally*. Note that figures K-O represent the sequence, with figures P and Q the same as figures N and O, but from an alternate angle. That said, in figure K Steve attempts to start moving behind Ed, in part by pulling on Ed's arm. By working against Ed's muscle instead of going through the available *Voids*, Steve ends

Figure K

Figure L

Figure M

Figure N

Figure O

Figure P

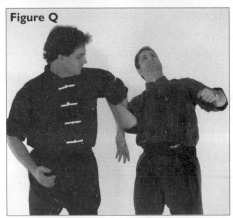

Figure Q

up pushing against Ed's right leg, which only allows Ed to be stable. In some cases, it might be possible to draw someone in Ed's position into a hammerlock position with this tactic, but doing so exposes the person in Steve's position to the counterpunch depicted in figure L. That strike could be delivered to Steve's mid-section since reaching for Ed's arm leaves his torso unprotected.

In figures M and N, Steve attempts to move towards Ed's rear left. Note how much Steve moves relative to how much Ed moves. Whereas Ed remains nearly stationary, Steve must cover a great deal of ground, hardly the *Efficient*, positive *Ratio* of *Spatial Relativity* we seek. It affords Ed ample space to exercise counter-movements, especially considering that each person gets *Equal Rights*. Not only that, positing himself as he does at Ed's left rear, Steve's force automatically will seek out Ed's right leg, offering Ed tremendous stability with which to resist. Contrast this against Steve's proper alignment with Ed's rear *Triangulation Point* in figure 12. Worse still, figure N depicts Steve applying pressure directly into Ed's arm in an effort to force it to bend and/or force Ed to bend at the waist. By applying direct pressure in the local joint, Steve tips Ed off as to the nature of the technique and will fail to allow the force to naturally seek out the *Weak Link* joint. Consider as well that Ed becomes the dominant *Sphere* that Steve decides to move around, and that were Steve able to start executing a lock from position figure N, it would be purely *Centrifugal*, casting Ed away and thus decreasing Steve's power in the process.

Finally, figure O depicts the difficulty Steve will encounter in forcing Ed's arm into the hammerlock position. Locked in a battle of direct pressure and strength without *Void, Triangulation Point, Centripetal Force, positive Spatial and Temporal Relativity,* and *Ratios, etc.* as allies, Ed simply can exercise strength and size and resist Steve's technique. In fact, you might note that Ed's feet actually align roughly with Steve's rear *Triangulation Point.*

Furthermore, as figure P reveals, Steve has lost his *Triangle Guard* and has turned his *Angling* away from the application of the technique, effectively leaving his own arm behind. While it might look as though Steve can direct the technique to Ed's *Triangulation Point,* which would roughly be below Ed's left shoulder, note that the angle of Ed's left arm will lead force to his right (stable) leg, and that because Steve is pushing against his arm,

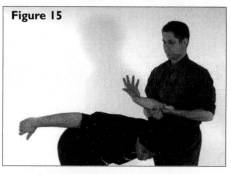

Figure 15

Figure 14

Figure 16

Ed's weight actually hovers more over the real leg than the "missing" one.

Figures 14-16 show Steve executing the hammer lock. Note the positioning of his hands in Figures 14-15, which exercise *Torsion* rather than grabbing to pin Ed's arm to his body. This sends fewer signals to Ed's *Body-Mind.* Of course, Steve applies that *Torsion* with *Indirect Pressure.* Additionally, note that Ed is falling directly into his *Triangulation Point* and that Steve remains aligned with Ed's body in such a way that he could strike it. Meanwhile Ed's alignment points tangentially away from Steve, thus keeping Steve safe. At this point, Steve also has *Sequentially Locked* Ed all the way to his hips, if not his legs, and Steve exercises *Centripetal* force, drawing Ed into his *Center* and power structure rather than moving him away from it. Doing so permits Steve to use *Heaviness, Structure, Relaxation, Spinal Alignment* and other factors to exercise *Centripetal Force* and drop Ed *down* rather than in some arbitrary direction that would be longer and cause less impact. What cannot be seen in the pictures but would be present in application is Steve's exercise of *Complex Force* against Ed's arms by both *Carving* and *Sheering* against them. Clearly, were Steve to apply *Live Energy* to this technique at this point, he could dislocate Ed's shoulder without difficulty. In terms of *Rhythm*, it should be clear as to who has established control of the pacing of the technique.

Figure 17

Figure R

Meanwhile, figure 17 demonstrates that Steve could insert a knee to Ed's face in the process of taking him to the floor. This insert, which could be to the shoulder to dislocate or to one of Ed's legs in the form of a kick, uses *Economical Motion* by impacting against Ed's own falling motion.

By contrast figure R depicts what might happen if Steve attempts to throw Ed down through more *Centrifugal* means. Note that Steve has turned his *Triangle Guard* and body structure away from Ed in an effort to trip him. As such, he will end up pulling from behind himself, hardly a powerful way to apply force. Not only that, he literally has to move Ed around himself in order to get him down, which only works to Ed's advantage. Ed can use any contact with Steve to resist the turning motion. Furthermore, because he is standing in Ed's *Triangulation Point* and using that as the center of the *Centrifugal* circle, Steve cannot possibly throw Ed to that spot. Finally, we also see Steve once again doing more movement than Ed, who has remained virtually motionless since having thrown the punch, making it exceptionally unlikely that Steve could get to this position at all.

Figure 18

This last position figure 18 shows Ed fully compromised and on his way to becoming prostrate. Note that Steve still exercises *Torsion* and would be applying *Extension and Penetration* directly *down* to Ed's *Triangulation Point*. As always, Steve also has available targets, such as hand strikes to Ed's head and ribs, and knee strikes to Ed's ribs and head. Steve remains in a solid *Structure*, fully able to maintain *Control* of Ed and use the same arm position as a finishing lock. All said, the combination, depicted again on the facing page, should take at most two seconds start to finish.

NOTES ON MY APPROACH TO THE TEXT

I AM NOT IN THE HABIT OF SETTING OUT A LIST OF QUALIFYING REMARKS about myself and my thoughts, but a text such as this one requires that certain statements be said outright. I find this especially important given the fierce and unfortunate contention in the martial arts community regarding who practices the better martial art.

1. I am no master.

While I might, at times, appear to be speaking with absolute certainty, I am only as certain as my perspective permits, and I recognize my perspective to be notably limited. I know that points have escaped my consideration. I am happy to learn. I am just a wanderer on the path.

2. Similarly, any uses of the word, "true," do not refer to absolute correctness but rather to consistently observable and verifiable factors. We deem gravity a "truth" because of the evidence that supports it and because of its omnipresence. While the "truth" of gravity varies—it is stronger at sea level than at 10,000 feet above—gravity remains predictable and measurable. That we deem it a "truth" does *not* mean we understand everything about it, it only means that it is consistently verifiable and ubiquitous, and it is in that spirit of reasoning that I will use "truth."

3. I intend for nothing in this text to suggest that my "style" of martial arts, my Way, is superior to any other style. Maybe it is stronger in some respects. Maybe it is weaker in others. I really do not know. I do not believe myself in a position to make such a judgment. And in final honesty, I really do not care. I have no interest in rivalry. I am honored if you can learn from this and I am honored to learn from you.

Essentially, this book emerges from the belief that all martial arts resonate with more similarities than differences, that each exercises the *same* principles, though to varying degrees and in varying ways. Do I believe that some methods of applying certain principles are superior to other methods? Actually, I do.

4. Every style operates in its own context and becomes functional because of many compounded factors within that context. Techniques function because of training method, teaching method, principles, range, tools, philosophical underpinnings, and martial objective (sport, self-defense, artistic expression, etc.). For example, is the *Muay Thai* round kick superior to *Tae Kwon Do's*? For certain objectives, perhaps so, and from other objectives, perhaps not. What is most important to remember, however, is that the *Muay Thai* kick works in accordance with a certain stance, footwork, posture, training method, martial objective, etc. Thus, even if we determine the *Muay Thai* kick to possess certain advantages over the *Tae Kwon Do* kick, it cannot *necessarily* be placed in a *Tae Kwon Do* context because the latter style does not possess the foundations of stance, footwork, posture, etc. to make the *Muay Thai* kick functional. And vice versa.

5. Therefore, this book will not advocate certain techniques. If by reading this text you hope to learn another joint lock or a different kick, you will be disappointed. However, this book will help you *improve the techniques you already practice by examining the principles that make them function*. This is an instruction manual of principles, not of techniques, but with the understanding that *principles govern techniques*.

6. *My* observation should be tested in *your* own practice. I ask only that you exercise great patience, practice, and reflection.

7. Furthermore, I typically see people acquire little success with practicing just one principle. Principles must be practiced *collectively*. *Principles build on principles*. Many principles only function, or at least only function well, when compounded with other principles. For better or worse, we cannot be selective about which principles we adopt. Every principle is a link in a chain. If one principle is weak, to say nothing of absent, then other principles will be useless. While there might be some give and take in interpretation and expression, we ultimately cannot pick and choose a principle here and a principle there. Each one depends on the others. They all interrelate.

8. Not only do they interrelate, they overlap and they blur. It would be easier if each were an entirely distinct entity unto itself, but such is not the case. Consequently, there are some principles I could have named individually that seemed to be covered well enough through the discussion of other principles. Similarly, some martial artists might find their own principles here under different names. I simply do not see how I could have avoided that. Naming and categorizing principles, though problematic, seems imperative if they are to be discussed. Yet if I named them differently, I could have had more or fewer principles.

9. Which brings me to the writing of this book, or more specifically, its

structure. I find no optimal way to organize a discussion of martial principles; I would have more success unscrambling an egg. Therefore, I had to devise an organization and the one I selected will suffice, though I recommend and request that readers read the book forwards first and then again backwards, chapter by chapter. I suggest and request as much because much of what I say at the beginning of the book will not make complete sense until the end, and what I write in the end will make greater sense when reviewed in the context of the beginning. Furthermore, reads in opposite directions will better provide a sense of the inter-relationship between the principles involved.

By the same rationale, I humbly request some patience from my readers. The final section of this book demonstrates one technique, step by step, *principle by principle*. Until principles become grounded in such a context, their essential and powerful nature might remain aloof.

Furthermore, when I do incorporate examples from particular styles in the body of the book, I do so only to demonstrate a particular point, not to advocate or denigrate the style in question. Nor is that meant to suggest that I am an instructor of that style. I'm not.

10. Lastly, *this book is an incomplete listing of principles*. There are too many martial principles to discuss in one text, and some are a bit too abstract for this format. Future texts will address additional principles.

All said, I have much to learn, and so I hope this book will stimulate dialogue in the martial arts community as a whole, and certainly between me and my readers. I welcome all of my readers to contact me at stevenpearlman@gmail.com with any questions, queries, comments, criticisms, conjecture, and/or insights they might have.